understanding
MICROECONOMICS

For NCEA Level Three
EXTERNALS/INTERNALS

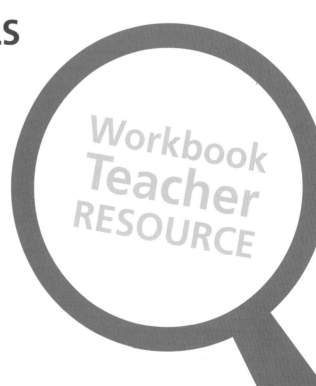

Workbook
Teacher
RESOURCE

Dan Rennie

T0360341

NELSON
A Cengage Company

Australia • Brazil • Mexico • Singapore • United Kingdom • United States

Understanding Microeconomics for NCEA L3 Teacher Resource
1st Edition
Dan Rennie

Typeset by : *Book*NZ

Any URLs contained in this publication were checked for currency during the production process. Note, however, that the publisher cannot vouch for the ongoing currency of URLs.

For product information and technology assistance,
in Australia call **1300 790 853**;
in New Zealand call **0800 449 725**

For permission to use material from this text or product, please email
aust.permissions@cengage.com

National Library of New Zealand Cataloguing-in-Publication Data
A catalogue record for this book is available from the National Library of New Zealand

ISBN 978 0 17 043810 0

Cengage Learning Australia
Level 7, 80 Dorcas Street
South Melbourne, Victoria Australia 3205

Cengage Learning New Zealand
Unit 4B Rosedale Office Park
331 Rosedale Road, Albany, North Shore 0632, NZ

For learning solutions, visit **cengage.co.nz**

Printed in Singapore by 1010 Printing Group Limited
1 2 3 4 5 6 7 22 21 20 19 18

Contents

For more information:

Email: nz.sales@cengage.com

Website: www.cengage.co.nz.

MICRO-ECONOMIC CONCEPTS
Marginal utility and demand

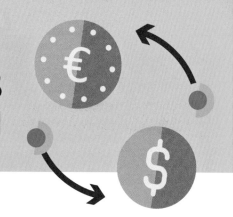

Utility and demand

As people consume goods or services they gain satisfaction (termed **utility**). Utility is measured in units of satisfaction termed utils. **Total utility (TU)** is the aggregate satisfaction gained from consuming successive quantities of a good. **Marginal utility (MU)** is the change or additions to total utility resulting from consumption of one extra unit of a good or service. MU equals TU2 minus TU1.

When making purchases, rational consumers aim to maximise their total satisfaction. If a consumer finds that the consumption of a good or service provides less satisfaction or utility than the price they paid to obtain the good or service, then this is not a rational or wise decision.

Tony Gordon's utility schedule for chewing gum each day		
Quantity consumed (packs)	Total utility (TU) (cents)	Marginal utility (MU) (cents)
1	80	80
2	144	64
3	192	48
4	224	32
5	244	20
6	244	0
7	230	−14

Tony Gordon's demand schedule for chewing gum each day	
Price (cents)	Quantity demanded (packs)
80	1
64	2
48	3
32	4
20	5
0	6

From the table we can observe that if a consumer's purchases increase, then the marginal utility will decrease. Therefore if a consumer was to decrease his or her purchases of a product, then marginal utility would increase.

As more of a product is consumed (as shown in the table), total satisfaction (total utility) increases but this will be at a decreasing rate. This is known as the **law of diminishing marginal utility**, that is, as more of a good or service is consumed holding all else constant, total utility increases but at a decreasing rate.

The rational consumer attempting to maximise his or her total utility should purchase more goods until price **(P) equals MU**; this is the **optimum purchase rule**. The individual demand curve is derived from the individual's marginal utility (MU) curve, because consumers receive less extra satisfaction as consumption increases they will only buy more of a good or service if the price falls. Therefore, the demand curve will slope downwards to the right. It follows that a rational consumer who finds that the price of a good or service was greater than the additional satisfaction (MU) obtained from consuming it, will decide it was not worth buying the good or service.

A demand schedule can be derived from a utility schedule. Marginal utility determines the price consumers are willing to pay for a good or service. When constructing a demand schedule or graph using a utility table the quantity is taken from the quantity figure given while the corresponding marginal utility figure is the price that consumers are willing to pay. For example, Tony is willing to pay 80 cents for the first packet of chewing gum and 64 cents for the second packet. The price he is willing to pay for each additional packet of chewing gum matches the falling marginal utility in the table.

Consumer equilibrium – two or more goods

To maximise total utility with limited income a consumer will be in equilibrium where MU Good A/Price Good A = MU Good B/Price Good B = MU Good C/Price Good C. This is where the marginal utility spent on the goods or services is equal.

	Kyle's utility table					
	Movies ($10)			Pizza ($5)		
Quantity	TU	MU	MU per dollar	TU	MU	MU per dollar
1	100	100	10	70	70	14
2	180	80	8	130	60	12
3	230	50	5	170	40	8
4	250	20	2	200	30	6
5	260	10	1	210	10	2

Kyle has an income of $35 and is deciding on which combination of pizza ($5 each) and movies ($10 each) will give him the highest total utlity and therefore the greatest satisfaction. His equilibrium is where the MU of Pizza/Price of Pizza equals MU of Movies/Price of Movies. In this instance it will be three pizzas and two movies. At this equilibrium Kyle's total utility is 350 utils (170 utils plus 180 utils), there is no other combination of pizza or movies that would result in a higher total utility for Kyle.

The order of purchases of pizza and movies is dependent on the MU per dollar. Kyle will purchase the products with the highest MU per dollar given his limited income.The first purchase is therefore a pizza because it has a MU per dollar of 14 (70/$5), next is another pizza because it has a MU per dollar of 12 (60/$5). Next is a movie because the MU per dollar is 10 (100/$10). The next purchase will be either a pizza or movie because the MU per dollar for both is 8. Kyle will be indifferent to consuming either, and since Kyle has $35 to spend he is able to purchase both.

Student notes: Marginal utility and demand

Utility – means satisfaction, consumers aim to maximise satisfaction. The table below shows that as more units are consumed the marginal utility (MU) decreases. If the price of a product rises there will be a resulting decrease in the amount purchased and an increase in the MU as a result.

Units consumed	Total utility (cents)	Marginal utility (cents)
1	500	500
2	900	400
3	1 000	100
4	1 050	50

Demand schedule using MU	
Price (cents)	Quantity demanded
500	1
400	2
100	3
50	4

Total utility (TU)   The aggregate satisfaction gained from consuming successive quantities of a good.

Marginal utility (MU)   The change in total utility resulting from the consumption of one extra unit of a given commodity.

Explaining why MU leads to the downward-sloping demand curve: As consumption increases, MU decreases. The rational consumer attempting to maximise his/her satisfaction will be prepared to purchase to where P = MU. Consumers will only purchase additional units at a lower price. The individual demand curve is therefore derived from the individual MU curve.

Optimum purchase rule: A consumer desiring to maximise total utility should purchase more goods and services until price equals marginal utility.

The law of diminishing marginal utility – As more of a good or service is consumed, the total utility will increase at a decreasing rate.

   ISBN: 9780170438100

Consumer equilibrium – two or more goods

For a consumer aiming to maximise total satisfaction and achieve consumer equilibrium they must satisfy these conditions:

1   spend all their income and

2   the marginal utility per dollar must be equal

i.e., $\dfrac{MU\ a}{price\ a} = \dfrac{MU\ b}{price\ b} = \dfrac{MU\ c}{price\ c}$

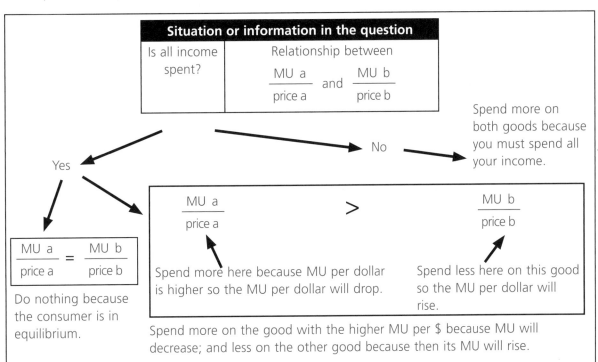

Situation or information in the question	
Is all income spent?	Relationship between $\dfrac{MU\ a}{price\ a}$ and $\dfrac{MU\ b}{price\ b}$

No → Spend more on both goods because you must spend all your income.

Yes

$\dfrac{MU\ a}{price\ a} = \dfrac{MU\ b}{price\ b}$

Do nothing because the consumer is in equilibrium.

$\dfrac{MU\ a}{price\ a}$ > $\dfrac{MU\ b}{price\ b}$

Spend more here because MU per dollar is higher so the MU per dollar will drop.

Spend less here on this good so the MU per dollar will rise.

Spend more on the good with the higher MU per $ because MU will decrease; and less on the other good because then its MU will rise.

Order of purchases						
	Pizza ($5)			Wedges ($5)		
Quantity	TU	MU	MU per dollar	TU	MU	MU per dollar
1	100	100	20	50	50	10
2	180	80	16	80	30	6
3	210	30	6	100	20	4
4	220	10	2	100	0	0

Purchase of pizza or wedges in order of preference. Consumer income is $20.

1st   Pizza

2nd   Pizza

3rd   Wedges

4th   Wedges or pizza (indifferent to these two products because they have the same MU per dollar).

At this equilibrium of 3 pizza/1 wedges or 2 pizza/2 wedges the total utility in both instances is 260 utils, there is no other combination of products that will give a higher total utility.

QUESTIONS & TASKS

1 a Explain the difference between total utility and marginal utility.

Total utility is the aggregate satisfaction gained from consuming successive quantities of a good.

Marginal utility is the change in total utility resulting from the consumption of a given commodity.

MU = TU2 – TU1

b Explain the law of diminishing marginal utility.

As more of a good/service is consumed, the total utility will increase at a decreasing rate (i.e. MU will

fall) or successive equal additions to consumption result in smaller amounts of extra utility.

c Complete the table that shows Ian's total and marginal utility from buying cans of soft drink per week.

Quantity consumed (cans)	Total utility (cents)	Marginal utility (cents)
1	200	200
2	360	160
3	460	100
4	524	64
5	564	40

d Use the concept of marginal utility to explain why the demand curve for the product slopes downward.

As consumption increases, the marginal utility gained by consuming the product will fall. As the

marginal utility falls, a rational consumer will be less willing to make the same sacrifice to buy the goods/

producers will only sell more by reducing price.

e Use the information in the table above to complete Ian's demand schedule for cans of soft drink per week and draw a demand curve in the grid provided.

Ian's demand schedule for cans of soft drink per week	
Price (cents)	Quantity demanded
200	1
160	2
100	3
64	4
40	5

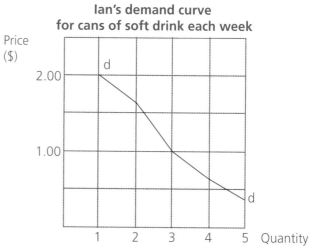

Ian's demand curve for cans of soft drink each week

2 a Complete the table and use it to complete the sentences.

Quantity consumed (pies)	Total utility	Marginal utility
0	0	– (or 0)
1	24	24
2	44	20
3	56	12
4	60	4

A decrease in the amount of a good purchased would <u>decrease</u> total utility, and marginal utility will <u>increase</u>.

b Look at the values in the marginal utility column above and state the law of economics they show.

<u>The law of diminishing marginal utility.</u>

c State the optimum purchase rule.

<u>P = MU</u>

d State the consumer equilibrium rule (or formula) a consumer should use to ensure they maximise total utility they receive from purchasing two products.

$$\frac{MU\ a}{price\ a} = \frac{MU\ b}{price\ b}$$

e The price of good A is $2 and the price of good B is $1.50. If a consumer evaluates the marginal utility of B to be 30 and he or she is in equilibrium with respect to purchases of A and B, then he or she must consider the marginal utility of A to be what?

$$\frac{MU\ a}{price\ a} = \frac{MU\ b}{price\ b} \quad \frac{?}{2} = \frac{30}{1.50} \quad MUa = 40$$

f Explain the significance of the law of diminishing marginal utility in deriving the individual demand curve.

<u>As consumption increases, MU decreases. The rational consumer attempting to maximise his/her satisfaction will be prepared to purchase to where P = MU. Consumers will only purchase additional units at a lower price. The individual demand curve is therefore derived from the individual MU curve.</u>

g Indicate if the following statements are correct or incorrect.

(i) The consumer gains the maximum utility for the money available when the quantity purchased is at a point where P > MU. <u>Incorrect</u>

(ii) The consumer gains the maximum utility for the money available when the quantity purchased is at a point where P = MU. <u>Correct</u>

(iii) When a consumer increases consumption of a good or service the MU tends to decrease and they will be prepared to pay less. <u>Correct</u>

(iv) The consumer's equilibrium occurs when the marginal utility per dollar of all goods and services is equal (this is the equi-marginal rule). <u>Correct</u>

3 Alan is a Year 13 Economics student who likes drinking flavoured milk. Explain the concept of utility. In your answer you should:

- Complete the table below by calculating the missing values.
- Draw Alan's demand schedule for flavoured milk per day in the schedule provided.
- Define the law of diminishing marginal utility.
- Explain, using the law of diminishing marginal utility, why Alan's demand curve will slope downwards to the right. Refer to the table in your answer.

Alan's utility schedule for flavoured milk (per day)		
Number of bottles consumed	Total utility (cents)	Marginal utility (cents)
1	600	600
2	1 000	400
3	1 300	300
4	1 500	200
5	1 600	100

Alan's demand schedule for flavoured milk per day	
Price ($)	Quantity demanded
1.00	5
2.00	4
3.00	3
4.00	2
6.00	1

The law of diminishing marginal utility states that as quantity consumed increases the extra satisfaction (MU) from consuming an extra unit decreases.

The price consumers are prepared to pay for a good depends on the marginal utility they receive from it (i.e., there is a relationship between price and marginal utility/consumer will continue to consume up to the point where P = MU).

Since MU falls as quantity increases (i.e., the law of diminishing MU) consumers will only buy larger quantities if the price falls to match their lower MU. A drop in price from $2 to $1 is required for Alan to buy an additional unit of flavoured milk. So a demand curve must slope downward to the right with lower prices matching lower MUs of larger quantities consumed.

4 Mark Cambo enjoys hitting golf balls and often goes to the driving range to hit a basket of golf balls. He gives you the following information about his utility.

Explain the concept of utility. In your answer you should:

- Complete the table below by filling in the missing numbers.
- Plot Mark Cambo's demand curve for golf balls on the grid below.
- Name the law that explains why Mark gains less satisfaction with every basket of balls purchased.
- Use marginal utility to explain why Mark Cambo purchases more baskets of golf balls when the price of a basket of golf balls falls.

Mark Cambo's utility schedule for baskets of golf balls		
Quantity consumed (basket of balls)	Total utility (cents)	Marginal utility (cents)
1	600	600
2	1 000	400
3	1 200	200
4	1 250	50

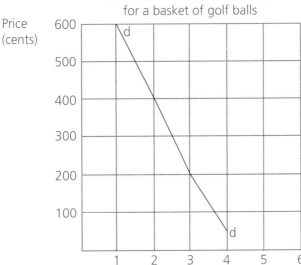

Mark Cambo's demand curve for a basket of golf balls

The law of diminishing marginal utility explains why Mark gains less satisfaction with every basket of golf balls purchased.

Mark will purchase a basket of golf balls until he reaches the point where P = MU (optimal purchase rule). When the price of a basket of golf balls falls, P < MU, there is an incentive for Mark to increase his consumption of baskets of golf balls. As he consumes additional units, MU will fall. Consequently, consumer equilibrium will be restored at a lower price and a corresponding lower marginal utility (P′ = MU′). A rational consumer (like Mark) will therefore increase the quantity he purchases when the price of a good falls.

5 Julian likes to hire videos or video games at the local store. Videos are $10 each and video games $8.

a Complete the table given.

Quantity of each product	Marginal utility of videos (utils)	MU per $ videos	Marginal utility of video games (utils)	MU per $ video games
1	80	8	56	7
2	40	4	40	5
3	20	2	32	4
4	10	1	24	3

b State the law of economics that the changing values of marginal utility show in the table.

The law of diminishing marginal utility.

c State the consumer equilibrium rule Julian needs to apply to maximise the total utility he receives from buying videos and video games.

$$\frac{MU\ videos}{price\ videos} = \frac{MU\ video\ games}{price\ video\ games}$$ and all income is spent

d How many videos and video games should Julian purchase to maximise his total utility?

Number of videos 2

Number of video games 3

e Explain using the optimum purchase rule why Julian would buy fewer videos if their price increased.

The optimum purchase rule states P = MU, if the price of a video increases then price will exceed the MU, and therefore the price paid for one more video would outweigh the satisfaction derived from it. Julian would therefore purchase fewer videos, this will cause MU to rise (the law of diminishing marginal utility) until it equals the new increased price.

   ISBN: 9780170438100

6 A consumer, Jacob, assigns the following utility to successive levels of consumption.

Units consumed	Utility					
	Pizza	MU per $	Drink	MU per $	Wedges	MU per $
1	120	12	22	11	40	10
2	90	9	20	10	36	9
3	60	6	18	9	32	8
4	40	4	14	7	28	7
5	20	2	12	6	24	6
Price per unit	$10		$2		$4	

Help Jacob maximise the total utility he receives from purchasing pizza, drinks and wedges. In your answer you should:
- Complete the MU per $ column for each product in the table.
- State the consumer equilibrium rule (or formula) Jacob should use to ensure he maximises the total utility he receives.
- Assume Jacob has $20 to spend. What combination of goods will he buy?
- In what order will Jacob purchase pizza, drinks and wedges? Justify your answer for Jacob's fifth purchase.

$$\frac{MU\ pizza}{price\ pizza} = \frac{MU\ drinks}{price\ drinks} = \frac{MU\ wedges}{price\ wedges}$$

Jacob will purchase 1 pizza, 3 drinks and 1 lot of wedges.

Order of purchases	Price $	Total income spent
1st pizza	10	10
2nd drink	2	12
3rd= wedges	4	16
3rd= drink	2	18
5th drink	2	20

Jacob will buy a drink for his fifth purchase instead of another lot of wedges because at that stage he has only $2 left out of $20 income and therefore cannot afford to buy the wedges at a price of $4 or pizza at $10 each.

2 MICRO-ECONOMIC CONCEPTS
Elasticity of demand

Price elasticity of demand

Price elasticity of demand (Ep) measures the responsiveness of quantity demanded of a good or service to changes in its price.

Inelastic demand (ep < 1)

Goods or services that are inelastic in nature have the following characteristics, they tend to have **no, or few, close substitutes** and are often considered **necessities**, for example bread, milk, medical services. The products may be **addictive**, such as cigarettes or alcohol. When the relative cost of the commodity is a **small fraction of total spending** then demand will be inelastic, for example a newspaper.

For goods or services that are inelastic in nature (Ep < 1) **a given change in price causes a less than proportionate change in quantity demanded**. As the price of a product increases total revenue will increase, while a price decrease will cause total revenue for firms to decrease.

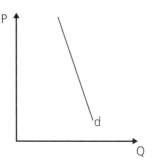

Inelastic demand curve

Elastic demand (ep > 1)

Goods and services that are **elastic** in nature have the following characteristics:-they tend to have **many substitutes** and are often considered **luxuries** such as designer clothing, eating out at a five star Michelin restaurant or staying in a penthouse suite at a hotel. When the relative cost of the commodity is a **high proportion of total spending** then demand will be elastic, for example a new car.

For goods and services that are elastic in nature (Ep > 1) **a given change in price causes a more than proportionate change in quantity demanded**. As the price of a product increases total revenue for a firm will decrease, while a price decrease will cause total revenue for firms to increase.

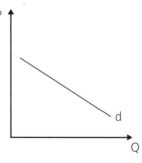

Elastic demand curve

Tax and elasticity

The incidence of a tax refers to who actually pays the tax. In most cases, part of a tax is paid by the consumer and part is paid by the firm. The incidence of a tax falls mainly on consumers when a good or service is inelastic. When demand is inelastic, a given increase in price will see a less than proportionate decrease in quantity demanded, meaning that producers are more able to pass on most of the tax to consumers. Consumers pay to the extent of the price rise, this will be the greatest incidence of the tax. Any amount of the tax not covered by the price increase has to be absorbed by the firm.

Taxes placed on goods that are price inelastic can raise significant revenue. The reason for this is that the price rise caused by the imposition of the tax on goods or services that are inelastic in nature will cause a proportionately small decrease in quantity demanded. This results in a relatively large number of goods or services on which the tax is imposed, and therefore greater tax revenue is collected. Given this, a government is more likely to impose taxes on products such as cigarettes and alcohol that are inelastic in nature, than products such as new cars.

Taxes placed on goods that are price elastic may raise less revenue than a tax placed on goods that are price inelastic. The reason for this is that the price rise caused by the imposition of the tax on goods or services that are elastic in nature will cause a proportionately large decrease in quantity demanded. This can leave only a relatively small number of goods or services on which the tax is imposed, and therefore less tax revenue is collected.

       ISBN: 9780170438100

Calculating price elasticity of demand

Price elasticity of demand can be calculated using the revenue method, which compares the change in price (P) with the change in total revenue (TR). Total revenue (TR) equals price (P) multiplied by the quantity sold (Q). If a firm desires to increase revenue it would increase price if the product was inelastic in nature and decrease price if the product was elastic in nature.

Revenue method for price elasticity of demand			
Price change	Inelastic $EP < 1$	Unitary $Ep = 1$	Elastic $Ep > 1$
P ⬆	TR ⬆	TR ⬌	TR ⬇
P ⬇	TR ⬇	TR ⬌	TR ⬆
	TR/P changes are in the same direction	TR remains the same with price changes	TR/P changes are in the opposite direction

Midpoint method

The midpoint method to calculate price elasticity of demand (Ep) uses the averages of the quantity demanded and price to work out the elasticity coefficient.

To calculate the price elasticity of demand using the midpoint method, the following formula is used (the change in quantity demanded/the midpoint of the quantity demanded) divided by (the change in price of/the midpoint of the prices indicated). Note the final number (coefficient) will always be a negative number because price and quantity demanded always occur in opposite directions. To be strictly accurate the coefficient should be written as a negative number. However, it is common practice in economics to ignore the negative sign.

For example, the price of coffee rose from $15 per kg to $20 per kg and sales fell from 100kg to 80kg per week. The price elasticity of demand for coffee equals (–20/90) divided by ($5/$17.5) is –0.777 which is 0.78, therefore the price elasticity of demand for coffee is inelastic.

$$Ep = \frac{\left[\dfrac{\text{change in quantity demanded}}{\text{midpoint of quantity demanded}}\right]}{\left[\dfrac{\text{change in price}}{\text{midpoint of the prices indicated}}\right]} = \frac{\left[\dfrac{\dfrac{\Delta Qd}{Q1 + Q2}}{2}\right]}{\left[\dfrac{\dfrac{\Delta P}{P1 + P2}}{2}\right]}$$

Price elasticity of demand is a point concept so a demand curve can have a range of elasticities, typically relatively elastic (Ep greater than 1) at the top end and relatively inelastic (Ep less than than 1) at the lower end.

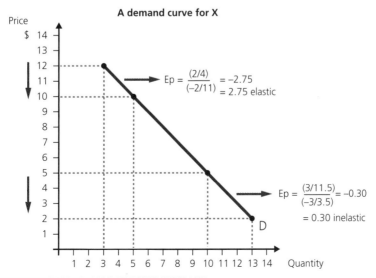

A demand curve for X

$$Ep = \frac{(2/4)}{(-2/11)} = -2.75$$
$$= 2.75 \text{ elastic}$$

$$Ep = \frac{(3/11.5)}{(-3/3.5)} = -0.30$$
$$= 0.30 \text{ inelastic}$$

ISBN: 9780170438100

Student notes: Elasticity of demand

Price elasticity of demand (Ep) – measures the responsiveness of quantity demanded of a good (or service) to changes in its price.

Goods (or services) that are elastic in nature (Ep > 1) – often considered luxuries, many substitutes, takes a high percentage of income spent, e.g., new cars, houses. A given change in price evokes a more than proportionate change in quantity demanded.

Goods (or services) that are inelastic in nature (Ep < 1) – necessities, few (if any) substitutes, takes a small percentage of income spent, can be addictive in nature, e.g., cigarettes, alcohol, bread, milk. A given change in price evokes a less than proportionate change in quantity demanded.

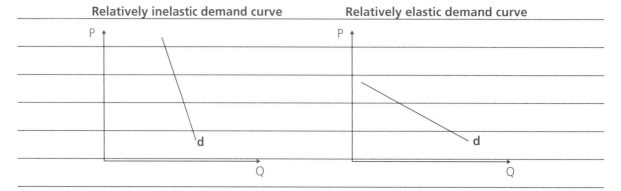

Relatively inelastic demand curve   Relatively elastic demand curve

Revenue method for Ep – Ep = 1 (unitary) P ↕ TR unchanged

Ep > 1 (elastic) P ↑ TR ↓

Ep < 1 (inelastic) P ↑ TR ↑

Formula to calculate price elasticity of demand midpoint method

$$Ep = \dfrac{\left[\dfrac{\text{change in quantity demanded}}{\text{midpoint of quantity demanded}}\right]}{\left[\dfrac{\text{change in price}}{\text{midpoint of the prices indicated}}\right]} = \dfrac{\left(\dfrac{\Delta Q}{\dfrac{Q1 + Q2}{2}}\right)}{\left(\dfrac{\Delta P}{\dfrac{P1 + P2}{2}}\right)}$$

        ISBN: 9780170438100

QUESTIONS & TASKS

1 **a** Define price elasticity of demand and give the formula to calculate Ep.

Ep measures the responsiveness of quantity demanded of a good or service to changes in its price.

$$Ep = \frac{\dfrac{\Delta QD}{\text{midpt QD}}}{\dfrac{\Delta P}{\text{midpt price}}} \quad \text{or} \quad Ep = \frac{\%\Delta QD}{\%\Delta P}$$

b Work out price elasticity of demand for each question below. Show your working (round to two decimal places). Use the midpoint method.

(i)

Price ($)	Quantity demanded
1.50	100
1.70	95

$$Ep = \frac{\left(\dfrac{-5}{97.5}\right)}{\left(\dfrac{.20}{1.60}\right)} = -0.410 = 0.41 \text{ inelastic}$$

(ii) Work out the Ep on the curve at the positions indicated.

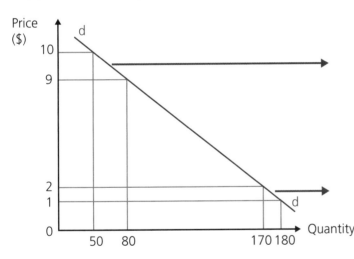

$$Ep \text{ is } \frac{\left(\dfrac{30}{65}\right)}{\left(\dfrac{-1}{9.5}\right)} = -4.384 = 4.38 \text{ elastic}$$

$$Ep \text{ is } \frac{\left(\dfrac{10}{175}\right)}{\left(\dfrac{-1}{1.5}\right)} = 0.085 = 0.09 \text{ inelastic}$$

c Explain what a price elasticity of demand coefficient of less than one indicates about a good or service.

A price elasticity of demand less than one indicates that the good or service is inelastic in nature. Goods or services that are inelastic in nature have the following characteristics, they tend to have no, or few, close substitutes and are often considered necessities, for example bread, milk, medical services. The products may be addictive, such as cigarettes or alcohol. When the relative cost of the commodity is a small fraction of total spending then demand will be inelastic, for example a newspaper.

For goods or services that are inelastic in nature (Ep < 1) a given change in price causes a less than proportionate change in quantity demanded.

2 Calculate price elasticity of demand for each of the following questions (to two decimal places). Work out Ep using the midpoint method.

a

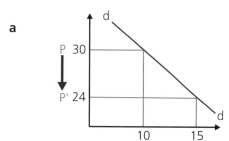

$$Ep = \frac{\left(\dfrac{5}{12.5}\right)}{\left(\dfrac{-6}{27}\right)} = -1.80 = 1.80 \text{ elastic}$$

b

	Price $	Quantity demanded
Old situation	25	100
New situation	30	60

$$Ep = \frac{\left(\dfrac{-40}{80}\right)}{\left(\dfrac{5}{27.5}\right)} = -2.75 = 2.75 \text{ elastic}$$

c Complete the table.

	Relative changes in price/revenue	Elasticity – unitary, inelastic, elastic
(i)	Price increases and total revenue remains unchanged	unitary
(ii)	Price increases and total revenue increases	inelastic
(iii)	Total revenue increases when price rises from $10 to $12	inelastic
(iv)	P ↓ TR ↓	inelastic
(v)	P ↓ TR remains the same	unitary
(vi)	Price decreases and total revenue increases	elastic
(vii)	TR ↑ when price falls	elastic
(viii)	Revenue remains the same when price falls	unitary
(ix)	Change in price and total revenue are in the same direction	inelastic
(x)	TR ↑ P ↑ or P ↓ TR ↓	inelastic
(xi)	Changes in TR and P go in the opposite direction	elastic

d (i) Give reasons why the price elasticity of demand coefficient of wiper blades is 0.19.

A small percentage of income is spent on wiper blades. There are few, if any, substitutes for wiper blades. Wiper blades are a necessity.

(ii) Indicate what will happen to a firm's revenue if they increase the price. Explain why.

Total revenue will increase because the given change in price will cause a less than proportionate change in quantity demanded.

3 a Indicate the price elasticity of demand indicated by the situation outlined in the table below.

Situation		Elasticity of demand
(i)	The response to a given change in price is an exactly proportionate change in quantity demanded	Unitary
(ii)	The response to a given change in price is a more than proportionate change in quantity demanded	Elastic demand
(iii)	The response to a given change in price is a less than proportionate change in quantity demanded	Inelastic demand
(iv)	Price elasticity of demand is greater than 1	Elastic demand
(v)	%Δ price < %Δ quantity demanded	Elastic demand
(vi)	%Δ price = %Δ quantity demanded	Unitary
(vii)	%Δ QD < %Δ price	Inelastic demand

b Doctor visits fell from 10 000 to 9 000 when price increased from $25 to $30. What is the price elasticity of demand for doctor visits? Give a possible reason for doctor visits, relating it to the Ep you calculated.

$$Ep = \frac{\left(\frac{-1\,000}{9\,500}\right)}{\left(\frac{5}{27.5}\right)} = -0.578 = 0.58$$

Inelastic. Doctors are a necessity/few substitutes if you are sick.

c The brewery decides to increase the price of a jug of beer from $4.50 to $5.00 and the quantity sold decreases from 7 500 to 7 300.

(i) Work out the change in revenue from the price increase. Was this an increase or decrease in revenue?

P	Q	TR		
$4.50	7 500	$33 750	P ↑	TR ↑
$5.00	7 300	$36 500	revenue increased by $2 750	

(ii) Work out Ep using the midpoint method.

$$Ep = \frac{\left(\frac{-200}{7\,400}\right)}{\left(\frac{0.50}{4.75}\right)} = -0.256 = 0.26 \text{ inelastic}$$

d Explain what a price elasticity of demand coefficient of greater than one indicates about a good or service.

A price elasticity of demand greater than one indicates that the good or service is elastic in nature. Goods and services that are elastic in nature have the following characteristics: they tend to have many substitutes and are often considered luxuries such as designer clothing, eating out at a five star Michelin restaurant or staying in a penthouse suite at a hotel. When the relative cost of the commodity is a high proportion of total spending then demand will be elastic, for example a new car.

For goods and services that are elastic in nature (Ep > 1) a given change in price causes a more than proportionate change in quantity demanded.

4 Price elasticity of demand is a point concept.

Explain price elasticity of demand using the graph below. In your answer you should:

- Define 'price elasticity of demand'.
- Calculate price elasticity of demand along the demand curve. Use the midpoint method and show your working.
- Describe how a knowledge of price elasticity will assist a firm to increase total revenue.

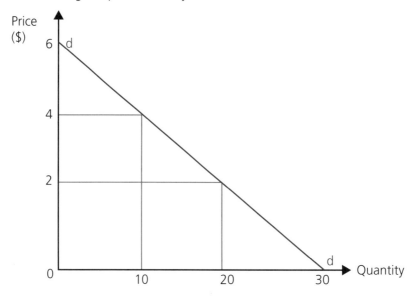

Price elasticity of demand measures the responsiveness of quantity demanded of a good or service to changes in its price.

Ep between $6 and $4: Ep = $\dfrac{\left(\dfrac{-10}{5}\right)}{\left(\dfrac{2}{5}\right)}$ = −5 = 5   elastic

Ep between $4 and $2: Ep = $\dfrac{\left(\dfrac{-10}{15}\right)}{\left(\dfrac{2}{3}\right)}$ = −1 = 1   unitary

Ep between $2 and $0: Ep = $\dfrac{\left(\dfrac{-10}{25}\right)}{\left(\dfrac{2}{1}\right)}$ = −0.2 = 0.2   inelastic

The calculations show that a demand curve can have a range of elasticity, typically elastic at the top end of a demand curve and inelastic at the bottom end.

Firms are aware that when price elasticity of demand is inelastic that a given change in price causes a less than proportionate change in quantity demanded and if a product is elastic in nature this means that a given change in price causes a more than proportionate change in quantity demanded. Therefore, if a firm desires to increase revenue it would increase price if the product was inelastic in nature and decrease price if the product was elastic in nature.

5 Various factors determine the price elasticity of demand for a product. The demand coefficient of water is 0.15, coffee 0.56 and meals out at a restaurant 1.35. Firms use this knowledge in their pricing decisions.

Explain factors that determine price elasticity of demand and how firms use this knowledge. In your answer you should:

- Explain factors that influence price elasticity of demand with reference to the information above.
- Explain how firms will use a knowledge of price elasticity of demand in their pricing decisions.

Factors that determine a product's elasticity include if it is a necessity or a luxury, the availability of substitutes and proportion of total income spent. Inelastic demand includes products that tend to have no or few close substitutes and are often considered necessities such as bread, milk, medical services. The products may be addictive such as cigarettes or alcohol. When the relative cost of the commodity is a small fraction of total outlay then the demand will be inelastic, for example a newspaper. Elastic demands include products that have many substitutes and are often considered luxuries such as fashion clothing and cars as there are substitutes such as walking, catching a bus, etc.

Water is inelastic in nature because water is a necessity. There are no substitutes for water and it takes a small proportion of total income spent.

Coffee is inelastic in nature because coffee is addictive/necessity. There are few or no substitutes for coffee and it takes a small proportion of total income spent.

Meals out at a restaurant are elastic in nature because they are a luxury. There are many substitutes. Can take a high proportion of total income spent.

Firms are aware that when price elasticity of demand is inelastic that a given change in price causes a less than proportionate change in quantity demanded and if a product is elastic in nature this means that a given change in price causes a more than proportionate change in quantity demanded. Therefore, if a firm desires to increase revenue it would increase price if the product was inelastic in nature and decrease price if the product was elastic in nature.

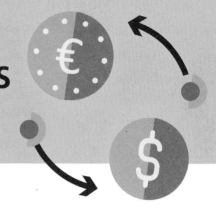

3 MICRO-ECONOMIC CONCEPTS
Elasticity of supply

Price elasticity of supply

Price elasticity of supply (Es) measures the **responsiveness of quantity supplied** of a good or service to **changes in price**.

Supply over time

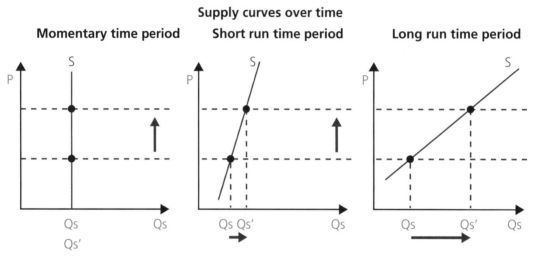

Momentary supply is supply at a given point in time and is sometimes referred to as supply on a given day. The quantity supplied is fixed regardless of price (illustrated by the perfectly inelastic supply curve shown, drawn as a vertical line). The curve reflects that firms have only a fixed amount of stock on hand available to meet demand and are **unable to alter any factors**, for example tickets to a school social, or the lots available for sale at an auction. There is no responsiveness in the quantity supplied to a change in price and the coefficient of elasticity of supply is zero.

In the **short-run time period, at least one input is fixed**. The firm is restricted in its ability to change output. In the short run the supply of all goods is inelastic because the quantity supplied is limited to the quantity of finished goods on hand or easily available. Supply **elasticity** is said to **lower**.

In the **long run period** firms have **time to expand their use of all factors** and so increase their total output capacity. Shortages and profits will attract more firms to the industry, which will increase total market supply. Over time, supply will be more responsive to price (elastic) as existing producers are able to increase production levels, new producers can enter the market, and improvements in technology increase productivity. **Elasticity** is then said to be **higher**.

Supply is inelastic, or relatively unresponsive to price changes in the short run, and elastic, or relatively responsive, in the long run. In response to a price change output will change by more in the long-run than short-run time period, as shown in the diagram above.

Factors that determine elasticity of supply

Manufacturers who are able to quickly increase (decrease) output in response to higher (lower) prices because they are able to have longer (shorter) production runs with an increase (decrease) in overtime have a more responsive elasticity of supply. A company that has excess capacity should be able to increase its output without a rise in costs. In this situation the supply curve is elastic because it can respond to changes in demand. When economies are in recession it is assumed that resources (land, capital and labour) are not being fully utilised and elasticity can be higher.

       ISBN: 9780170438100

The **ability** of a firm to be able to **store stock (inventory)** influences the elasticity of supply. If a company has finished products in stock it is able to respond quickly to increases in demand, therefore supply will be elastic. The opposite applies when there is less inventory, in this situation supply will be more inelastic.

The longer the duration that a firm is allowed to adjust its production levels the more elastic the supply curve is. However, agricultural producers tend to have either inelastic supply or momentary supply (perfectly inelastic) because producers have made decisions about what crops to plant and have limited land, further they are often subject to climate conditions that influence output.

Calculations price elasticity of supply

$$Es = \frac{\left[\dfrac{\text{change in quantity supplied}}{\text{midpoint of quantity supplied given}}\right]}{\left[\dfrac{\text{change in price}}{\text{midpoint of the prices indicated}}\right]} = \frac{\left[\dfrac{\Delta Qs}{\dfrac{Q1 + Q2}{2}}\right]}{\left[\dfrac{\Delta P}{\dfrac{P1 + P2}{2}}\right]}$$

The midpoint method to calculate price elasticity of supply (Es) uses the averages of the quantity supplied and price to work out the elasticity coefficient.

To calculate the price elasticity of supply using the midpoint method, the following formula is used (the change in quantity supplied / the midpoint of the quantity supplied) divided by (the change in price / the midpoint of the prices indicated).

For example: the price of X increases from $9 to $11 and quantity supplied increases from 300 to 500. The price elasticity of supply equals (200/400) divided by ($2/$10) equals 2.50, therefore the price elasticity of supply for X is elastic.

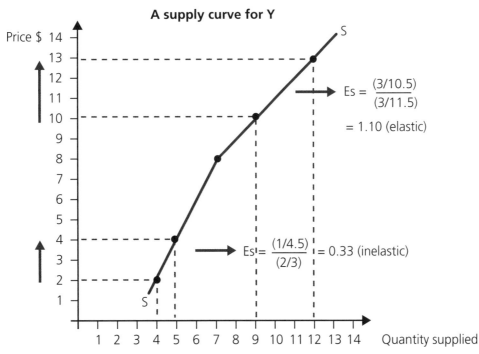

Price elasticity of supply is a **point concept** so a supply curve can have a range of elasticities, typically relatively elastic (Es greater than 1) at the top end and relatively inelastic (Es less than than 1) at the lower end. When price elasticity of supply equals one it is termed unitary.

When **price elasticity of supply is less than one** this means that a **given change in price causes a less than proportionate change in quantity supplied** and indicates **inelastic supply** (Es less than one).

When **price elasticity of supply is greater than one** this means that **a given change in price causes a more than proportionate change in quantity supplied** and indicates **elastic** supply (Es greater than one).

Student notes: Price elasticity of supply

Price elasticity of supply (Es) – measures the responsiveness of quantity supplied of a good or service to a change in its price.

Price elasticity of supply coefficient – enables us to classify supply curves as inelastic (Es < 1) or elastic (Es > 1) which helps us understand the response a firm will have to a change in price for its output.

Momentary supply – (perfectly inelastic supply Es = 0) supply curve is drawn as a vertical line this is because there can be no responsiveness in the quantity supplied to a change in price. The quantity supplied is fixed.

Short-run supply – (relatively inelastic) firms have at least one fixed factor and therefore the firm is restricted in its ability to change supply/output levels. Supply in the short run will be lower or more inelastic.

Long-run supply – (relatively elastic) firms can alter all factors therefore firms can be adaptable, supply is higher or more elastic.

Inelastic supply – (Es < 1) a given change in price evokes a less than proportionate increase in quantity supplied.

Elastic supply – (Es > 1) a given change in price evokes a more than proportionate increase in quantity supplied.

Formula to calculate price elasticity of supply, midpoint method

$$Es = \frac{\text{change in quantity supplied}}{\text{midpoint of quantity supplied given}} \div \frac{\text{change in price}}{\text{midpoint of the prices indicated}} = \frac{\dfrac{\Delta Qs}{\dfrac{Q1 + Q2}{2}}}{\dfrac{\Delta P}{\dfrac{P1 + P2}{2}}}$$

QUESTIONS & TASKS

1 a Define 'price elasticity of supply'.

Measures the responsiveness of the quantity supplied of a good to a change in its price.

b Work out the price elasticity of supply for each question below (show your working). Use the midpoint method.

(i)

Price ($)	Quantity demanded
1.00	17
0.95	10

$$Es = \frac{\left(\frac{-7}{13.5}\right)}{\left(\frac{-0.05}{0.975}\right)} = 10.11 \text{ elastic}$$

(ii) Work out the Ep on the curve at the positions indicated.

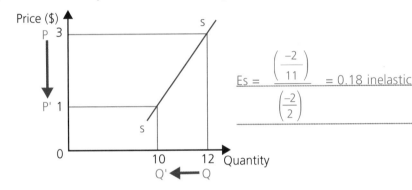

$$Es = \frac{\left(\frac{-2}{11}\right)}{\left(\frac{-2}{2}\right)} = 0.18 \text{ inelastic}$$

c Use the diagram to match up the curves with the description below. Write the letter of your choice.

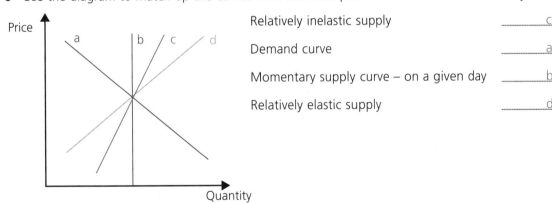

Relatively inelastic supply	c
Demand curve	a
Momentary supply curve – on a given day	b
Relatively elastic supply	d

d Complete the table below.

Situation	Elasticity
(i) The response to a given change in price is a more than proportionate change in quantity supplied.	Elastic supply
(ii) The response to a given change in price is a less than proportionate change in quantity supplied.	Inelastic supply
(iii) A given price change causes no change in quantity supplied.	Perfectly inelastic
(iv) %Δ price > %Δ quantity supplied	Inelastic supply
(v) %Δ quantity supplied > %Δ price	Elastic supply

2 Calculate the price elasticity of supply for each question below (show your working). Use the midpoint method.

a

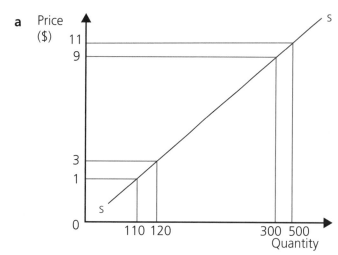

(i) Between $11 and $9:

$$Es = \frac{\left(\dfrac{200}{400}\right)}{\left(\dfrac{-2}{10}\right)} = 2.50 \text{ elastic}$$

(ii) Between $3 and $1:

$$Es = \frac{\left(\dfrac{-10}{115}\right)}{\left(\dfrac{-2}{2}\right)} = 0.09 \text{ inelastic}$$

b Briefly explain why there is a difference in the short-run and long-run supply curves for bottled water.

Idea that supply can adjust in response to situations over a period of time. In the short run there is at least one fixed factor of production and therefore the firm is restricted in its ability to change supply/ output levels. In the long run all inputs can be varied, therefore the firms can be more adaptable and more efficient in the production of bottled water.

c Complete the table using the following phrases and ideas; momentary time period, able to alter all factors, the firm has at least one fixed factor, long-run, short-run, a firm is unable to alter any factors, A, B and C.

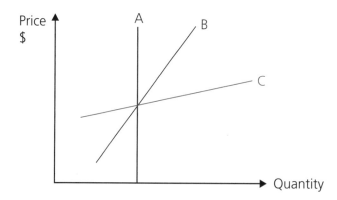

Supply elasticity	Curve	Features	Time period
Es > 1	C	able to alter all factors	long-run
Es < 1	B	the firm has at least one fixed factor	short-run
Es = 0	A	a firm is unable to alter any factors	momentary time period

3 **a** Below are the correct supply curves in the short-run and long-run time periods. Use these graphs and your own knowledge to complete the sentences that follow.

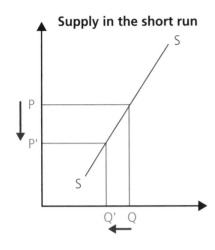

Supply in the short run

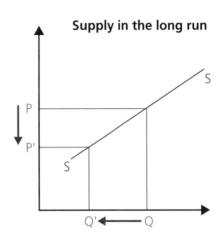

Supply in the long run

(i) Supply in the short run is relatively <u>inelastic</u> and in the long run relatively <u>elastic</u>.

(ii) 'In response to a price <u>decrease</u> the output will fall by more in the <u>long</u> run than it does in the <u>short</u> run.'

(iii) In the short run supply is relatively <u>unresponsive/inelastic</u> and in the long run more <u>responsive/elastic</u>.

(iv) Supply on a given day is <u>perfectly</u> <u>inelastic</u> and the curve is drawn as a <u>vertical</u> line.

(v) When a given price change causes a more than proportionate change in quantity supplied this indicates <u>elastic supply</u>. The short-run supply curve is relatively <u>inelastic</u>.

(vi) Inelastic supply occurs when a given change <u>in price causes a less than proportionate change</u> <u>in quantity supplied</u>. The long-run supply is relatively <u>elastic</u>.

b Calculate price elasticity of supply for each question below (show your working). Use the midpoint method.

(i)

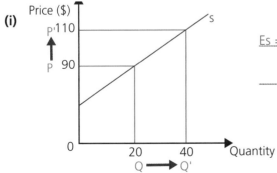

$$Es = \frac{\left(\frac{20}{30}\right)}{\left(\frac{20}{100}\right)} = 3.33 \text{ elastic}$$

(ii)

Price ($)	Quantity supplied
1.00	30
1.50	34

$$Es = \frac{\left(\frac{+4}{32}\right)}{\left(\frac{+.50}{1.25}\right)} = 0.31 \text{ inelastic}$$

4 Supply over time

Supply is inelastic, or relatively unresponsive to price changes in the short run, and elastic, or relatively responsive, in the long run.

Explain supply over time. In your answer you should use diagrams and:

- Explain the momentary time period.
- Explain the short-run time period.
- Explain the long-run time period.

Momentary supply is supply at this moment in time and is sometimes referred to as supply on a given day when quantity supplied is fixed regardless of price.

This is illustrated by the perfectly inelastic supply curve shown, drawn as a vertical line.

The curve reflects that firms have only a fixed amount of stock on hand available to meet demand and are unable to alter any factors, for example tickets to a school social, or the lots available for sale at an auction.

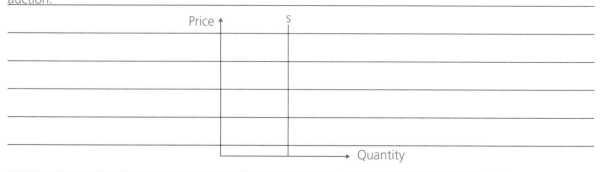

In the short-run time period, at least one input is fixed. The firm is restricted in its ability to change output.

In the short run the supply of all goods is inelastic because the quantity supplied is limited to the quantity of finished goods on hand or easily available. Supply elasticity is said to be lower.

In the long run firms have time to expand their use of all factors and so increase their total output capacity. Shortages and profits will attract more firms to the industry, which will increase total market supply. Over time, supply will be more responsive to price (elastic) as existing producers are able to increase production levels, new producers can enter the market, and improvements in technology increase productivity. Elasticity is then said to be higher.

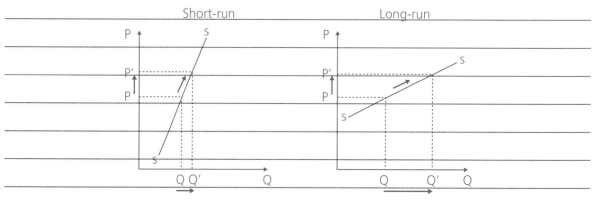

In response to a price change output will change by more in the long-run than short-run time period, as shown in the two diagrams.

5 Alfred Marshall developed the economic theory that price elasticity of supply for a good or service is linked to time periods.

Graph 1: The market supply of fish

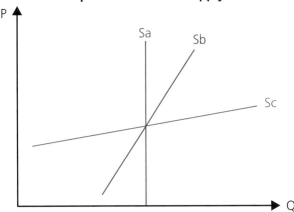

Explain price elasticity of supply. In your answer you should:

- Define price elasticity of supply and explain the difference between inelastic and elastic supply.
- Assume that fish prices have increased. With reference to Graph 1, explain which of the three supply curves for fish is most appropriate for a period of one year. Justify your answer.

Price elasticity of supply measures the responsiveness of quantity supplied of a good or service to a change in its price.

When price elasticity of supply is less than one this means that a given change in price causes a less than proportionate change in quantity supplied and indicates inelastic supply.

When price elasticity of supply is greater than one this means that a given change in price causes a more than proportionate change in quantity supplied and indicates elastic supply.

The most appropriate supply curve for a year is Sb (or Sc).

Sb – idea that there is some ability to increase supply of fish in one year/some inputs are variable, others are fixed. Sc – idea that in the longer run all inputs are variable.

4 MICRO-ECONOMIC CONCEPTS
Diminishing returns and supply

Inputs in the production process

Resources (or factors of production) are the economic inputs used by producers in the production process. Resources can be classified as natural resources, capital goods, human resources and entrepreneurship. Depending on the business some factor inputs are unable to be changed in the short run and are considered to be fixed, other factor resources or inputs are able to be used in greater quantities, these would be considered to be variable inputs in the production process. However, in the **short run** every firm will have **at least one fixed factor**. This could be skilled workers (human resources) or the land (natural resources) used in the production process. For firms involved in manufacturing, the fixed input in the production process is most likely to be the building (factory, office or premises) from which the firm operates. It could also be other capital resources such as equipment, machinery or vehicles. The variable input that may be easier for some firms to change in the short run could be the ability to hire or employ additional workers or the ability to use more raw materials or power. In the **long-run** firms **can change all inputs** (the factors of production) and the firm can be more adaptable and change the size of its operations.

Diminishing returns

The law of **diminishing returns** refers to the idea that as more and more of a factor (input) is used, with at least one fixed factor, there is some point at which the increase in output will be at a decreasing rate.

Diminishing returns occurs in the **short run** when there is **at least one fixed input** and the **increase in a firms output is at a decreasing rate**. In the table, we assume that workers are the only variable factor in the production process. The first worker adds 10 units to total output, the second worker adds 20 units to total output and the third worker adds 10 units to total output. Diminishing returns set in after the second worker (with the employment of the third worker). The additions to output (marginal output) increased between the first and second workers, thereafter the additional output falls as diminishing returns set in.

Firms will experience diminishing returns in the short run because, in the short run, at least one factor input is fixed. If additional quantities of other (variable) factors are added into the production process, the total output will increase at a diminishing rate (marginal product must eventually fall). This is because each factor has less of the fixed factor to work with, reducing its ability to produce (extra) output.

Workers	Total output	Marginal output
1	10	10
2	30	20
3	40	10
4	46	6
5	48	2
6	46	-2

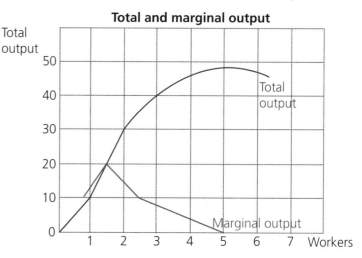

Diminishing returns will cause a firm's marginal costs to increase because as each additional variable unit produces less when diminishing returns are occurring, **the production of extra units of output will require more and more of variable inputs to produce them** (compared with earlier units). Therefore, it follows that the cost of each additional unit produced (i.e., MC) must increase because more inputs are being used to produce it. So, marginal cost must rise as output increases.

       ISBN: 9780170438100

Increasing returns to a factor reflect that a firm's short-run average costs would be falling. The increased input of a factor results in increasing additions to output, or a decreased input results in a smaller decrease in output. If a firm decreases an input by 5% but output falls by only 4%, the addition to outputs is actually increasing. The production process must be more efficient than before and costs must be falling (in the short run).

Decreasing returns to a factor (or diminishing returns) reflect that the increase of one input results in decreasing additions to output. The firm increases an input by 5% but output rises by only 3%. Similarly a decrease in an input would result in a larger decrease in output. An input falls by 10% and output decreases by 12%. Both these examples show that the production process has become inefficient. The short-run average costs (SAC) will eventually rise.

Break-even and shut-down points for a firm

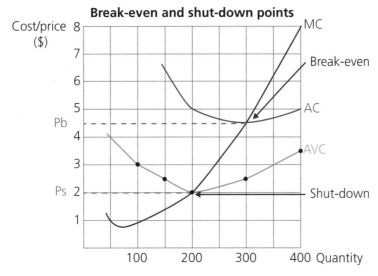

Break-even is the **price** at which **revenue covers all economic costs**. On the graph the value of break-even is shown as the value of Pb ($4.5). The two cost curves equal to the price at the break-even point are the marginal cost curve and average cost curve (MC and AC).

Between Pb and Ps a firm is operating below its break-even point and above its shut-down point. It has a price which covers all its average variable costs (AVC) and is paying some of its fixed costs. It should continue producing in the short run because if it shuts-down it still must pay fixed costs.

Shut-down is the **price** where **revenue just covers variable costs**. Shut-down is shown as the value Ps on the graph ($2). The shut-down point is at a level where price is just equal to average variable costs (AVC). At this point the firm is indifferent to whether it continues to produce or shuts-down. The two cost curves equal to the price at the shut-down point are the marginal cost curve and average variable cost curve (MC and AVC).

Firms will shut down if the price falls below the minimum average variable cost (AVC). At any price below its minimum average variable cost, a firm is not covering its variable costs or making any contribution to fixed costs. Therefore, a firm is better off by shutting down and ceasing operations. It will no longer use variable inputs (raw materials, power) and therefore no longer have to pay any variable costs but will still have to pay fixed costs from some other source.

Fixed costs (FC) are independent of output, they must be paid whether or not the firm is producing, e.g., rent, mortgage repayments, rates. These are costs that a firm cannot avoid and must pay because they involve contractual arrangements with other parties, even if the firm has closed down (ceased producing). **Variable costs (VC)** represent costs directly related to production and if there is no production, variable costs are zero, for example, power, raw materials, postage, wages. As a firm starts producing a firm will begin to incur and pay variable costs.

Deriving the supply curve from the marginal cost curve

Supply is the amount of a good/service producer's offer for sale at each price (ceteris paribus). **Marginal cost** is the addition to total cost resulting from the production of an extra unit of output. A firm will only offer a good/service for sale if the price they receive covers the cost of producing it (i.e., the marginal cost).

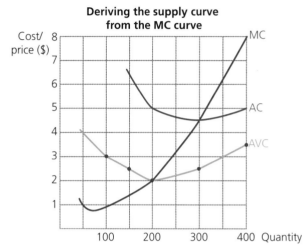

Deriving the supply curve from the MC curve

A firm's supply schedule from the MC curve	
Price	**Quantity supplied**
1.00	0 (zero)
2.00	200
4.50	300
8.00	400

At $8 the quantity supplied is 400 and at $3 the quantity supplied is 240 because the marginal cost curve (MC) above AVC or shut-down is a firm's supply curve. At $1 the quantity supplied is zero (0) because the price is below the shut-down point and the firm has ceased operating and is not producing.

The firm's **short-run supply curve** is derived from the marginal cost curve and starts from the minimum of the average variable cost curve. A firm's short-run supply curve is that part or portion of the **marginal cost curve above AVC (or shut-down)**.

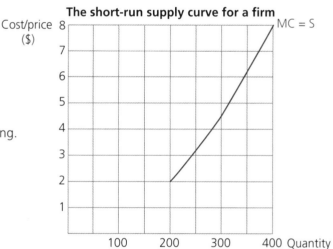

The short-run supply curve for a firm

Since a firm's supply curve is the marginal cost curve, it will shift to the right (outward) if costs decrease or shift to the left (inward) if costs increase.

Student notes: Diminishing returns and supply

Diminishing returns will occur in the short run when there is at least one fixed input; the additions to output at some stage start to decrease.

Firms experience diminishing returns in the short run because in the short run, at least one factor input is fixed. If additional quantities of other (variable) factors are added into the production process, the total output will increase at a diminishing rate (marginal product must eventually fall). This is because each factor has less of the fixed factor to work with, reducing its ability to produce (extra) output.

ISBN: 9780170438100

Diminishing returns cause a firm's marginal costs to increase because as each additional variable unit produces less when diminishing returns are occurring, the production of extra units of output will require more and more variable inputs to produce them (compared with earlier units). Therefore, it follows that the cost of each additional unit produced (i.e., MC) must increase because more inputs are being used to produce it. So, marginal cost must rise as output increases. A firm will only supply a product if it covers the marginal costs of producing it. As MC increase as output increases, firms will require a higher price to increase the quantity supplied of a product.

Increasing returns to a factor mean that a firm's short-run average costs are falling (efficient output-to-input change). This means that an increase in input causes a larger increase in output; or that a decrease in input causes a smaller decrease in output. Initially, increasing returns to a factor cause MC to fall.

Break-even point is at a price at which revenue covers all economic costs. The two cost curves equal to the price at the break-even point are MC and AC.

Shutdown point is at a price at which revenue only just covers variable costs. The two cost curves equal to the price at the shutdown point are MC and AVC.

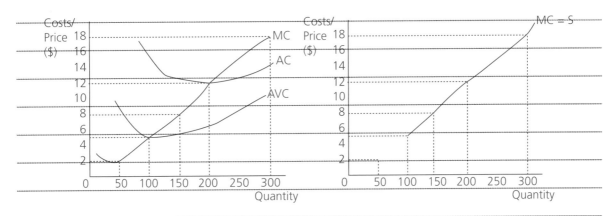

A firm's supply curve is that part of MC above AVC (or shutdown). The firm's supply curve starts from the minimum of the AVC (shutdown) so below this position quantity supplied is zero.

| Supply schedule for a firm using MC curve ||
Price ($)	Quantity supplied
2	0
8	150
12	200
18	300

QUESTIONS & TASKS

1 a Explain why firms experience diminishing returns in the short run.

<u>In the short run, at least one factor input is fixed. If additional quantities of other (variable) factors are</u>

<u>added into the production process, the total output will increase at a diminishing rate (marginal product</u>

<u>must eventually fall). This is because each factor has less of the fixed factor to work with, reducing its</u>

<u>ability to produce (extra) output.</u>

b Explain why diminishing returns cause a firm's marginal costs to increase.

<u>Since each additional variable unit produces less when diminishing returns are occurring, the production</u>

<u>of extra units of output will require more and more of variable inputs to produce them (compared with</u>

<u>earlier units). Therefore, it follows that the cost of each additional unit produced (i.e., MC) must increase</u>

<u>because more inputs are being used to produce it. So, marginal cost must rise as output increases.</u>

c For each table indicate when diminishing returns sets in **(i)** after the … **(ii)** with the ….

Output	10	100	250	450	550
Machines	1	2	3	4	5

(i) after the <u>fourth machine</u> **(ii)** with the <u>fifth machine</u>

Output	20	50	90	150	**250**	**260**	265
Workers	1	2	3	4	**5**	**6**	7

(i) after the <u>fifth worker</u> **(ii)** with the <u>sixth worker</u>

Machine	Output
1	50
2	150
3	160
4	165
5	167

(i) after the <u>second machine</u> **(ii)** with the <u>third machine</u>

d Why does the marginal cost curve initially fall and then rise?

<u>Initially increasing returns and the more efficient use of resources leads to falling MC but eventually, in</u>

<u>the short run, diminishing returns will occur causing MC to increase.</u>

    ISBN: 9780170438100

Output	200	300	400	500	600
Marginal costs	30	25	60	78	100

2 Explain the relationship between ouput and marginal costs. In your answer you should:
- Draw a sketch diagram of a marginal cost curve and explain its shape.
- Explain why diminishing returns cause a firm's marginal costs to increase.
- Describe the relationship between marginal cost and the quantity supplied of a product by a firm.

The marginal cost curve will initially fall and then rise because initially increasing returns to a factor and the more efficient use of resources leads to falling MC but in the short run eventually diminishing returns will occur causing MC to increase.

MC

Because each additional variable unit produces less when diminishing returns are occurring, the production of extra units of output will require more and more variable inputs to produce them (compared with earlier units). Therefore, it follows that the cost of each additional unit produced (i.e., MC) must increase because more inputs are being used to produce it. So, marginal cost must rise as output increases.

A firm will only supply a product if it covers the marginal costs of producing it. Because MC increase as output increases firms will require a higher price to increase the quantity supplied of a product.

3 Use the diagram to answer the questions below.

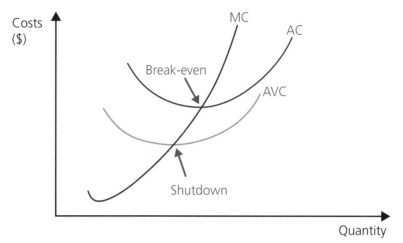

a Label the curves and identify and label the break-even and shutdown points.

(i) What is the vertical distance between AC and AVC equal to? <u>AFC</u>

(ii) Is this gap a constant? <u>No</u>

(iii) When the firm is not producing it must still pay what types of costs? <u>FC</u>

(iv) What costs are directly related to production? <u>VC</u>

(v) If the firm is not producing, what is the value of these costs? <u>zero</u>

b Write fixed costs or variable costs for the following terms.

Rent <u>fixed</u>   Wages <u>variable</u>

Raw materials <u>variable</u>   Debt servicing <u>fixed</u>

Interest <u>fixed</u>

c What is debt servicing?

<u>Interest payments and repayments of principal on loans.</u>

d Define the following terms.

Break-even: <u>A price at which revenue covers all economic costs.</u>

Shutdown: <u>A price at which revenue only just covers variable costs.</u>

e Complete this statement.

If a firm ceases its operation it must still pay <u>fixed</u> costs. If market price is above the level of average variable cost, it can cover its <u>variable</u> costs and still have something left over to pay its fixed costs, it may as well <u>continue</u> operating. If price falls below AVC, there is nothing left over to contribute to <u>fixed</u> costs and variable costs are not fully covered, then the firm should <u>shut down</u>

4 a Write if the following statements are correct or incorrect.

(i) A firm's supply curve is equal to its AC curve.   _____ incorrect

(ii) A firm's supply curve is equal to its MC curve above AVC.   _____ correct

(iii) When revenue covers all economic costs it is at shutdown.   _____ incorrect

(iv) Break-even is when revenue covers variable costs only.   _____ incorrect

(v) At any revenue below shutdown, the firm will save paying variable costs

by not operating but will still have to pay fixed costs.   _____ correct

(vi) Break-even is when revenue covers all economic costs.   _____ correct

b Label the curves on the diagram and clearly label the break-even point (label B) and the shutdown point (label SD).

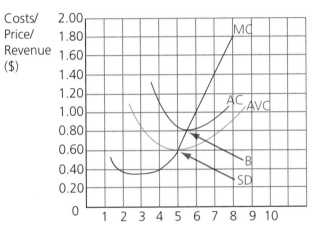

c Give the value of: **(i)** Shutdown $0.60_____   **(ii)** Break-even $0.80_____.

d What cost concept is represented by the vertical gap between AVC and AC? _AFC_____

e Why does this gap narrow as output rises?

AFC declines with increasing output because the FC are spread over a greater number of units of output. Therefore because ATC = AFC + AVC, a higher proportion of TC will be made up of VC as output rises so the gap narrows.

_____

_____

_____

f Which two cost curves are equal to the price at:

(i) shutdown point? MC and AVC_____   **(ii)** break-even point? MC and AC_____.

g Explain why the firm can continue producing in the short run at $0.70.

Firm has a price which covers AVC and makes some contribution towards FC._____

_____

_____

_____

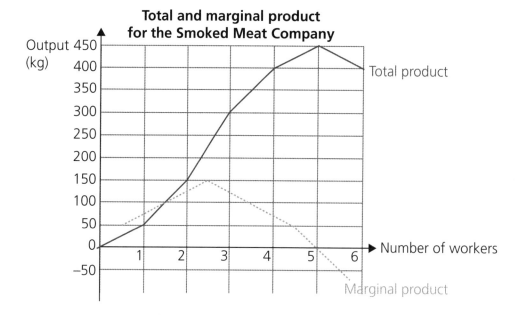

Total and marginal product for the Smoked Meat Company

5 Explain the relationship between diminishing returns and a firm's marginal costs.
In your answer you should
- State when diminishing returns set in, after/with.
- Explain why firms experience diminishing returns in the short run.
- Explain why diminishing returns cause a firm's marginal costs to increase.

Diminishing returns set in after the employment of the third worker (with the fourth worker).

In the short run, at least one factor input is fixed. If additional quantities of other (variable) factors are added into the production process, the total output will increase at a diminishing rate (marginal product must eventually fall). This is because each factor has less of the fixed factor to work with, reducing its ability to produce (extra) output.

Because each additional variable unit produces less when diminishing returns are occurring, the production of extra units of output will require more and more variable inputs to produce them (compared with earlier units). Therefore, it follows that the cost of each additional unit produced (i.e., MC) must increase because more inputs are being used to produce it. So, marginal cost must rise as output increases.

6 The average variable cost curve is important in determining the short-run supply curve for the perfectly competitive producer.

Explain the relationship between a firm's average variable cost curve and its supply curve. In your answer you should:

- Label the curves in Graph one and complete the supply schedule next to it.
- Label the shutdown point (label S) and break-even point (label B) on Graph one.
- Define the terms break-even and shutdown and indicate which two cost curves are equal to the price at each point.
- Explain how a firm's supply curve is derived from MC

Graph one

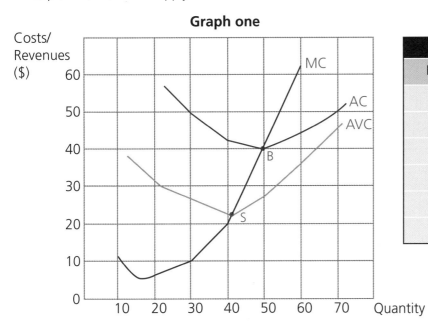

Supply schedule	
Price ($)	**Quantity**
10	0
20	0
30	45
40	50
50	55
60	58

Break-even is a price at which revenue covers all economic costs. The two cost curves equal to the price at the break-even point are MC and AC.

Shutdown is a price at which revenue only just covers variable costs. The two cost curves equal to the price at the shutdown point are MC and AVC.

The short-run supply curve for the perfect competitor is the MC curve above the minimum AVC curve. At any price less than the minimum of the AVC curve the firm will shut down in the short run.

MICRO-ECONOMIC CONCEPTS
Role of prices:
Market equilibrium

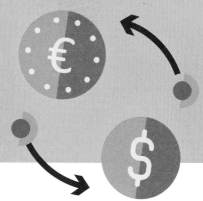

Establishing market equilibrium

Market for pizza weekly				
Price $	Quantity demanded	Quantity supplied	Market situation	Pressure on price
14	0	12000	Surplus 12000	Downward
12	2000	10000	Surplus 8000	Downward
10	4000	8000	Surplus 4000	Downward
8	6000	6000	Equilibrium	None/Stable
6	8000	4000	Shortage 4000	Upward
4	10000	2000	Shortage 8000	Upward
2	12000	0	Shortage 12000	Upward

Equilibrium is a term to denote a balance between forces involved. The **equilibrium price and equilibrium quantity** in a market is determined by the interaction of the forces of demand and supply. Equilibrium in a market is the price at which the quantity demanded by consumers equals the quantity supplied by producers. At the equilibrium, both parties involved in the market are completely satisfied, with consumers having purchased all they want to buy, and producers having sold all they want to sell.

At the market equilibrium the **market will clear** and there will be neither a surplus (excess supply) or a shortage (excess demand). Therefore, all stock is sold (i.e., no stock is unsold) and consumers do not want to buy any more of the good or service. As long as the conditions of demand and conditions of supply remain unchanged (ceteris paribus) then the equilibrium price and equilibrium quantity will remain unchanged.

On a schedule the equilibrium can be found where the quantity demanded by consumers and the quantity supplied by producers are equal at one particular price.

On the diagram, the equilibrium price for pizza is $8 (Pe) and the equilibrium

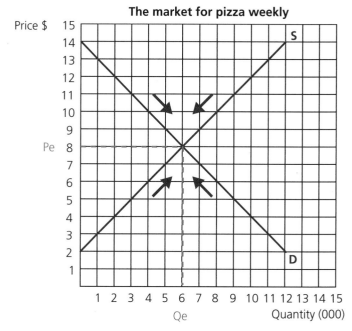

quantity for pizza is 6 000 (Qe) because this is where the demand curve and the supply curve intersect, with the quantity demanded by consumers equal to the quantity supplied by firms.

Shortage (excess demand)

A **shortage (excess demand)** will occur at any price below the equilibrium where the quantity supplied by producers is less than the quantity demanded by consumers. When there is a shortage the market will react with consumers bidding up the price. As the price of a good or service increases quantity supplied increases because selling the good or providing that service becomes relatively more profitable for firms because the revenue (income) they earn is higher and firms will be more able to cover costs. As the price of a good or service increases consumers' real incomes fall and the good or service becomes relatively less affordable, consumers will be less willing and able to purchase the good or service with their limited incomes and look to buy more of a relatively cheaper substitute.

A shortage of 8 000 will occur at $4 (P1) because at this price the quantity supplied by producers (Qs, 2 000) is less than the quantity demanded by consumers (Qd, 10 000). As price increases the quantity demanded by consumers decreases from 10 000 (Qd) to 6 000 (Qe), while the quantity supplied by producers increases from 2 000 (Qs) to 6 000 (Qe). Equilibrium is restored at $8 (Pe) where quantity supplied equals quantity demanded of 6 000 (Qe) and the market clears.

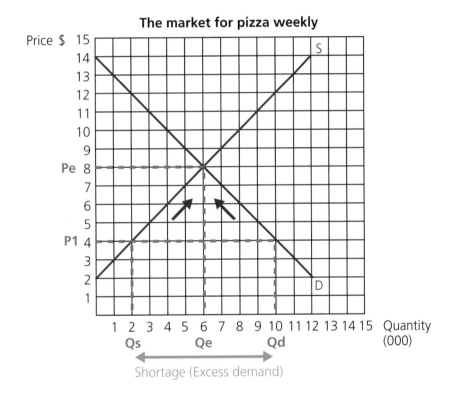

At any price below the equilibrium the quantity sold in the market equals the quantity supplied by producers. There is no unsold stock at any price below the equilibrium.

Surplus (excess supply)

A **surplus (excess supply)** will occur at any price above the equilibrium where the quantity supplied by producers is greater than the quantity demanded by consumers. When there is a surplus the market will react with firms willing to accept a lower price to get rid of unsold stock. As the price of a good or service decreases quantity supplied decreases because selling the good or providing that service becomes relatively less profitable for firms because the revenue (income) they earn is lower and firms will be less able to cover costs. As the price of a good or service decreases consumers' real incomes rise and the good or service becomes relatively more affordable, consumers will be more willing and able to purchase the good or service with their limited incomes and look to buy less of a relatively more expensive substitute.

A surplus of 4 000 will occur at $10 (P2) because at this price the quantity supplied by producers (Qs, 8 000) is greater than the quantity demanded by consumers (Qd, 4 000). As the price decreases the quantity demanded by consumers increases from 4 000 (Qd) to 6000 (Qe), while the quantity supplied by producers decreases from 8 000 (Qs) to 6 000 (Qs). Equilibrium is restored at $8 (Pe) where quantity supplied equals quantity demanded of 6 000 (Qe) and the market clears.

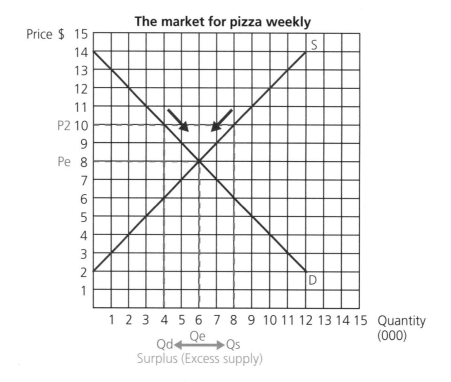

At any price above the equilibrium the quantity sold in the market equals the quantity demanded by consumers. The quantity of the stock unsold in the market equals the size of the surplus.

Shortage (excess demand) and shifts of the demand and/or supply curves

A shortage (excess demand) will occur where the quantity supplied by producers is less than the quantity demanded by consumers. When the condition of ceteris paribus is relaxed and there is either an increase in demand (an outward shift of the demand curve) and/or a decrease in supply (an inward shift of the supply curve), this will create a shortage (excess demand) at the original price.

The market will react to a shortage with consumers bidding up the price. Price rises, until equilibrium price and quantity is reached and the market clears.

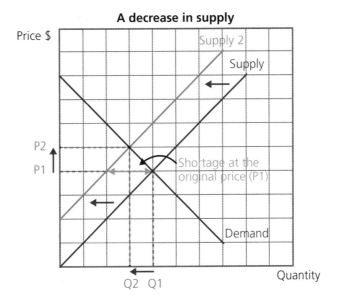

A decrease in supply

Surplus (excess supply) and shifts of the demand and/or supply curve

A surplus (excess supply) will occur where the quantity supplied by producers is greater than the quantity demanded by consumers.

When the condition of ceteris paribus is relaxed and there is either a decrease in demand (an inward shift of the demand curve) and/or an increase in supply (an outward shift of the supply curve), this will create a surplus (excess supply) at the original price.

When there is a surplus, firms will accept a lower price to get rid of unsold stock. The price falls, until the equilibrium price and quantity is reached and the market clears.

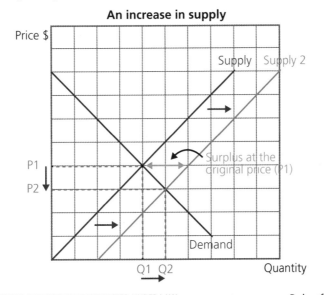

An increase in supply

Student notes: Role of prices: market equilibrium

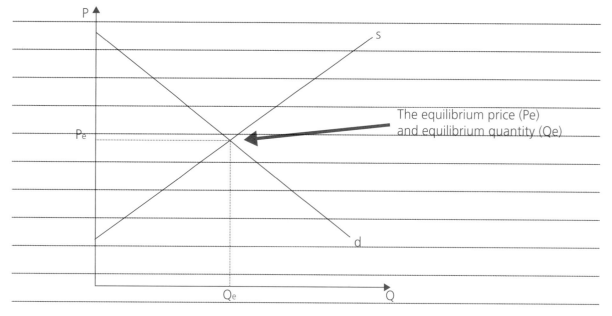

The equilibrium price (Pe) and equilibrium quantity (Qe)

• The equilibrium is the price at which quantity demanded by consumers equals the quantity supplied by producers. At the equilibrium the market will clear and there will be neither a surplus or shortage, all stock is sold (i.e., no stock is unsold).

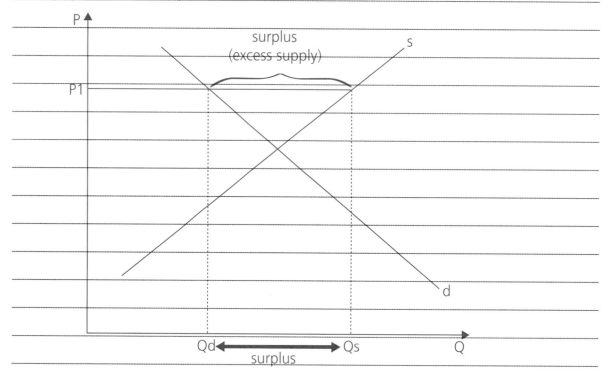

• A surplus (excess supply) will occur at any price above the equilibrium where the quantity supplied by producers is greater than the quantity demanded by consumers.

• At P1 the market will react to a surplus with the producers (firms) accepting a lower price to get rid of unsold stock.

As price falls quantity supplied decreases and quantity demanded increases until equilibrium is restored.

       ISBN: 9780170438100

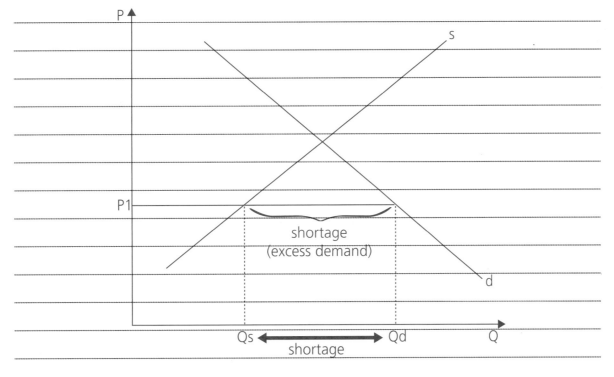

- A shortage (excess demand) will occur at any price below the equilibrium where the quantity supplied by producers is less than the quantity demanded by consumers.

- At P1 the market will react to a shortage with consumers bidding up price. As price increases the quantity supplied increases and quantity demanded decreases until equilibrium is restored.

- When ceteris paribus is broken and the conditions of demand or supply change then there will be a new equilibrium price and equilibrium quantity as one or both curves (demand and/or supply) shift.

- To illustrate a change in the market due to a shift of a curve, these conventions are followed:

  – The new demand and/or supply curves are drawn parallel to the original curves, with appropriate labels for the new curves including direction arrows.

  – The new equilibrium price is labelled p' and the new equilibrium quantity is labelled q'. Direction arrows are used to show the increase or decrease in price and/or quantity that result in the market.

- An increase in supply or a decrease in demand will cause a surplus at the original equilibrium price. The market will react with the price falling.

- A decrease in supply or an increase in demand will cause a shortage at the original equilibrium price. The market will react with the price increasing.

QUESTIONS & TASKS

1 At a price of $6.00, the market supply of DVD movies each week is 250. As the price falls to $5.00 the quantity supplied falls by 20%. If the price is $2.00 the supply is 100 and 120 at $3.00.

a Draw the market for DVD movie rentals each week from the information provided.

Price ($)	Market demand
6.00	100
5.00	120
3.00	200
2.00	250

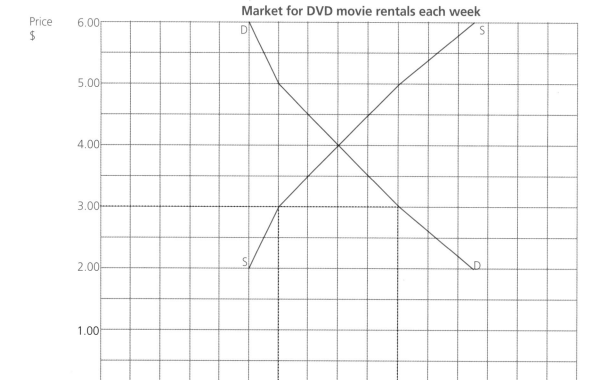

b Identify the equilibrium price and quantity.   price = $4.00_____   quantity = 160_____

c **(i)** On your graph, show the market situation if the price of a DVD movie rental was $3.00. Fully label the graph and explain why the price of a DVD is likely to rise in this situation.

At $3 there is a shortage and the price will rise because consumers will bid up the price to obtain

DVD movies._____

(ii) Explain fully how the equilibrium quantity is restored when the price increases. Use the terms 'quantity supplied' and 'quantity demanded' in your answer.

Price increases from $3.00 to $4.00. Quantity demanded decreases from 200 to 160, quantity

supplied increases from 120 to 160 until Qd = Qs or equilibrium._____

44   Role of prices: Market equilibrium   PHOTOCOPYING OF THIS PAGE IS RESTRICTED UNDER LAW.   ISBN: 9780170438100

2 Study the graph and answer the questions that follow.

a Work out the missing quantity supplied and write them in the space provided.

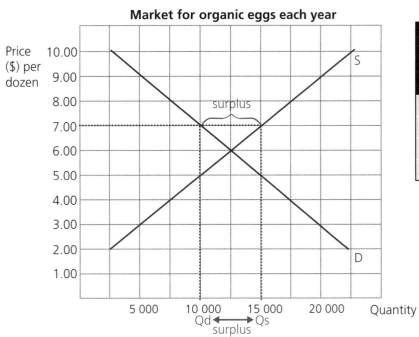

Market for organic eggs each year

Price $ per dozen	Fresh eggs quantity supplied	Natures Ways quantity supplied
2.00	1 000	1 500
4.00	3 250	4 250
8.00	6 500	11 000
9.00	8 000	12 000

b What is the equilibrium price and quantity?

Price <u>$6.00 per dozen</u>   Quantity <u>12 500</u>

c Identify the price where a surplus of 5 000 will occur. Also identify at this price the quantity demanded and the quantity supplied.

Price <u>$7.00 per dozen</u>   Quantity demanded <u>10 000</u>   Quantity supplied <u>15 000</u>

d How will the market react to a surplus of 5 000?

<u>Producers will be willing to accept a lower price to get rid of unsold stock. Price falls from $7.00 to</u>

<u>$6.00 per dozen to the equilibrium and quantity demanded increases from 10 000 to 12 500 and</u>

<u>quantity supplied decreases from 15 000 to 12 500.</u>

e Explain how the quantities for a market supply curve are derived.

<u>Horizontal summation of all firms' supply curves/schedules at each price.</u>

f Explain why firms supply more as the price increases.

<u>Costs increase so higher price needed/higher profits or revenue increased resource scarcity so higher</u>

<u>price needed (not more money).</u>

3 **a** Draw the change indicated by the TITLE of each graph and label each diagram fully. Label the original price and quantity as P and Q respectively. Label the new price and quantity as P' and Q' respectively.

(i) **A decrease in supply**

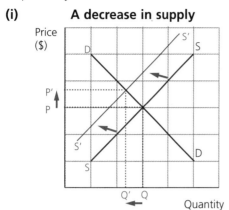

(ii) **An increase in supply**

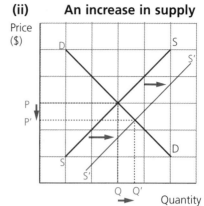

(iii) **An increase in demand**

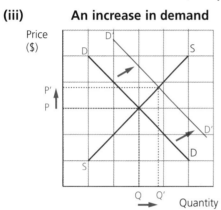

(iv) **A decrease in demand**

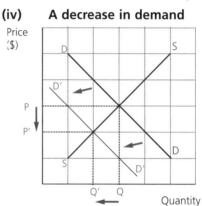

b Write 'demand' or 'supply' for each idea below depending on what condition each statement represents. The first one is done for you.

(i)	income is a condition of	demand	**(ix)**	price of a substitute is a condition of	demand
(ii)	sales tax is a condition of	supply	**(x)**	price of a complement is a condition of	demand
(iii)	subsidy is a condition of	supply	**(xi)**	GST is a condition of	supply
(iv)	tariff is a condition of	supply	**(xii)**	indirect tax is a condition of	supply
(v)	advertising is a condition of	demand	**(xiii)**	direct tax is a condition of	demand
(vi)	cost of raw materials is a condition of	supply	**(xiv)**	productivity is a condition of	supply
(vii)	technology is a condition of	supply	**(xv)**	flood, strike, disease is a condition of	supply
(viii)	fashion/taste is a condition of	demand	**(xvi)**	price of a related good is a condition of	supply

c Complete the table.

Situation	Causes
(i) Shift of demand curve to the right	↑ income/change in tastes in favour of product/ ↓ price complement/ ↑ price substitute/ ↑ advertising of product ↓ direct tax
(ii) Shift of supply curve to the right	↓ costs of production/new improved technology/ ↑ productivity/ ↓ price related good/subsidy/change of goals ↑ S/ ↓ indirect tax/good growing season/trade restrictions ↓

4 a Students are encouraged to bring their own laptops, smartphones or tablets to use in schools. Show the change this has had on the market for smartphones. Label the new equilibrium price and quantity as P1 and Q1 respectively.

New Zealand market for smartphones

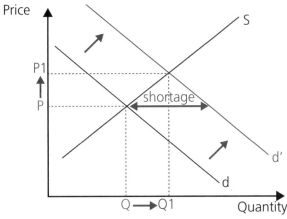

b (i) State the situation that would exist in the market if the price remained at the original equilibrium P.

Shortage or excess demand

(ii) Explain the market forces that result in the new equilibrium price and quantity, at P1 and Q1.

The increase in demand creates excess demand or a shortage at the original equilibrium P. Consumers will bid prices up to price P1. The increase in price to P1 causes an increase in quantity supplied to Q1. Equilibrium is restored at P1 because quantity demanded equals quantity supplied.

c (i) There has been a decrease in the cost of coal extraction. Use the sketch graph below to show the effect of this decrease on the market for coal.

Market for coal

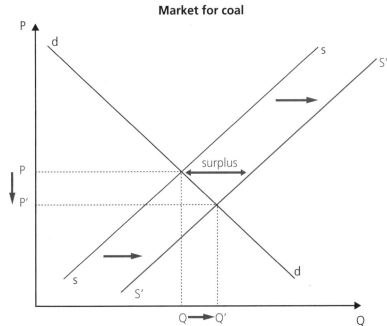

(ii) Explain how equilibrium is restored after the change.

The increase in supply creates a surplus at the current price (P). Producers are willing to accept a lower price to get rid of unsold stock. Price falls to the new equilibrium. Quantity supplied falls and quantity demanded rises and the equilibrium is restored at P' Q'.

> The health benefits of eating apples has just been published in a medical journal, they contain a range of vitamins.

5 **a** On the graph below, show the impact that is likely to result from the resource material above. Use dotted lines to show the new price and quantity. Fully label the changes.

Market for apples monthly

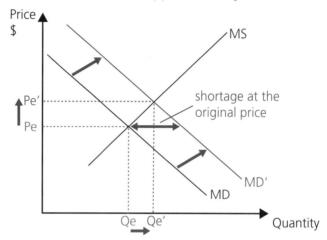

b Discuss how this information affects market demand. In your answer you should explain how market demand is determined and explain the effects this report will have on market demand.

Market demand is the horizontal sum of all individual demand curves and/or schedules at each price. In this case, it is those individuals who eat apples at each price. With the report that there are health benefits associated with eating apples it is likely that consumers will buy more apples at each and every price, causing the market demand curve to shift outward (to the right) as indicated by the change from MD to MD'.

c Discuss the effect this change will have on the market for apples monthly. In your answer you should:
- explain the effect on apple consumers
- explain the effect on apple producers.

As the market demand curve shifts outward (to the right) this will cause a shortage at the current price Pe and the equilibrium price will rise (to Pe'). Consumers are consuming more apples at each and every price as indicated by the shift of the market demand curve from MD to MD'.

As the equilibrium price rises, apple growers are more able to cover costs and earn higher revenues and the quantity supplied of apples increases because it is more profitable. Apple growers will switch more resources into producing apples.

Sunrise and sunset industries

A firm is a single business while an industry is the sum of all firms which produce one type of product. The dairy industry in New Zealand includes all those firms involved in producing dairy products for sale from the farmers who milk cows, firms who process the milk into final or intermediate products, and firms who market the final product.

If prices for dairy products in world markets rise, the industry as a whole will prosper and grow. Dairy farmers will be encouraged to invest more in milk production. For example, farmers may purchase land, converting sheep farms to dairy production. This will involve the purchase of capital items such as milking sheds, tractors and equipment. Milk production will increase, farmers' incomes will rise and they may employ extra workers.

Factories processing milk and firms marketing the final product will also increase output and sales. Employment will rise and spending will increase beyond the dairy industry.

The hospitality and travel industry may well benefit as individuals with increased disposable incomes take holidays and travel. Regions whose economies are dependent on the dairy industry are likely to benefit the most from the expansion in economic activity.

As domestic and global economies go through the trade cycle of recession, recovery and boom, it is likely that the part of the trade cycle that the New Zealand economy is in will differ from a number of its trading partners. If there is a downturn in overseas demand, there are likely to be reduced incomes and possibly business closures for firms that rely heavily on export orders. Unemployment is likely to rise and living standards in the affected areas and communities will be lower.

The converse applies for a recovery and increase in overseas demand. While some industries may be experiencing a decline in activities it is possible that other industries are experiencing growth, e.g., while the car and shoe manufacturing industries have declined, other industries such as tourism, wine, education and dairying have grown in size and importance in the New Zealand economy.

The changing demand for a product in local or world markets may be temporary or permanent. Resources will switch from declining industries (**sunset**) into growth industries (**sunrise**) where prospects and profits are likely to be better.

There is always likely to be a change in the fortune of various industries within an economy at any given point in time. The change will mean some individuals losing jobs in some industries, while new opportunities arise in other industries, some firms' profits declining while others are growing, firms may close down or may go through a process of restructuring.

Student notes: Role of prices and profits

An increase in sales and revenue will encourage New Zealand firms to increase production as stock levels fall. To satisfy the increase in demand firms will need to hire additional workers or pay existing workers overtime. An increase in business confidence will mean that firms will invest in new capital. Resources may switch out of less profitable ventures/industries and into growth industries, for example, the growth of the dairy industry.

New Zealand firms import products because the price is lower than the New Zealand price. As New Zealand firms import goods and services, local (domestic) firms must match the world (overseas) price or lose sales. As the price falls, some domestic producers may be unable to cover the costs of production so decide to close down or produce another good or service. The fall in price will cause the quantity demanded in the local market to increase.

A firm's profit depends on earning revenue from sales while keeping costs as low as possible.

    ISBN: 9780170438100

QUESTIONS & TASKS

Government economic reform and changes in domestic and international demand patterns have transformed the New Zealand economy. Businesses have shifted from old 'sunset' industries to innovative 'sunrise' industries.

1 **a** Indicate if the following industries are 'sunset' or 'sunrise' industries.

(i) boat building	_____sunrise_____	**(ii)** organics	_____sunrise_____

(i) boat building _____sunrise_____   **(ii)** organics _____sunrise_____

(iii) car manufacturing _____sunset_____   **(iv)** wine _____sunrise_____

(v) education _____sunrise_____   **(vi)** tourism _____sunrise_____

(vii) film making _____sunrise_____   **(viii)** shoe manufacturing _____sunset_____

(ix) dairying _____sunrise_____   **(x)** wool and sheep _____sunset_____

b The difficulty with economic reform is the short-term losses, and long-run gains. Outline some possible short-term losses and long-run gains that were a result of reform policies that liberalised trade in New Zealand.

(i) Short-term losses: Idea of businesses making less profit or closing down, workers made redundant, unemployment and the lowering of living standards in the affected communities and areas.

(ii) Long-term gains: Idea of more efficient resource use, development of new industries and new employment opportunities as sunrise industries develop.

c Indicate if the following statements are facts or opinions. Justify your answers.

(i) A 'sunset' industry will always be a 'sunset' industry. _____opinion_____

Justification: While an industry may be in decline for a certain time period, demand domestically and internationally may change and cause a sunset industry to grow at a later date.

(ii) The growth and contraction of some New Zealand industries will depend on what goes on in the global economy. _____fact_____

Justification: New Zealand is part of a worldwide (global) economy with exports contributing 30% to New Zealand GDP. Recessions and booms in overseas economies and changes in international demand will therefore impact on many New Zealand industries. For some industries it will mean contraction while for others expansion.

2 The ski industry continues to grow as more tourists visit during the New Zealand winter.
Explain the impact of the ski industry on the New Zealand economy. In your answer you should:
- Explain the effect of increased tourist numbers on the ski industry in New Zealand.
- Explain the effect on prices and profit.

As tourist numbers increase during the ski season, ski operaters' revenue and profits will increase because of the higher turnover due to the increased demand. Ski operators may have to hire additional staff and train them, or pay existing staff overtime to satisfy the extra demand from increased numbers of tourists. Ski operators may extend the ski season, open up new ski areas or invest in new snow machines, etc. As ski operators become more confident about the future they may borrow funds to invest in plant and machinery to increase profit, because they have higher expectations about the returns and profits they will make.

Increased tourist numbers will cause demand for ski industry goods and services to increase which will increase the price firms receive. Firms are receiving a higher price and the quantity sold has increased, higher revenues will be generated. If the revenue firms receive exceeds the cost to provide the additional services, profits will increase as a result. New firms will be attracted into the tourism industry seeking to earn profit.

3 Foreign fee-paying student numbers continue to decline as the recession continues and the dollar appreciates.

Explain, using the education industry, the effect on an industry when it is in decline. In your answer you should:

- Explain the effect on providers of education.
- Explain the flow-on effects to other industries, profits and resource use.

When the New Zealand dollar appreciates against other currencies the cost of an education in New Zealand for foreign students increases and is more expensive. Since New Zealand is less price competitive, fee-paying students look for a relatively cheaper option. As fewer students come to New Zealand, providers of education services in New Zealand will hire fewer teachers and support staff and put investment plans on hold. Some firms may find that they generate insufficient revenue and may have to close down or switch resources into producing something else that is more profitable.

Other industries will be affected, such as providers of accommodation, meals and essential services, e.g., health, because of the decrease in demand the profits of these firms are likely to fall as revenue decreases. Firms may decide to switch resources into other activities that are more profitable.

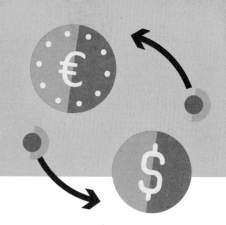

Consumer surplus (CS)

Consumer surplus (CS) is the difference between the maximum amount that a person is willing to pay for a good or service and its current market price. It represents the benefit consumers receive over and above what they actually pay (Pe) for a good or service. The earlier units purchased provide more satisfaction (utility) than the price paid.

On the diagram, consumer surplus is the shaded area because consumers only pay the market equilibrium price (Pe) for all purchases (of a hard copy book), therefore they enjoy a surplus in terms of what they would be willing to pay (demand) rather than go without on the earlier units. To calculate the value of consumer surplus, it is the value of the area above the equilibrium price paid (Pe) and below the demand curve, i.e. the shaded triangle on the diagram PeAP5. The area of a triangle equals a half (0.5) multiplied by the base multiplied by the height. In this instance the value of consumer surplus equals 0.5 multiplied by 3m books multiplied by $10 which equals $15m.

The value of consumer spending (or expenditure) equals the price paid (Pe) multiplied by the quantity purchased (Qe), $40 multiplied by 3m books which equals $120m. The value of total utility or satisfaction from the consumption of Qe units, is the area QeAP50 which equals $135m.

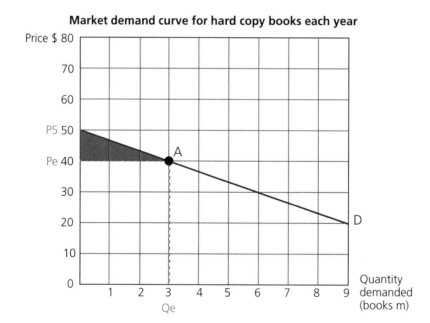

Market demand curve for hard copy books each year

If the market equilibrium price fell to $30 per book the new quantity demanded would increase to 6m books. The new value of consumer surplus would be 0.5 multiplied by 6m books multiplied by $20 which equals $60m, because this is the area above the new price paid and below the demand curve. The change in consumer surplus would be an increase of $45m because this is the difference between the value of the original consumer surplus ($15m) and the value of the new consumer surplus ($60m). In this instance, consumer surplus on the original quantity is greater because equilibrium price has fallen. Since the quantity consumed has increased there are more units on which the consumer derives a surplus.

ISBN: 9780170438100

Producer surplus (PS)

Producer surplus (PS) is the difference between the total earnings of suppliers for a certain quantity sold and the total costs required to put that quantity on the market. Producer surplus occurs in the market for a good or service because firms are willing to supply each unit for a lower price than they receive in the market.

On the diagram, producer surplus is the shaded area because while producers receive the market equilibrium price (Pe) for all units sold they are willing to supply each unit for a lower price than what they are paid. To calculate the value of the producer surplus, it is the value of the area below the price firms receive (Pe) and above the supply, i.e. the triangle PeAP1. The area of a triangle equals a half (0.5) multiplied by the base multiplied by the height. In this instance, the value of producer surplus equals 0.5 multiplied by 3m books multiplied by $30 which equals $45m.

The total revenue received by the producer for Qe units is the price they receive (Pe) multiplied by the quantity sold (Qe), $40 multiplied by 3m books equals $120m. The total cost to the producer to supply Qe units is the area below the supply curve P1AQeO, which is $75m.

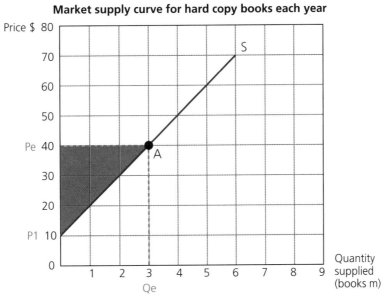

Market supply curve for hard copy books each year

If the market equilibrium price fell to $30 per book the new quantity supplied would decrease to 2m books. The new value of producer surplus would be 0.5 multiplied by 2m books multiplied by $20 which equals $20m, because this is the area below the new price received and above the supply curve. The change in producer surplus would be a decrease of $25m because this is the difference between the value of the original producer surplus ($45m) and the value of the new producer surplus ($20m).

Student notes: Consumer surplus/producer surplus

Consumer surplus (CS) represents the benefit consumers receive over and above what they actually pay for a good or service. The earlier units purchased provide more satisfaction (utility) than the price paid. To calculate the value of consumer surplus you need to work out the size of the area that is above the price paid and below the demand curve shown.

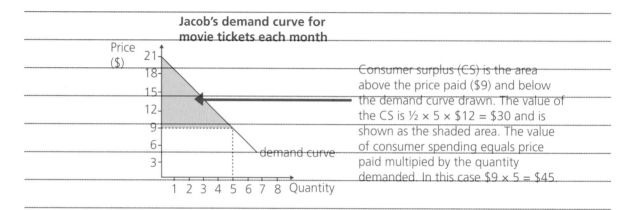

Jacob's demand curve for movie tickets each month

Consumer surplus (CS) is the area above the price paid ($9) and below the demand curve drawn. The value of the CS is ½ × 5 × $12 = $30 and is shown as the shaded area. The value of consumer spending equals price paid multipied by the quantity demanded. In this case $9 × 5 = $45.

Producer surplus (PS) represents the difference between the price a producer receives for a good or service and the cost to the producer to provide it.

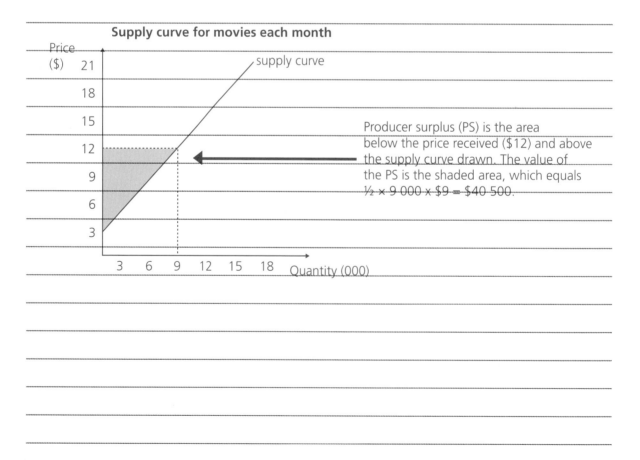

Supply curve for movies each month

Producer surplus (PS) is the area below the price received ($12) and above the supply curve drawn. The value of the PS is the shaded area, which equals ½ × 9 000 × $9 = $40 500.

      ISBN: 9780170438100

QUESTIONS & TASKS

1 a Draw up the demand curve of the schedule below.

Annabelle's demand schedule for new release DVDs each month	
Price ($)	**Quantity demanded**
10.00	11
11.00	9
12.00	7
13.00	5
14.00	3
15.50	0

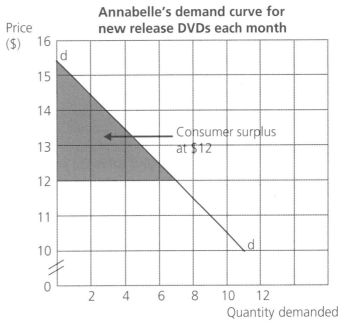

b Why does Annabelle buy more new release DVDs as the price falls?

Can afford more, willing and able to buy more.

c List two causes (other than changing the price of substitutes for DVDs) that could shift the demand curve for DVDs to the right, i.e., increase the demand for DVDs. For each cause, give the reason to explain why the demand curve will shift to the right.

Cause and reason: Increase in income/decrease in income (direct) tax. Can afford more/can buy more

DVDs at each and every price.

Cause and reason: Change in taste/fashion towards DVDs. Idea that watching DVDs becomes more

popular because they are better quality or have more features than videos so demand increases.

d What is demand?   Demand is a want (desire) backed up by the ability to pay.

e Explain why an increase in price does not result in a decrease in demand.

An increase in price results in a decrease in quantity demanded.

f Assume the market price is $12, calculate the value of:

(i) Consumer spending $12 × 7 = $84.00

(ii) Consumer surplus ½ × 7 × 3.5 = $12.25

g Shade in the area of consumer surplus at $12.

2 a (i) Use the diagram to calculate consumer surplus for both demand curves at a price of $10. Show your working.

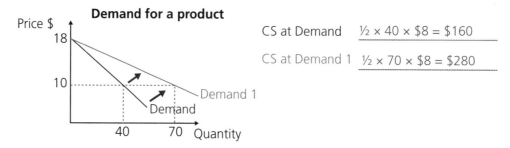

Demand for a product

CS at Demand   ½ × 40 × $8 = $160

CS at Demand 1   ½ × 70 × $8 = $280

(ii) Calculate the value of consumer spending for both demand curves.

Demand: $10 × 40 = $400

Demand 1: $10 × 70 = $700

b Use the demand curve shown to complete the table below. Show your working.

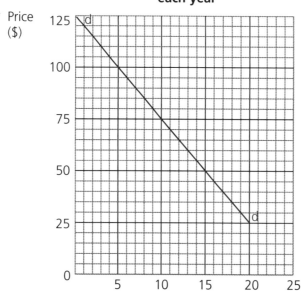

Jim's demand curve for restaurant meals each year

Price $	Value of consumer spending	Value of consumer surplus
(i) 25	$25 × 20 = $500	½ × 20 × $100 = $1 000
(ii) 50	$50 × 15 = $750	½ × 15 × $75 = $562.50
(iii) 100	$100 × 5 = $500	½ × 5 × $25 = $62.50

c Define consumer surplus.

The difference between what consumers are willing to pay and what they actually pay rather than go

without a commodity.

3 a Draw the supply curve for paperback books given the schedule below.

Supply schedule for paperback books each month	
Price ($ per book)	Quantity supplied
2	0
12	5 000
24	7 000

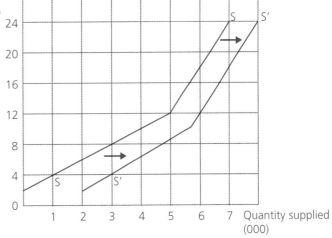

Supply curve for paperback books each month

b (i) Define producer surplus.

Producer surplus (PS) represents the difference between the price a producer receives for a good or service and the cost to the producer to provide it.

(ii) Describe the effects of a change in price of paperback books each month from $2 per book to $12 per book. Relate your answer to the change in producer surplus.

As the price rises from $2 per book to $12 per book the quantity supplied increases from zero books to 5 000 books. The producer surplus increases from zero to $25 000. (½ × 5 000 × $10)

c Calculate producer surplus at a price of

(i) $8 ½ × 3 000 × $6 = $9 000

(ii) $10 ½ × 4 000 × $8 = $16 000

d Illustrate on your graph an increase in supply. Label fully.

e Explain how the supply curve illustrates the law of supply.

A decrease in price will lead to a decrease in quantity supplied, ceteris paribus or other things being equal; an increase in price will lead to an increase in quantity supplied.

f Define individual supply.

The quantity of a good or service a (one) supplier will willingly bring to the market at a range of prices.

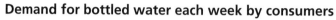

4 As price changes so will consumer spending and consumer surplus.

Explain the statement above with reference to the diagram below. In your answer you should:

- Define consumer surplus and calculate the change shown.
- Calculate the change in consumer spending.

Demand for bottled water each week by consumers

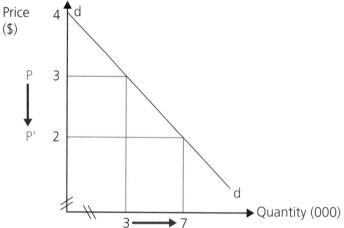

Consumer surplus is the difference between what consumers are willing to pay and what they actually pay rather than go without a commodity.

As price decreases from $3 to $2 the consumer surplus will increase from $1 500 (½ × 3 000 × $1) to $7 000 (½ × 7 000 × $2), i.e., an increase of $5 500. The quantity demanded increased by 4 000 as the price falls by $1, because consumers can afford more and are more willing and able to buy bottled water. Consumer surplus is greater because the price has fallen and since the quantity consumed has increased there are more units on which the consumer derives a surplus.

The change in consumer spending changes from $9 000 ($3 × 3 000) to $14 000 ($2 × 7 000), an increase of $5 000.

5 Producer surplus (PS) for a firm will change if there is a change in price and/or costs.

Explain producer surplus. In your answer you should refer to the graph and:
- Define supply and producer surplus.
- Calculate producer surplus at a price of $20 and $40.
- Show an increase in supply by 50%. Label this change fully.
- Discuss the resulting change in producer surplus at $20 and $40.

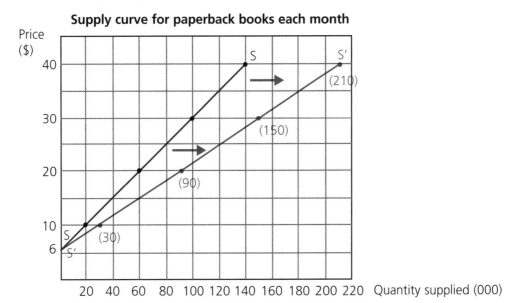

Supply curve for paperback books each month

Supply is the quantity of a good or service a supplier will willingly bring to the market at a range of prices.

Producer surplus (PS) represents the difference between the price a producer receives for a good or service and the cost to the producer to provide it.

At $20 the PS is $420 000 (½ × 60 000 × $14) and at $40 is $2.38m (½ × 140 000 × $34). When there is an increase in quantity supplied at each and every price as shown by S' (an increase in supply) then the size of producer surplus will change. The new PS at $20 is $630 000 (½ × 90 000 × $14) and at $40 is $3.57m (½ × 210 000 × $34). Therefore the increase in PS at $20 is $210 000 and at $40 is $1.19m.

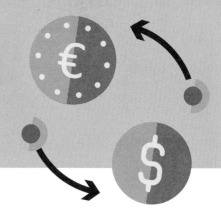

Allocative efficiency and a production possibility curve

Production possibility curves are drawn on the assumption that there are two goods only, fixed resources and a given level of technology. A **production possibility curve (PPC)** or production possibility frontier (PPF) shows the maximum output combination of two goods that can be produced given that existing resources and technology are used fully, that is, to their best possible use with the least cost.

The maximum output shown by any point on the PPC shows scarcity, because it is impossible to produce beyond the curve with existing resources or state of technology.

For the production possibility curve to shift outwards, the firm or economy needs to find new resources, or develop new technology.

Production possibility curve

Good Y

200 — A

150 — B

90 — C

• D

E

0   1000   1200   1300 1350

Good X

Any point inside the curve (for example point D) is production inefficient, which means resources are not being fully utilised or put to their best possible use.

All points on a PPC are production efficient but only one position can be allocatively efficient, that is, it is the position that represents what consumers actually want.

Any point on a PPC frontier shows production efficiency because this is where resources are fully employed and resources put to their best possible use.

The point of **allocative efficiency** is a single point on the production possibility frontier which represents that combination of goods that consumers actually want, or when it is not possible to make someone better off without making someone else worse off.

Any point inside the PPC graph such as D shows that some resources are not fully used; this is termed **production inefficiency**. The economy could possibly have an increase in its standard of living without incurring an opportunity cost.

Allocative efficiency

Allocative efficiency requires production efficiency, and it is not possible for one person to be made better off without making anyone else worse off. This means there is no possible reallocation of resources that will make someone better off without making someone else worse off. Allocative efficiency occurs at the free market equilibrium where the total consumer surplus and the total producer surplus are maximised.

The market system operates automatically to allocate our economic resources to the most efficient socially desirable use, it is said to be allocatively efficient. This point, where the demand curve and supply curve intersect, is the point of allocative efficiency. This is shown in the diagram as point AE. Note, the areas of consumer surplus and producer surplus do not have to be equal. At the market equilibrium price of $40 per book the value of consumer surplus is $15m and the value of the producer surplus is $45m.

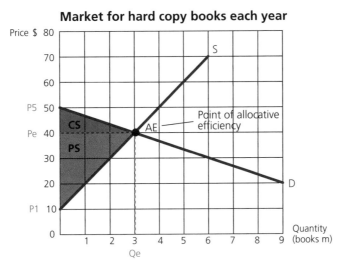

If the market automatically shifts away from the equilibrium, the consumer surplus and producer surplus will change and a new allocative efficiency will be established.

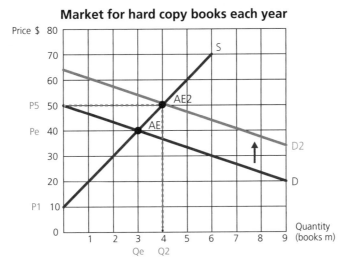

If the market equilibrium price rose to $50 per book the value of the consumer surplus and producer surplus will change. The new value of consumer surplus would be 0.5 multiplied by 4m books multiplied by $15 which equals $30m because this is the area above the new price paid ($50/P5) and below the new demand curve (D2). The change in consumer surplus would be an increase of $15m because this is the difference between the value of the original consumer surplus ($15m) and the value of the new consumer surplus ($30m). The new value of producer surplus would be 0.5 multiplied by 4m books multiplied by $40 which equals $80m, because this is the area below the new price received ($50) and above the supply curve. The change in producer surplus would be an increase of $35m because this is the difference between the value of the original producer surplus ($45m) and the value of the new producer surplus ($80m).

Student notes: Allocative efficiency

Allocative efficiency – requires production efficiency, also it is not possible to make someone better off without making someone else worse off. The sum of CS and PS is maximised.

Production efficiency – resources are fully employed and put to their best possible use, any point on the PPC.

    ISBN: 9780170438100

1 Allocative efficiency requires production as well as that combination of goods and services that consumers actually want.

Explain allocative efficiency. In your answer you should:

- Explain how the production possibility curve (PPC) in Graph 1 illustrates the concepts of scarcity and opportunity cost.
- Explain how the market would move the economy from Point A to Point B on Graph 1 as peoples' tastes changed from organic flowers to organic vegetables and illustrate the opportunity cost of this change.
- Explain how the move from Point A to Point B on Graph 1 reflects a move from productive efficiency to allocative efficiency.

Graph 1
A production possibility curve for organic crops

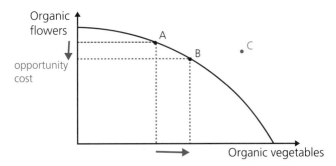

Scarcity is shown by not being able to go beyond the PPC, e.g., point C is unattainable. There is a limit to the amount of organic produce that can be produced because economic resources are scarce, or because resources are scarce the producers cannot operate beyond the PPC. Opportunity cost is the next best alternative foregone when a decision is made, you can only have more organic flowers (vegetables) if the producers forego/sacrifice organic vegetables (flowers).

As tastes change from organic flowers to organic vegetables it will mean less demand for organic flowers and this will lead to a fall in prices, and vice versa for organic vegetables. Price signals will lead to producers moving resources from organic flowers to organic vegetables.

To remain at Point A would mean that the economy is producing at productive efficiency, i.e., all available resources and technology are being used, and the output is being produced at the lowest possible cost for that level of output.

Moving to Point B means that allocative capacity is also being met, i.e., that productive efficiency is being met, and markets are in equilibrium, so that it is impossible to change the allocation of resources in such a way as to make someone better off without making someone else worse off, and the sum of consumer and producer surplus is maximised.

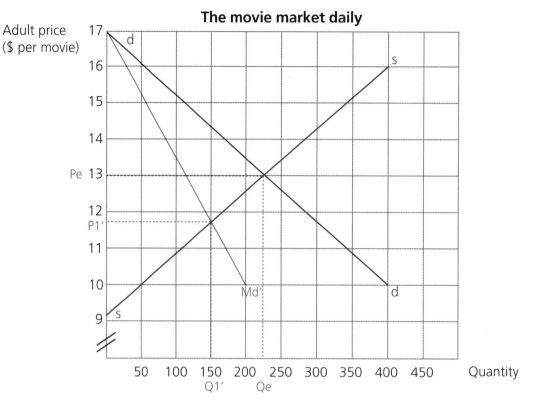

The movie market daily

2 **a** From the information contained in the graph above, construct a market demand and market supply schedule in the table below. On the graph above, identify the market price as Pe and the market quantity as Qe.

The movie market daily		
Adult price ($)	**Market supply**	**Market demand**
10	50	400
12	160	280
14	270	170
16	400	50

b As a result of increased competition from cheaper DVD rentals, there is a 50% decrease in the number of people going to the movies. Draw a new market demand curve, labelled Md′. Identify the new market price as P1′ and new market quantity as Q1′.

c What is the new equilibrium price and quantity? $ <u>11.75 (+/– 0.25)</u>   <u>150 (+/– 12.5)</u>

d Complete your table (show your working).

	Original equilibrium	**New equilibrium**
(i) CS	½ × 225 × $4 = $450	½ × 150 × $5.25 = 393.75
(ii) PS	½ × 225 × $3.75 = $421.88	½ × 150 × $2.50 = $187.50
(iii) Consumer spending	$13 × 225 = $2 925	$11.75 × 150 = $1 762.50

       ISBN: 9780170438100

3 a Explain the difference between consumer surplus and producer surplus.

Consumer surplus: the difference between what consumers are willing to pay and what they actually pay rather than go without.

Producer surplus: the difference between the total earnings of suppliers for a certain quantity sold and the total costs required to put that quantity on the market.

b Use numbers to indicate the answers asked for.

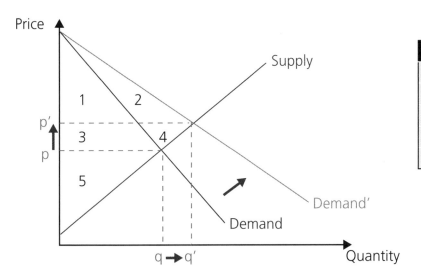

Question	Area
CS before	13
CS after	12
PS before	5
PS after	345
Change in PS	34

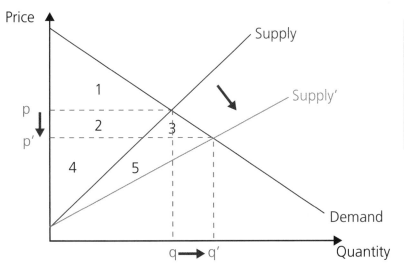

Question	Area
CS before	1
CS after	123
Change in CS	23
PS before	24
PS after	45

4 Use the graph to answer the following questions.

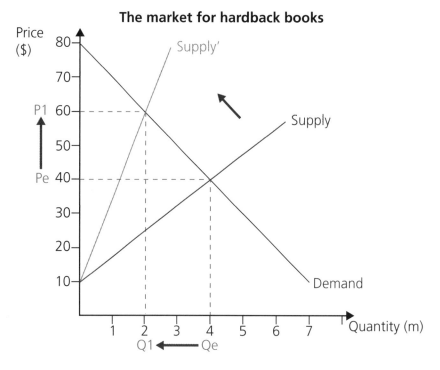

The market for hardback books

a Complete the table.

Calculate	Working and answer
(i) CS before	½ × 4m × $40 = $80m
(ii) CS after	½ × 2m × $20 = $20m
(iii) Change in CS	CS vs CS′ = $60m decrease
(iv) PS before	½ × 4m × $30 = $60m
(v) PS after	½ × 2m × $50 = $50m
(vi) Change in PS	PS vs PS′ = $10m decrease

b Define allocative efficiency.

Requires production efficiency as well as that combination of goods/services that consumers actually

want. It is not possible to make someone better off without making someone else worse off.

c Explain how market forces move the market for hardback books to the new equilibrium price P1 and quantity Q1.

The decrease in supply will cause a shortage (excess demand) at the original price Pe. Consumers will

bid up the price to P1 to gain the hardback books they want. The price will increase from Pe to P1 and

the quantity will fall from Qe to Q1. At Q1 the quantity demanded equals quantity supplied so the

equilibrium is restored.

d Define consumer surplus (CS).

The difference between what consumers are willing to pay and what they actually pay rather than do

without a commodity.

5 Use the graph to answer the following questions.

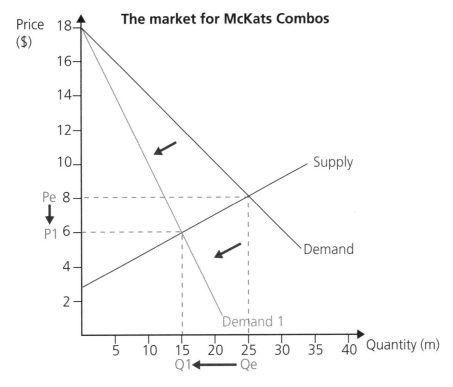

The market for McKats Combos

a Complete the table.

Calculate	Working and answer
(i) CS before	½ × 25m × $10 = $125m
(ii) CS after	½ × 15m × $12 = $90m
(iii) Change in CS	CS vs CS' = $35m decrease
(iv) PS before	½ × 25m × $5 = $62.5m
(v) PS after	½ × 15m × $3 = $22.5m
(vi) Change in PS	PS vs PS' = $40m decrease

b Explain how market forces move the market for McKats Combos back to the new equilibrium price P1 and quantity Q1.

The decrease in demand causes a surplus (excess supply) at the original price Pe. Producers are willing to accept a lower price to get rid of unsold stock. The price will fall from Pe to P1 and the quantity will fall from Qe to Q1. At Q1 the quantity demanded equals the quantity supplied so the equilibrium is restored.

c Define producer surplus (PS).

The difference between the total earnings of suppliers for a certain quantity sold and the total costs required to put that quantity on the market.

6 If the market shifts away from the equilibrium, the CS and PS will be reduced and/or redistributed.

Fully explain changes in consumer spending and producer surplus. In your answer you should refer to the graph and:

- Explain the changes in consumer surplus, producer surplus and AE.
- Explain how the market forces restore the equilibrium.

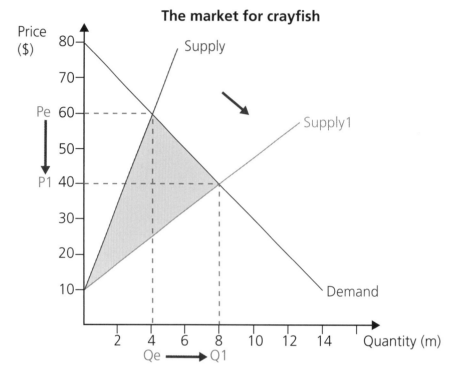

The market for crayfish

The original CS was $40m (½ × 4m × $20) and the new CS is $160m (½ × 8m × $40), therefore an increase of $120m, because the price is lower and quantity of crayfish consumed has increased and there are more units on which consumers derive a surplus.

The original PS was $100m (½ × 4m × $50) and the new PS is $120m (½ × 8m × $30), therefore there is an increase of $20m.

The shaded area on the diagram represents the change in AE.

The increase in supply causes a surplus (excess supply) at the original price Pe. Producers are willing to accept a lower price to get rid of unsold stock. The price will fall from Pe to P1 and the quantity will fall from Qe to Q1. At Q1 the quantity demanded equals the quantity supplied so the equilibrium is restored.

7 Resources should be allocated according to consumer demand.

Fully explain how a change in demand will affect consumer surplus and producer surplus. In your answer you should refer to the graph and:

- Define the terms 'consumer surplus' and 'producer surplus'.
- Explain how market forces restore the equilibrium.
- Explain how the change in demand affects CS and PS.

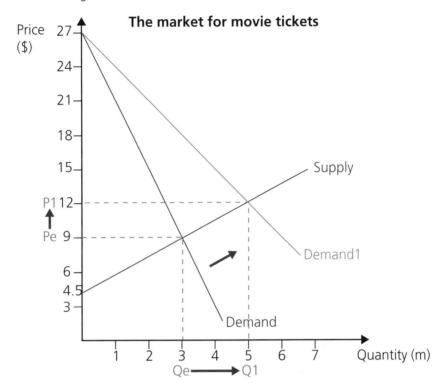

Consumer surplus is the difference between what consumers are willing to pay and what they actually pay rather than go without.

Producer surplus is the difference between the total earnings of suppliers for a certain quantity sold and the total costs required to put that quantity on the market.

The increase in demand will cause a shortage (excess demand) at the original price Pe. Consumers will bid up the price to P1 to gain the movie tickets they want. The price will increase from Pe to P1 and the quantity will increase from Qe to Q1. At Q1 the quantity demanded equals quantity supplied so the equilibrium is restored.

CS = $27m (½ × 3m × $18) CS′ = $37.5m (½ × 5m × $15)

Δ CS = $10.5m increase ($27m vs $37.5m)

PS = $6.75m (½ × 3m × $45) PS′ = $18.75m (½ × 5m × $7.5)

Δ PS = $12m increase ($6.75 vs $18.75m)

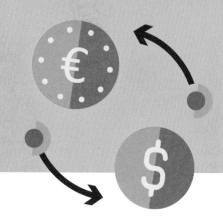

9 EFFICIENCY OF MARKET EQUILIBRIUM
Sales tax and allocative efficiency

Sales tax and allocative efficiency

An **indirect tax** (such as sales tax or VAT) is a tax collected by firms (a third party) and then passed on to the government. An indirect tax will decrease supply causing the equilibrium price to rise and equilibrium quantity to decrease. To **illustrate the effects of a per unit (dollar) sales** tax requires shifting the original supply curve upward to the left by the per unit tax amount. For example, if the per unit tax is $5 and $5 equates to 5 spaces on the graph, you must shift the entire supply curve vertically upwards by this distance. It is important to note that the increase in the price will not be as much as the amount of the tax because the curves are sloping. Therefore, the producer is able to pass some of the tax on to the consumer.

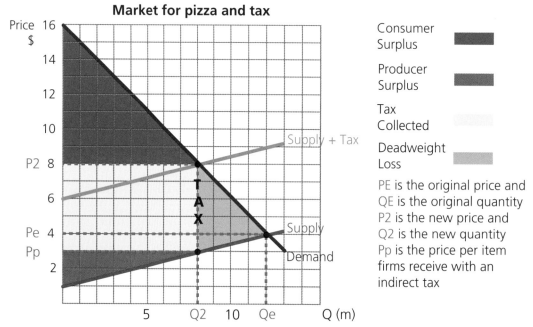

Market for pizza and tax

Consumer Surplus

Producer Surplus

Tax Collected

Deadweight Loss

PE is the original price and QE is the original quantity
P2 is the new price and Q2 is the new quantity
Pp is the price per item firms receive with an indirect tax

The tax per unit is the gap between the supply curves. Note the price does not rise by the full amount of the tax per unit. In this case the tax per unit is $5 but the price has gone up by $4.

	Original equilibrium	New equilibrium
(i) Consumer surplus (CS)	0.5 × 12m × $12 = $72m	0.5 × 8m × $8 = $32m
(ii) Producer surplus (PS)	0.5 × 12m × $3 = $18m	0.5 × 8m × $2 = $8m
(iii) Deadweight loss (DWL)	Nil (zero)	0.5 × 4m × $5 = $10m

With a tax consumer surplus will decrease because consumers pay more and buy less. Producer surplus will decrease because producers receive a lower price and sell less. There is a deadweight loss from the tax that represents the loss of allocative efficiency because part of the original consumer surplus and producer surplus is not picked up as part of the tax.

 ISBN: 9780170438100

The impact of a sales tax worked example

	Before the tax	After the tax
Quantity sold	Qe, 12m	Q2, 8m
Price consumers pay	Pe, $4	P2, $8
Consumer spending	Pe x Qe, $48m	P2 x Q2, $64m
Price producers receive	Pe, $4	Pp, $3
Producer revenue	Pe x Qe, $48m	Pp x Q2, $24m
Change in the value of sales	(Pe x Qe) difference (P2 x Q2). An increase of $16m	
Change in producers' revenue	(Pe x Qe) difference (Pp x Q2). A decrease of $24m	
How much is the tax per unit?	The size of the gap between the supply curves. $5	
Government revenue from the tax	Tax per unit x Q2. $5 x 8m = $40m	

The **incidence of a tax** refers to who actually pays the tax. In most cases, part of a tax is paid by the consumer and part is paid by the firm. **Consumers** pay to the extent of the price rise from the original price paid (Pe) to the new price paid (P2). Any amount of the tax not covered by the price increase has to be absorbed by the firm (from Pe to Pp on the diagram opposite).

The change in the value of consumer spending that results from the tax equals the difference between the original price a consumer pays (Pe) multiplied by the original quantity purchased (Qe) and the new price paid (P2) multiplied by the new quantity purchased (Q2). Since a tax results in a price increase there will be a decrease in quantity demanded because fewer consumers are willing and able to purchase with their limited incomes.

The value of consumer spending may remain unchanged, decrease or increase because the new value of consumer spending depends on the relative changes in both the new price paid and the new quantity purchased. Consumers may look to buy a substitute good or service that is relatively cheaper.

Producers will find that the tax adds to their costs so they will decrease supply, meaning that there will be a decrease in quantity supplied at each and every price. The firm will collect the tax revenue and pass this onto the government. Therefore, the price per item firms receive with a tax will be lower than the price consumers pay for them.

To identify how much producers earn per item for the product at the new equilibrium you track down from the new equilibrium position until you hit the original supply curve, this gives the price per item firms receive with a tax (shown on the diagram as the letter Pp).

The change in the firm's income or revenue will be the difference between the firm's original income, which was the original price (Pe) received multiplied by the original quantity (Qe) and the new value of the firm's income, which equals the price per item the firm now receives (Pp) multiplied by the new quantity sold (Q2). The producer's total income with the sales tax will fall because the price per item that the firm receives will be lower and the quantity sold will fall.

The revenue that the **government** collects from the tax equals the tax per unit multiplied by the new quantity (tax per unit x Q2).

The incidence of a sales tax

The **incidence of a tax** refers to who actually pays the tax. In most cases, part of a tax is paid by the consumer and part is paid by the firm.

When the demand curve is relatively inelastic the producer is able to pass on most of the tax to the consumer as shown in the diagram. The shaded area is the consumer incidence of the tax.

The incidence of a tax falls mainly on consumers when a good or service is inelastic. When demand is inelastic, a given increase in price will see a less than proportionate decrease in quantity demanded, meaning that producers are more able to pass on most of the tax to consumers. Consumers pay to the extent of the price rise (from P to P'), this will be the greatest incidence of the tax. Any amount of the tax not covered by the price increase has to be absorbed by the firm (from P to A).

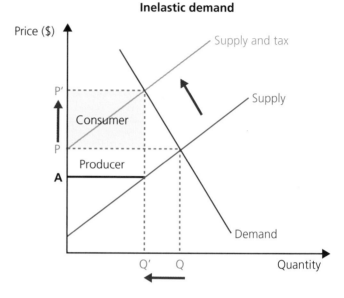

Taxes placed on goods that are price inelastic can raise significant revenue. The reason for this is that the price rise caused by the imposition of the tax on goods or services that are inelastic in nature will cause a proportionately small decrease in quantity demanded. This results in a relatively large number of goods or services on which the tax is imposed, and therefore greater tax revenue is collected. Given this, a government is more likely to impose taxes on products such as cigarettes and alcohol that are inelastic in nature, than products such as new cars.

The incidence of a tax falls more heavily on the producer when a good or service is elastic. When demand is elastic, a given increase in price will see a more than proportionate decrease in quantity demanded, meaning that producers are less able to pass the tax on to consumers. Consumers pay to the extent of the price increase that results from the tax. However, the greatest portion of the tax is not covered by the price increase and has to be absorbed by the firm.

Taxes placed on goods that are price elastic may raise less revenue than a tax placed on goods that are price inelastic. The reason for this is that the price rise caused by the imposition of the tax on goods or services that are elastic in nature will cause a proportionately large decrease in quantity demanded. This can leave only a relatively small number of goods or services on which the tax is imposed, and therefore less tax revenue is collected.

The incidence of a tax is dependent on the relative elasticities of demand and supply and can be seen on the two graphs.

When the demand curve is relatively elastic the producer is less able to pass on the tax to the consumer as shown in the diagram.

     ISBN: 9780170438100

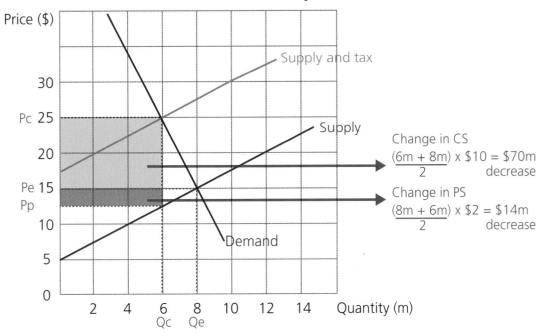

Sales tax and allocative efficiency

Change in CS
$\dfrac{(6m + 8m)}{2} \times \$10 = \$70m$ decrease

Change in PS
$\dfrac{(8m + 6m)}{2} \times \$2 = \$14m$ decrease

1 **a** Assume the government has placed a **per unit sales tax of $12**. On the graph above label:
- the original equilibrium price (Pe) and quantity (Qe)
- the new equilibrium price (Pc) and quantity (Qc)
- the new price producers receive as (Pp).

b Complete the table.

(i) Change in total consumer spending	($15 x 8m) vs ($25 x 6m) = $30m increase
(ii) Change in suppliers' revenue	($15 x 8m) vs ($13 x 6m) = $42m decrease
(iii) Change in consumer surplus	($10 x 6m) plus (0.5 x $10 x 2m) = $70m decrease
(iv) Change in producer surplus	($2 x 6m) plus (0.5 x $2 x 2m) = $14m decrease
(v) Government revenue from the tax	$12 x 6m = $72m
(vi) The deadweight loss	0.5 x $12 x 2m = $12m

2 Study the graph and answer the questions that follow.

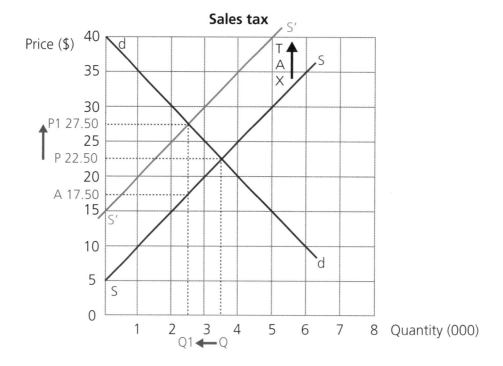

Sales tax

a On the above diagram label the original price P and original quantity Q. Label P1 and Q1 as the new equilibrium price and new equilibrium quantity respectively. Label the price firms receive with the sales tax as A.

b What is the value of the tax shown? <u>$10</u>

c Complete the table.

Question	Formula or letter	Value from graph
(i) Price paid by consumer before	P	$22.50
(ii) Price paid by consumer after	P1	$27.50
(iii) Price firms receive after	A	$17.50
(iv) Value of sales before	P × Q	$22.50 x 3 500 = $78 750
(v) Value of sales after	P1 × Q1	$27.50 × 2 500 = $68 750
(vi) Change in the value of sales	(P × Q) vs (P1 × Q1)	$10 000 decrease
(vii) Firms' revenue (income) after	A × Q1	$17.50 × 2 500 = $43 750
(viii) Change in the firms' revenue	(A × Q1) vs (P × Q)	$35 000 decrease
(ix) Tax revenue collected by government	tax × Q1	$10 x 2 500 = $25 000
(x) Consumer surplus before	½ × b × h	½ × $17.5 × 3 500 = $30 625
(xi) Consumer surplus after	½' × b' × h'	½ × $12.5 × 2 500 = $15 625
(xii) Change in consumer surplus	CS vs CS'	$30 625 v $15 625 = $15 000 decrease
(xiii) Deadweight loss	½ × b × h	½ × 1 000 × $10 = $5 000

 ISBN: 9780170438100

3 Study the graph below and answer the questions that follow.

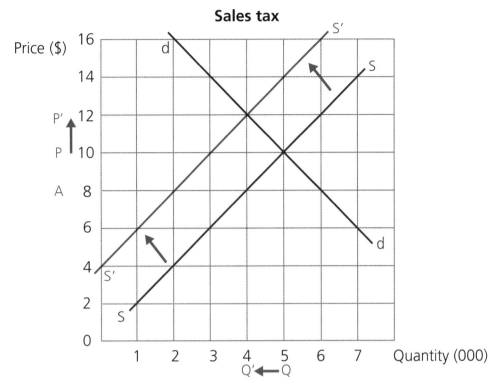

Sales tax

a Show on the above diagram a sales tax of $4 per item. Label the curve fully, showing the new price as P' and the new quantity as Q'. Label the new price firms receive as A.

b Calculate the change in consumer spending following the imposition of the sales tax. Show your working.

(P x Q) vs (P' x Q') = ($10 x 5 000) vs ($12 x 4 000) = $2 000 decrease

c What is the new equilibrium price? P' = $12

d At the new equilibrium how much do firms earn per item? A = $8

e Calculate the change in firms' revenue following the imposition of the sales tax.

(P x Q) vs (A x Q') = ($10 x 5 000) vs ($8 x 4 000) = $18 000 decrease

f Calculate the tax revenue collected by government. tax x Q' = $4 x 4 000 = $16 000

g Consumers receive a certain amount of consumer surplus before and after a tax is imposed. Explain what the surplus represents.

The amount (measured in $ terms) of utility (or satisfaction) that consumers enjoy without having to pay for when consuming a quantity of goods. The market price for all units consumed is equal to the $ utility value of the last marginal unit consumed, therefore earlier units give surplus satisfaction over and above what has to be paid for.

4 Use the diagram to answer the questions in the table.

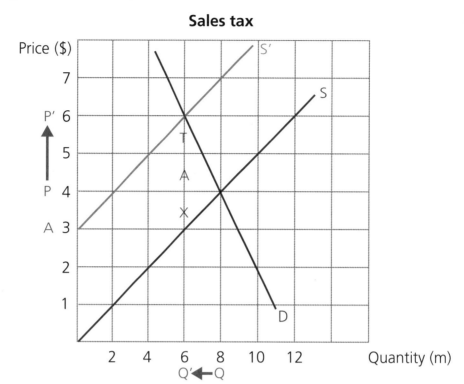

Sales tax

Question	Working and answer
a What price is paid by consumers before and after?	P = $4 before/P' = $6 after
b What is consumer expenditure before?	P x Q = $4 x 8m = $32m
c What is consumer expenditure after?	P' x Q' = $6 x 6m = $36m
d What is the change in consumer expenditure?	An increase of $4m
e What is the government revenue from the tax?	Tax x Q' = $3 x 6m = $18m
f Work out price elasticity of demand. **P ($)** / **Q** 4 / 8m 6 / 6m	Ep = $\dfrac{\left(\frac{2}{7}\right)}{\left(\frac{2}{5}\right)}$ = 0.71 inelastic
g What is producer revenue before?	P x Q = $4 x 8m = $32m
h What is producer revenue after?	A x Q' = $3 x 6m = $18m
i What is the change in producer revenue?	decrease of $14m
j Work out the value of the deadweight loss.	½ x 2m x $3 = $3m
k What do the parallel lines on the diagram indicate?	A per unit sales tax of $3
l Calculate PS before.	½ x 8m x $4 = $16m
m Calculate PS after.	½ x 6m x $3 = $9m
n Calculate the change in PS.	PS vs PS' = $7m decrease
o Calculate the change in CS.	$\dfrac{(6m + 8m)}{2}$ x $2 = $14m decrease

5 Study the diagram below and answer the questions that follow.

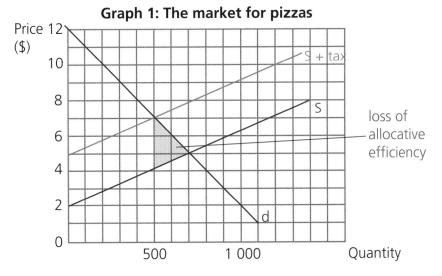

Graph 1: The market for pizzas

a Complete the table.

Question: Calculate	Working and answer
(i) CS before	½ x 700 x $7 = $2 450
(ii) CS after	½ x 500 x $5 = $1 250
(iii) Change in CS	CS vs CS' = $1 200 decrease
(iv) PS before	½ x 700 x $3 = $1 050
(v) PS after	½ x 500 x $2 = $500
(vi) Change in PS	PS vs PS' = $550 decrease

b (i) Calculate the tax per unit. $3 per pizza

(ii) Calculate the government revenue from the tax. $3 x 500 = $1 500

c Calculate:

(i) the incidence of the sales tax on consumers (show your workings). $2 x 500 = $1 000

(ii) the incidence of the sales tax on producers (show your workings). $1 x 500 = $500

d (i) How will the incidence of the sales tax change, the less price elastic the demand for pizzas becomes?

An increased consumers' incidence of the tax / greater proportion of the tax would have to be borne by the consumer.

(ii) Explain why the incidence of the sales tax will change.

As the lower price elasticity implies the product is more of a necessity, or has fewer substitutes, or is a small proportion of disposable income which means the producer is more able to 'pass on' the sales tax / consumer is prepared to pay a higher price.

e Shade the allocative efficiency that has been lost in the pizza market as a result of the sales tax being applied. Label this clearly.

6 The incidence of a tax is shared by buyers and sellers.

Fully explain the incidence of a tax. In your answer you should:

- Explain what is meant by the concept 'incidence of tax'.
- Explain, with the use of diagrams, how the incidence of tax is dependent on price elasticity of demand.

The incidence of taxation is a reference to who actually pays the tax imposed, as compared to the tax

impact which is a reference to the one on whom the tax is initially levied. The incidence of a sales tax is

shared by buyers and sellers. The consumer pays to the extent that the price rises from P to P'. Since the

tax is the vertical distance between the two supply curves, the producer must pay whatever part of the

tax that cannot be passed on to the consumer. The producer is forced to absorb the remainder of the tax

P to A.

The incidence of a tax is dependent on the relative elasticities of demand and supply and can be seen on

the two graphs.

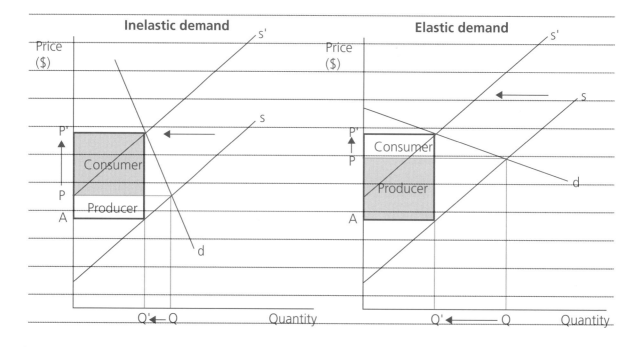

When the demand curve is relatively inelastic the producer is able to pass on most of the tax to the consumer as shown in the diagram. Bold rectangle is the total tax. Shaded area is the consumer incidence of the tax.

When the demand curve is relatively elastic the producer is unable to pass on most of the tax to the consumer as shown in the diagram, so the producer pays most of the tax. Bold rectangle is the total tax. Shaded area is the producer incidence of the tax.

PHOTOCOPYING OF THIS PAGE IS RESTRICTED UNDER LAW.   ISBN: 9780170438100

7 Cigarette smokers will be hit hard by new tax.

Explain the effect of a $4.50 tax per unit on cigarettes. In your answer you should:

- State or calculate the missing values to questions (i) to (viii) in the table below.
- Explain why the demand for cigarettes is likely to be relatively price inelastic.
- Using the elasticity theory identify and explain the group that the incidence of the tax will fall more heavily on.
- Shade the deadweight loss resulting from the tax and explain why it occurs.

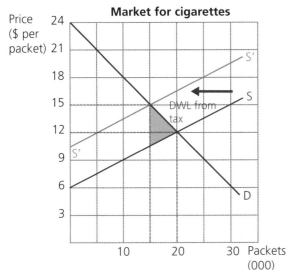

	Question	Answer
(i)	The new price consumers would pay per packet	$15
(ii)	The amount retailers will receive for themselves per packet	$10.50
(iii)	The new quantity sold per week	15 000
(iv)	The tax revenue received by the government	$67 500
(v)	The change in total consumer spending	$15 000 decrease
(vi)	The change in suppliers' after-tax revenue	$82 500 decrease
(vii)	The producer surplus before the tax	$60 000
(viii)	The change in consumer surplus due to the tax	$52 500 decrease

Cigarettes are price inelastic because cigarettes are addictive, so consumers will not be willing to stop consuming them when the price per packet increases, meaning that a given change in price will cause a less than proportionate change in quantity demanded.

The incidence of the sales tax of $4.50 per unit falls on the consumer – they pay $3.00 of the tax and the producer absorbs the remaining $1.50. Producers are more able to pass most of the tax on to the consumer because cigarettes are price inelastic, meaning the increase in price causes a less than proportionate fall in quantity demanded.

The deadweight loss (DWL) represents the loss of welfare or that part of consumer surplus and producer surplus that is not transferred to the government in tax, i.e., $11 250 (½ x 5 000 x $4.50).

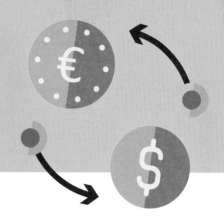

10 EFFICIENCY OF MARKET EQUILIBRIUM
Subsidy and AE

Subsidy and allocative efficiency

A **subsidy** is a payment by government to firms to keep their costs down, and as a result firms will increase supply. As supply increases the equilibrium price will decrease and the equilibrium quantity will increase. To **illustrate the effects of a per unit (dollar) subsidy** requires shifting the original supply curve downward to the right by the per unit subsidy amount. For example, if the per unit subsidy is $5 and $5 equates to 5 spaces on the graph, you must shift the entire supply curve vertically downwards this distance. It is important to note that the decrease in the price will not be as much as the amount of the subsidy because the curves are sloping. In most cases part of the subsidy will benefit the consumer and part will benefit the firm.

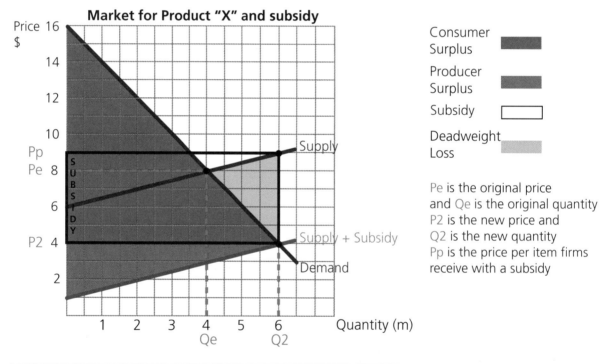

	Original equilibrium	New equilibrium
Consumer surplus (CS)	0.5 × 4m × $8 = $16m	0.5 × 6m × $12 = $36m
Producer surplus (PS)	0.5 × 4m × $2 = $4m	0.5 × 6m × $3 = $9m
Deadweight loss (DWL)	Nil (zero)	0.5 × 2m × $5 = $5m

With a subsidy, consumer surplus will increase because consumers pay less and buy more. Producer surplus will increase because producers receive a higher price and sell more. There is a deadweight loss from the subsidy that represents the loss of allocative efficiency because part of the original consumer surplus and producer surplus is not picked up as part of the subsidy.

The impact of a subsidy worked example

	Before the subsidy	After the subsidy
Quantity sold	Qe, 4m	Q2, 6m
Price consumers pay	Pe, $8	P2, $4
Consumer spending	Pe x Qe, $32m	P2 x Q2, $24m
Price producers receive	Pe, $8	Pp, $9
Producer revenue	Pe x Qe, $32m	Pp x Q2, $54m
Change in the value of sales	(Pe x Qe) difference (P2 x Q2). A decrease of $8m	
Change in producers' revenue	(Pe x Qe) difference (Pp x Q2). An increase of $22m	
How much is the subsidy per unit?	The size of the gap between the supply curves. $5	
Cost to the government of the subsidy	Subsidy per unit x Q2. $5 x 6m = $30m	

The subsidy per unit is the gap between the supply curves. Note the price does not fall by the full amount of the subsidy per unit. In this case the subsidy per unit is $5 but the price has gone down by $4.

The **incidence of a subsidy** is a reference to who actually benefits from the government paying a subsidy. **Consumers** benefit to the extent of the price decreases from the original price paid (Pe) to the new price they pay (P2). Any amount of the subsidy not covered by the price decrease to consumers goes to the firm (from Pp to P2 on the diagram opposite).

The change in the value of consumer spending that results from the subsidy equals the difference between the original price a consumer pays (Pe) multiplied by the original quantity purchased (Qe) and the new price paid (P2) multiplied by the new quantity purchased (Q2). Since a subsidy results in a price decrease there will be an increase in quantity demanded because more consumers are more willing and able to purchase the good or service with their limited incomes.

The value of consumer spending may remain unchanged, decrease or increase because the new value of consumer spending depends on the relative changes in both the new price paid and the new quantity purchased. Consumers may look to buy a complement to use in conjunction with the subsidied good or service. Consumers may also look to buy less of a substitute good or service that is relatively more expensive.

Producers will find that the subsidy reduces their costs so they will increase supply, meaning that there will be an increase in quantity supplied at each and every price. The price per item that firms receive with a subsidy will be higher than the price that consumers pay them. To identify how much producers earn per item for the product you track up from the new equilibrium position until you hit the original supply curve, this gives the price per item firms receive with a subsidy (shown on the diagram as the letter Pp).

The change in the firm's income or revenue will be the difference between the firm's original income, which was the original price (Pe) received, multiplied by the original quantity (Qe) and the new value of the firm's income, which equals the price per item the firm now receives (Pp) multiplied by the new quantity sold (Q2). The producer's total income with the subsidy will increase because the price per item that the firm receives will be higher and the quantity sold will increase.

The cost to the **government** of the subsidy equals the subsidy per unit multiplied by the new quantity (subsidy per unit x Q2).

Incidence of a subsidy

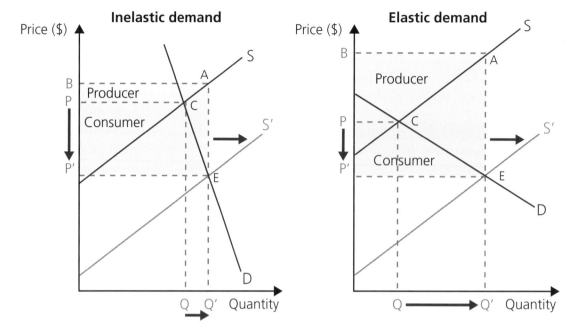

Interpreting the graph	Letter answer
Total cost to government of the subsidy	B P' E A
Gain consumer surplus from the subsidy	P P' E C increase
Gain producer surplus from the subsidy	B P C A increase
Total deadweight loss	A C E

The incidence of a subsidy falls mainly on consumers when a good or service is inelastic. When demand is inelastic, a given decrease in price will see a less than proportionate increase in quantity demanded. It will result in a relatively large decrease in price paid by the consumer, with a relatively small increase in the quantity sold, therefore consumers rather than producers gain the most from the subsidy. Consumers benefit to the extent of the price decrease (from P to P'), which will be the greatest incidence of the subsidy. Any amount of the subsidy not covered by the price decrease will benefit the firm (from P to B).

The incidence of a subsidy falls more heavily on the producer when a good or service is elastic. When demand is elastic, a given decrease in price will see a more than proportionate increase in quantity demanded. It will result in a relatively small decrease in price paid by the consumer, with a relatively large increase in the quantity sold, therefore producers rather than consumers gain the most from the subsidy.

When demand is inelastic consumers benefit more (as shown in the left hand diagram) and when demand is elastic the incidence benefits the producer or seller more (as shown in right hand diagram).

That part of the subsidy paid by the government that does not form part of the new producer surplus or new consumer surplus is termed the deadweight loss (DWL). The DWL of a subsidy is shown as an inwardly pointed triangle (ACE).

QUESTIONS & TASKS

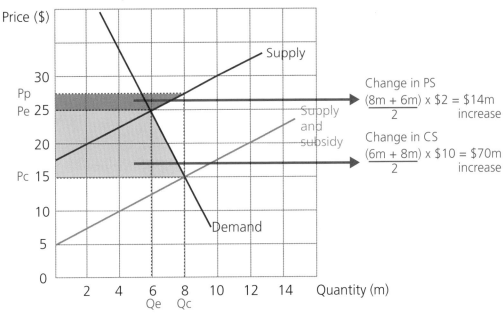

Subsidy and allocative efficiency

Change in PS

$$\frac{(8m + 6m)}{2} \times \$2 = \$14m \text{ increase}$$

Change in CS

$$\frac{(6m + 8m)}{2} \times \$10 = \$70m \text{ increase}$$

1 a Assume the government has placed a **per unit subsidy of $12**. On the graph above label:
- the original equilibrium price (Pe) and quantity (Qe)
- the new equilibrium price (Pc) and quantity (Qc)
- the new price producers receive as (Pp).

b Complete the table.

(i) Change in total consumer spending	($25 x 6m) vs ($15 x 8m) = $30m decrease
(ii) Change in suppliers' revenue	($25 x 6m) vs ($27 x 8m) = $66m increase
(iii) Change in consumer surplus	($10 x 6m) plus (0.5 x $10 x 2m) = $70m increase
(iv) Change in producer surplus	($2 x 6m) plus (0.5 x $2 x 2m) = $14m increase
(v) Government revenue from the tax	$12 x 8m = $96m
(vi) The deadweight loss	0.5 x $12 x 2m = $12m

2 Study the graph and answer the questions that follow.

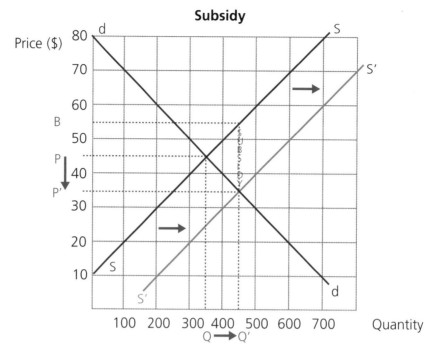

a On the above diagram label the original price P and new price P'. Label the original quantity Q and new quantity Q'. Label the price firms receive with a subsidy as B.

b What is the value of the subsidy shown per unit? <u>The gap between S and S' = $20</u>

c Complete the table below.

Question	Formula or letter	Value from graph
(i) Value of sales before	P × Q	$45 × 350 = $15 750
(ii) Value of sales after	P' × Q'	$35 × 450 = $15 750
(iii) Change in the value of sales	(P × Q) vs (P' × Q')	zero (0)
(iv) Firms' revenue before	P × Q	$15 750
(v) Firms' revenue after	B × Q'	$55 × 450 = $24 750
(vi) Change in firms' revenue	(P × Q) vs (B × Q')	$9 000 increase
(vii) Price per item received by firms with subsidy	B	$55
(viii) Cost to government of the subsidy	subsidy × Q'	$20 × 450 = $9 000
(ix) Consumer surplus before	½ x b x h	½ x 350 x $35 = $6 125
(x) Consumer surplus after	½ x b' x h'	½ x 450 x $45 = $10 125
(xi) Change in consumer surplus (CS)	(½ x b x h) vs (½ x b' x h')	$4 000 increase
(xii) Total deadweight loss	½ x b x h	½ x 100 x $20 = $1 000

3 **a** Use the diagram to answer the questions that follow in the table. Label the diagram appropriately.

Subsidy diagram

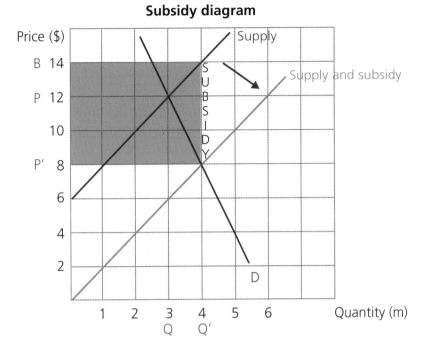

b What do the parallel lines on the diagram indicate? <u>A per unit subsidy of $6</u>

c Shade in the area of the cost to the government of the subsidy.

Give the value to represent the following		Working and answer
(i)	Price paid by consumer before	P = $12
(ii)	Price paid by consumer after	P′ = $8
(iii)	Consumer spending before	P × Q = $12 × 3m = $36m
(iv)	Consumer spending after	P′ × Q′ = $8 × 4m = $32m
(v)	Change in consumer surplus	$\frac{(3m + 4m)}{2}$ × $4 = $14m increase
(vi)	Change in producer surplus	$\frac{(4m + 3m)}{2}$ × $2 = $7m increase
(vii)	Cost to government of the subsidy	subsidy × Q′ = $6 × 4m = $24m
(viii)	Deadweight loss of the subsidy	0.5 × 1m × $6 = $3m

d Explain whether consumers or producers would receive the greater benefit of the subsidy. Use data in your answer.

<u>Consumers benefit the most from the subsidy. They pay $4 less, so receive 66.6% of the subsidy. The</u>

<u>gain in CS is $14m. Producers receive $2 of the $6 per unit subsidy (33.3%) and PS increases by $7m.</u>

4 Study the diagram below and answer the questions that follow.

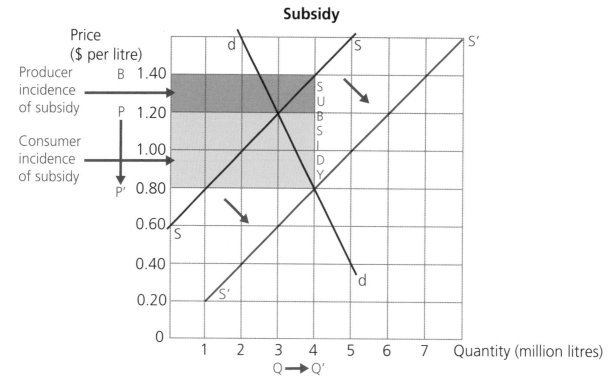

Subsidy

a Draw and label a new supply curve to show a subsidy of $0.60 per litre on the above diagram. Identify the new price paid by consumers as P′ and price received by producers as B.

b Work out the new equilibrium price and quantity. <u>P′ = $0.80 per litre   Q′ = 4 million litres</u>

c Work out the change in the value of sales.

   <u>(P x Q) vs (P′ x Q′) = ($1.2 x 3m) vs ($0.8 x 4m) = $0.4m decrease</u>

d At the new equilibrium how much do firms earn per item? <u>B = $1.40 per litre.</u>

e Calculate the change in firms' income.

   <u>(P x Q) vs (B x Q′) = ($1.2 x 3m) vs ($1.4 x 4m) = $2m increase</u>

f Calculate the cost to the government of the subsidy. <u>subsidy x Q′ = $0.6 x 4m = $2.4m</u>

g **(i)** Explain, with reference to the diagram, who benefits more from the subsidy, consumers or producers.

   <u>Consumers benefit more, price for consumers has changed by $0.40 per litre, while producers gain</u>

   <u>$0.20 per litre of $0.60 per litre subsidy.</u>

   (ii) Shade in consumer and producer incidence of the subsidy. Label clearly.

   (iii) Calculate the change in CS. <u>Gain of $1 400 000 (3m x $0.40 plus 0.5 x 1m x $0.40)</u>

   (iv) Calculate the change in PS. <u>Gain of $700 000 (3m x 0.20 plus 0.5 x 1m x $0.20)</u>

  ISBN: 9780170438100

5 Study the diagram and answer the questions that follow.

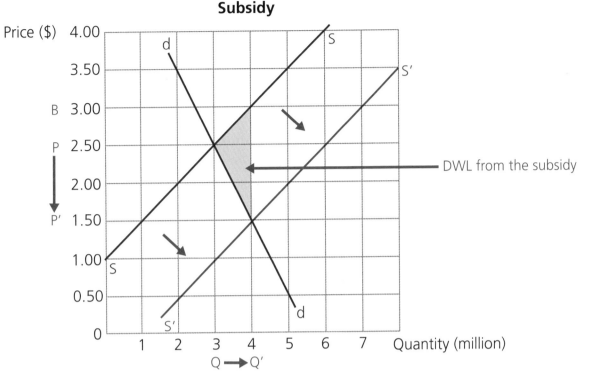

Subsidy

a What is the original:

(i) equilibrium price? <u>$2.50</u>

(iii) value of sales? <u>$7.5m</u>

(ii) equilibrium quantity? <u>3 million</u>

(iv) firms' income? <u>$7.5m</u>

b (i) Assume the government gives $1.50 subsidy on each item. Draw and label the new curve on the graph.

(ii) What is the new equilibrium price and quantity?

price <u>P' = $1.50</u> quantity <u>Q' = 4 million</u>

(iii) What is the value of sales now? <u>P' x Q' = $6m</u>

(iv) At the new equilibrium how much do firms earn per item? <u>B = $3.00</u>

(v) At the new equilibrium what is the firms' revenue? <u>B x Q' = $3.0 x 4m = $12m</u>

(vi) Calculate the cost of the subsidy to the government. <u>subsidy x Q' = $1.5 x 4m = $6m</u>

(vii) Calculate the change in consumer surplus. <u>$3.5m increase ($1 x 3m plus 0.5 x 1m x $1)</u>

c (i) Define allocative efficiency.

<u>A situation where CS and PS is maximised. A situation where production is at full capacity and no</u>

<u>one can be made better off without someone else being worse off.</u>

(ii) Shade in the deadweight loss resulting from the subsidy and explain why this deadweight loss occurs.

<u>The DWL (loss of allocative efficiency) represents the loss of welfare that is not transferred by the</u>

<u>subsidy, it is that part of CS and PS that is not gained by another party so is lost.</u>

6 Study the graph 'Market for school shoes' and answer the questions that follow.

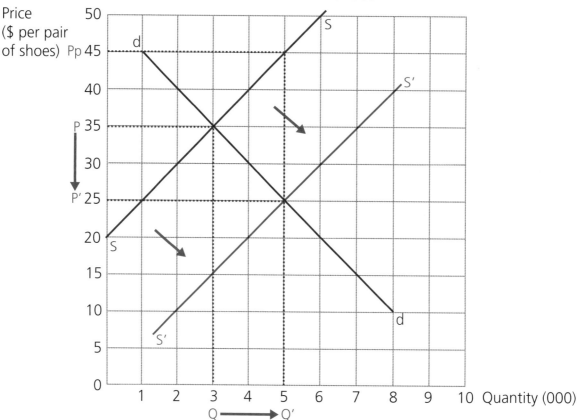

Market for school shoes

a (i) How much would the subsidy have to be per pair of shoes for the price to fall to $25?

$20 per pair of shoes

(ii) On the diagram show the effect of a subsidy that results in a price of $25 per pair of shoes. Label the new equilibrium quantity Q'.

b (i) What price does the producer receive after the subsidy?

$45

(ii) What is total consumer spending after the subsidy? $25 x 5 000 = $125 000

(iii) Calculate the cost to the government of such a subsidy. $20 x 5 000 = $100 000

(iv) Calculate the change in consumer surplus.

$40 000 increase ($10 x 3m plus 0.5 x 2m x $10)

(v) Calculate the change in producer surplus.

$40 000 ($10 x 3m plus 0.5 x 2m x $10)

(vi) Calculate the deadweight loss.

½ x $20 x 2 000 = $20 000

7 A subsidy will have different consequences for consumers, producers and government.

Explain the consequences of a subsidy on various groups. In your answer you should use data from the graph and:

- Explain the consequences of the subsidy on consumers.
- Explain the consequences of the subsidy on producers.
- Explain the consequences on government of the subsidy and the loss of allocative efficiency.

Bus trips per year

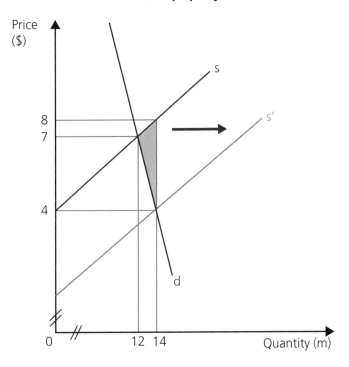

The consequences of the subsidy for the consumer are that the price falls from $7 to $4 and quantity demanded increases from 12m to 14m trips because it is relatively more affordable to take the bus. The spending by consumers falls from $84m to $56m per year. Consumer surplus increases by $39m (0.5 x (12m + 14m) x $3).

The consequences for the producers are that they receive a payment to keep costs down so supply will increase (i.e., at each and every price there is an increase in quantity supplied). Before the subsidy they received $7 per trip but now receive $8, the income for the bus company increases from $84m to $112m. Producer surplus increases by $13m (0.5 x (12m +14m) x $1).

The cost to government of the subsidy is $56m per year, there is a loss in allocative efficiency (shaded on the diagram) of $4m per year. This DWL represents that part of the subsidy that is not picked up as part of the consumer surplus and producer surplus, so represents a welfare loss.

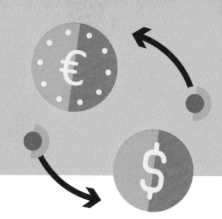
Maximum price control and allocative efficiency

A **price control** (maximum or minimum price) is imposed by government so that price cannot automatically move back to the equilibrium as it would in the free market because laws or regulations prohibit this.

A **maximum price** (or **ceiling price**) is a price control set by government prohibiting the charging of a price higher than a certain level. A maximum price is set in the interests of consumers to protect them from paying unreasonably high prices for essential goods and services, for example housing, petrol or certain food items such as bread and milk.

To illustrate the effects of a maximum price, draw a line at the price at which the maximum price is set and label this appropriately. Draw a dotted line to show the quantity demanded (Qd) and quantity supplied (Qs) at this price, than label the resulting shortage created. Show the decrease in price from the original price (Pe) to the maximum price (Pmax)

Market for bread and a maximum price

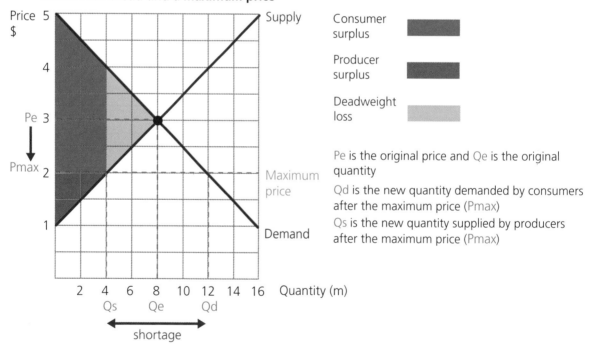

Pe is the original price and Qe is the original quantity

Qd is the new quantity demanded by consumers after the maximum price (Pmax)

Qs is the new quantity supplied by producers after the maximum price (Pmax)

	Original equilibrium	New equilibrium
Consumer surplus (CS)	0.5 × 8m × $2 = $8m	(0.5 × 4m × $1) plus (4m x $2) = $10m
Producer surplus (PS)	0.5 × 8m × $2 = $8m	(0.5 × 4m × $1) = $2m
Deadweight loss (DWL)	Nil (zero)	0.5 × 4m × $2 = $4m

There is a deadweight loss from a maximum price that represents the loss of allocative efficiency because part of the original consumer surplus and producer surplus is not picked up as part of the maximum price.

The impact of a maximum price worked example

	Before the maximum price	After the maximum price
Quantity sold	Qe, 8m	Q2, 4m
Price consumers pay	Pe, $3	Pmax, $2
Consumer spending	Pe x Qe, 24m	Pmax x Q2, $8m
Price producers receive	Pe, $3	Pmax, $2
Producer revenue	Pe x Qe, $24m	Pmax x Q2, $8m
Size of the shortage	The size of the gap between Q2 and Qd. 8m	

If the government sets a maximum price control of $2 for the market of bread this restricts the price that firms are legally allowed to charge. The diagram shows that imposing a maximum price at $2 for a loaf of bread will cause the price to fall from $3 to $2. As the price decreases the quantity demanded of bread made available by producers decreases from 8m (Qe) to 4m (Qs). This causes a shortage of 8m loaves of bread and could give rise to a black market where some people are willing to pay a higher price than the legally set price by government of $2 for bread.

The change in total value of sales after the maximum price is imposed is the difference between the original price multiplied by the original quantity (Pe multiplied by Qe) and the maximum price set multiplied by the quantity made available by suppliers (Maximum Price multiplied by Qs). In this instance, it is the difference between ($3 multiplied by 8m) and ($2 multiplied by 4m) which is a $16m decrease.

To assist individuals and families to buy affordable bread to eat the government could increase the supply of bread by offering producers a subsidy. A subsidy is a payment by government to suppliers (businesses) to keep costs down, as a result they will increase supply and the price will decrease. The advantage of a subsidy over a maximum price control is that there will be no shortage and the market will clear. The disadvantage of a subsidy is that it may be very expensive for the government, and the money spent on the subsidised good or service means this money cannot be spent elsewhere.

A maximum price set above the equilibrium price has no effect because a price above the equilibrium price creates a surplus (excess supply) where market forces automatically cause the price to decrease back to the equilibrium. Therefore, to be effective, a maximum price must be set below the equilibrium.

The **advantages of a maximum price** control is that it will lower the price of the good or service and make it more affordable for consumers, and there is no cost to the government. The problem of an effective maximum price set below the equilibrium is that it distorts the market because it does not allow the market to clear. A maximum price set below the equilibrium results in a shortage (excess demand), because at prices below the equilibrium the quantity demanded by consumers is greater than the quantity supplied by producers. This means that some consumers who had the good or service before the maximum price was imposed miss out because the quantity supplied decreases as the price falls. Solutions to overcome the shortage created by a maximum price could be first-come-first-served until supply runs out, or the government could issue ration cards giving an equal share to everyone.

A **black market** can arise with a maximum price. A black market is part of the underground or informal economy where activities that take place are illegal, unregulated and not taxed. In a black market, firms charge a price above the legally set government maximum price or well-off customers or consumers pay more than the government's legally set price to obtain the good or service that circumvents rationing measures put in place by the government.

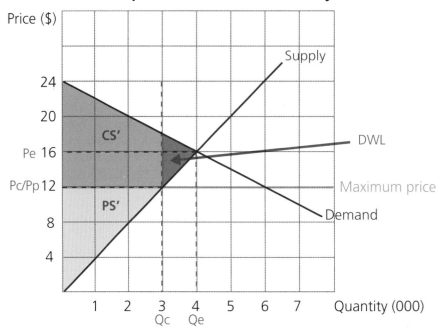

Maximum price and allocative efficiency

1 a Assume the government has placed a **maximum price control of $12**.
   On the graph above label:
   • the original equilibrium price (Pe) and quantity (Qe)
   • the new equilibrium price (Pc) and quantity (Qc)
   • the new price producers receive as (Pp).

b Complete the table.

(i) Change in total consumer spending	($16 x 4 000) vs ($12 x 3 000) = $28 000 decrease
(ii) Change in consumer surplus	($6 x 3 000) plus (0.5 x $6 x 3 000) vs (0.5 x $8 x 4 000) = $11 000 increase
(iii) Change in producer surplus	(0.5 x $12 x 3 000) vs (0.5 x $16 x 4 000) = $14 000 decrease
(iv) The deadweight loss	(0.5 x $6 x 1 000) = $3 000

2 a Show the effects of a maximum price of $3.20 per litre on the graph below (labelled as Pmax) on the market for milk each month.

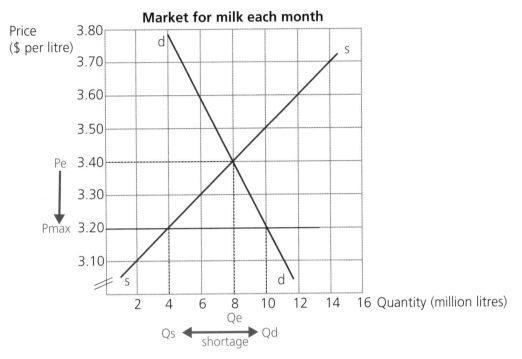

Market for milk each month

Price ($ per litre) axis values: 3.80, 3.70, 3.60, 3.50, 3.40 (Pe), 3.30, 3.20 (Pmax), 3.10

Quantity (million litres) axis values: 2, 4, 6, 8 (Qe), 10, 12, 14, 16

Qs ◄──── shortage ────► Qd

b Referring to the graph, identify:

- the price that consumers pay before and after: before: $3.40 per litre (Pe)

  after: $3.20 per litre (Pmax)

- the price that producers receive before and after: before: $3.40 per litre (Pe)

  after: $3.20 per litre (Pmax)

- the value of sales before and after: before: $3.40 x 8 million equals $27.2m

  after: $3.20 x 4 million equals $12.8m

c Discuss the effect on consumer spending and consumers of the maximum price.

A maximum price (Pmax) is a price control set by government, prohibiting the charging of a price higher than a certain level, in this case $3.20 per litre on milk. As the price of milk falls the quantity demanded increases from 8 million litres (Qe) to 10 million litres (Qd).

The change in consumer spending on milk falls from $27.2m to $12.8m.

Several flow-on effects include that consumers desire 10 million litres but can only purchase (legally) 4 million litres, that is, there is a shortage of 6 million litres of milk monthly, which is a problem. A black market may arise because some consumers who can afford to pay higher prices might offer to pay more than the legally set price. Some consumers may miss out, others may switch to a substitute good (e.g., milk powder).

Explains maximum price in depth. Values (figures) stated. Uses appropriate economic terms. Explains flow-on effects.

3 Use the diagram below to answer the questions that follow.

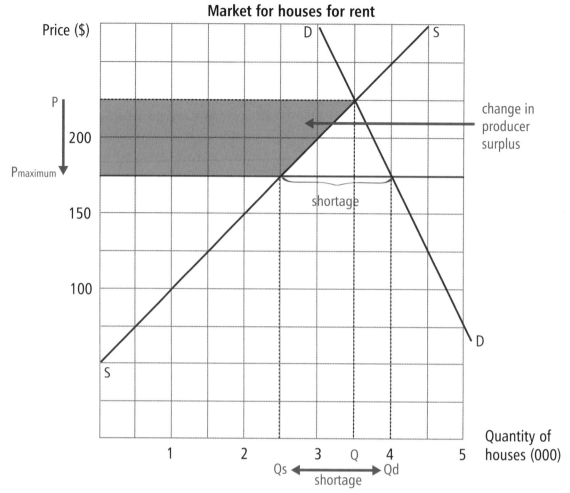

Market for houses for rent

The government wants to reduce the cost of houses for rent. One option is to impose a price control of $175.

a What is the correct economic term for this option? <u>Maximum price.</u>

b (i) Show the effect on the graph of the government imposing a price control of $175.

(ii) Calculate the change in producer surplus from the maximum price. Shade and label this area.

<u>(0.5 x 3 500 x $175) difference (0.5 x 2 500 x $125) = $150 000 decrease</u>

<u>OR (2 500 x $50 plus 0.5 x 1 000 x $50)</u>

c Alternatively, the government could achieve the same market price of $175 by offering a subsidy. How much would the subsidy on each house have to be?

<u>$75</u>

d Calculate the cost of the subsidy to the government.

<u>subsidy per unit x Q' = $75 x 4 000 = $300 000</u>

e Both price control and subsidy options achieve the same market price but have different effects on the quantity supplied. For each option calculate the change in quantity supplied.

(i) price control option <u>decrease 1 000 houses</u>　　　**(ii)** subsidy option <u>increase 500 houses</u>

f State one advantage of subsidies over price controls.

<u>Idea of no shortage, equilibrium found, market clears, no black market.</u>

4 Price controls can cause the market to be allocatively inefficient.

Explain the effects of a price control. In your answer you should use the graph and:

- Label the original equilibrium price and quantity as Pe and Qe respectively. Calculate the original value of CS and PS.
- Label the new equilibrium price and quantity as P1 and Q1 respectively. Calculate the new CS and PS after the increase in demand.
- Explain how the market restores the equilibrium.
- Assume the government fixes the price at Pe, shade the deadweight loss and explain why it occurs.

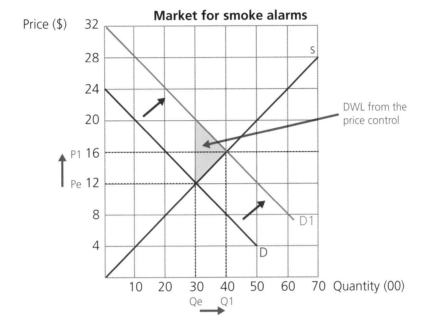

Market for smoke alarms

DWL from the price control

CS and PS at the original equilibrium is $18 000 and at the new equilibrium the CS and PS are both $32 000.

When there is an increase in demand it creates a shortage at the original price Pe. Consumers will bid up the price to P1. The equilibrium will be restored at P1 where the QD = QS.

The deadweight loss occurs because it represents the lost CS and PS that goes to no other party when the government fixes the price in the market at Pe.

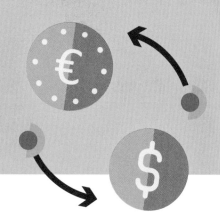
Minimum price control and allocative efficency

A **minimum price** (or **floor price**) is a price control set by government where the market price is not allowed to fall below a certain minimum (floor) level. A minimum price is set by the government in the interests of producers to protect them from volatile prices in world markets and ensure that they are not receiving an unreasonably low price for what they produce. At one time in New Zealand, the government set a minimum (floor) price on wool and butter.

To illustrate the effects of a minimum price, draw a line at the price at which the minimum price is set and label this appropriately. Draw a dotted line to show the quantity demanded (Qd) and quantity supplied (Qs) at this price, than label the resulting surplus created. Show the increase in price from the original price (Pe) to the minimum price (Pmin)

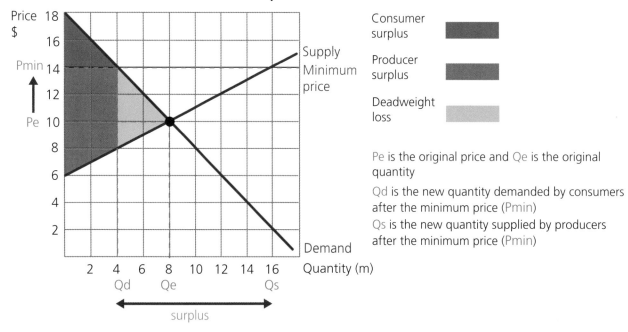

Market for wool and a minimum price

Pe is the original price and Qe is the original quantity

Qd is the new quantity demanded by consumers after the minimum price (Pmin)

Qs is the new quantity supplied by producers after the minimum price (Pmin)

	Original equilibrium	New equilibrium
Consumer surplus (CS)	(0.5 × 8m × $8) = $32m	(0.5 × 4m × $4) = $8m
Producer surplus (PS)	(0.5 × 8m × $4) = $16m	(4m × $6 plus 0.5 × 4m x $2) = $28m
Deadweight loss (DWL)	Nil (zero)	0.5 × 4m x $6 = $12m

There is a deadweight loss from a minimum price that represents the loss of allocative efficiency because part of the original consumer surplus and producer surplus is not picked up as part of the miniimum price.

The impact of a minimum price worked example

	Before the minimum price	After the minimum price
Quantity sold	Qe, 8 million	Qd, 4 million
Price consumers pay	Pe, $10	Pmin, $14
Consumer spending	Pe x Qe, $80m	Pe x Qd, $56m
Price producers receive	Pe, $10	Pmin, $14
Size of the surplus	The size of the gap between Qd and Qs. 12 million	

If the government sets a minimum price control of $14 on the market for wool, the diagram shows, the price of wool will increase from $10 to $14. As the price increases the quantity of wool demanded by consumers decreases from 8 million (Qe) to 4 million (Qd). There is a surplus of 12 million that the government has to buy and store.

The change in total value of sales after the minimum price is imposed is the difference between the original price multiplied by the original quantity (Pe multiplied by Qe) and the minimum price set multiplied by the quantity purchased by consumers (Minimum Price multiplied by Qd). In this instance, it is a $24m decrease.

The change in a firms revenue is the difference between the original price multiplied by the original quantity (Pe multiplied by Qe) and the minimum price set multiplied by the quantity produced by producers (Minimum Price multiplied by Qs) if the government purchases the excess supply of wool. Left to the free operation of the market this surplus goes unsold and creates a deadweight loss.

To be effective, a minimum price is set above the equilibrium price. This encourages producers to increase the quantity supplied because they are more able to cover their costs because they are earning higher revenue and it is more profitable to produce the good or service. The problem of an effective minimum price set above the equilibrium is that it distorts the market because it does not allow the market to clear. At the higher price the quantity demanded by consumers is less than the quantity supplied by producers resulting in excess supply (a surplus). The surplus (excess supply) is created because price is not allowed to fall below the controlled price to the equilibrium. The government then has to decide what to do with the surplus stock. In the past this surplus stock was stockpiled and sold at a later date.

A minimum price set below the equilibrium price has no effect because a price below the equilibrium price creates a shortage (excess demand) where market forces automatically cause price to increase back to the equilibrium. Therefore, to be effective, a minimum price must be set above the equilibrium.

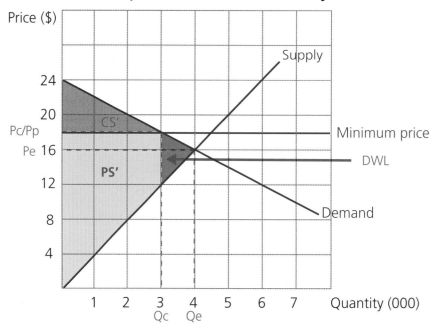

Minimum price and allocative efficiency

1 a Assume the government has placed a **minimum price control of $18**.
On the graph above label:
- the original equilibrium price (Pe) and quantity (Qe)
- the new equilibrium price (Pc) and quantity (Qc)
- the new price producers receive as (Pp).

b Complete the table.

(i) Change in total consumer spending	($16 x 4 000) vs ($18 x 3 000) = $10 000 decrease
(ii) Change in consumer surplus	(0.5 x $8 x 4 000) vs (0.5 x $6 x 3 000) = $7 000 decrease
(iii) Change in producer surplus	(0.5 x $16 x 4 000) vs ($6 x 3 000 plus 0.5 x $12 x 3 000) = $4 000 increase
(iv) The deadweight loss	0.5 x $6 x 1 000 = $3 000

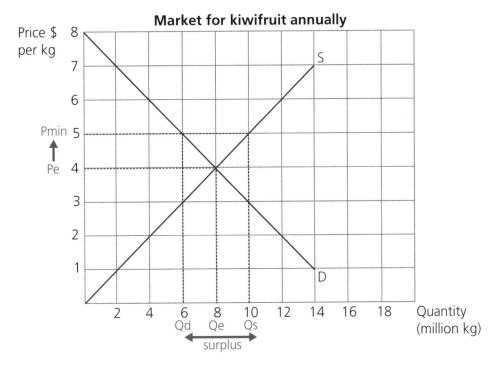

Market for kiwifruit annually

2 **a** Show a minimum price of kiwifruit set at $5 per kg.

b Referring to the graph above, identify and calculate:

	Before the minimum price	After the minimum price
Quantity sold	8m kg	6m kg
Price consumers pay	$4 per kg	$5 per kg
Consumer spending	$4 x 8m = $32m	$5 x 6m = $30m
Size of the surplus	4m kg	

c Referring to the graph above, identify and calculate:

	Before the minimum price	After the minimum price
Consumer surplus	0.5 x 8m x $4 = $16m	0.5 x 6m x $3 = $9m
Producer surplus	0.5 x 8m x $4 = $16m	6m x $2 plus 0.5 x 6m x $3 = $21m
Change in CS	Decrease of $7m	
Change in PS	Increase of $5m	
Deadweight loss	Nil (zero)	0.5 x 2m x $2 = $2m

Prices for avocados continue to vary.

3 The graph shows the effects of a minimum price on the market for avocados.

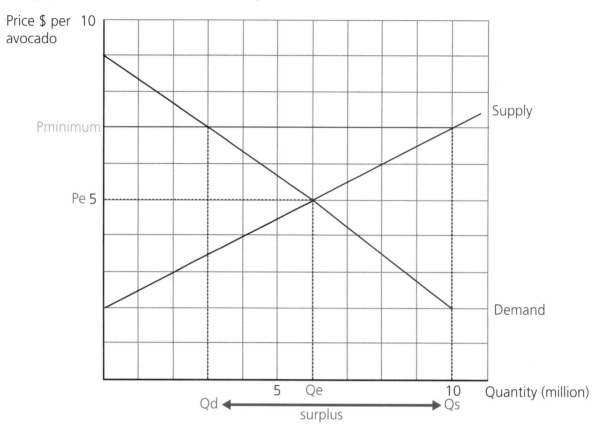

a On the graph above:

  (i) use dotted lines to show the original equilibrium price and quantity (label as **Pe** and **Qe**)

  (ii) use dotted lines to show the new quantity demanded (**Qd**) and supplied (**Qs**)

  (iii) label the resulting **surplus** or **shortage**.

b Referring to the graph above, identify and calculate:

	Before the price control	After the price control
(i) Consumer spending	$5 x 6m = $30m	$7 x 3m = $21m
(ii) Consumer surplus	0.5 x $4 x 6m = $12m	0.5 x $2 x 3m = $3m
(iii) Producer surplus	0.5 x $3 x 6m = $9m	(0.5 x $1.5 x $3m) plus ($3.5 x 3m) = $12.75m
(iv) Deadweight loss	nil (zero)	(0.5 x $3.5 x 3) = $5.25m

4 a Show the effects of a minimum price of $12 per kg on the graph below (labelled as Pmin) on the market for cheese each month. Shade and label the new consumer surplus **(i)**, producer surplus **(ii)** and any loss of allocative efficiency **(iii)**.

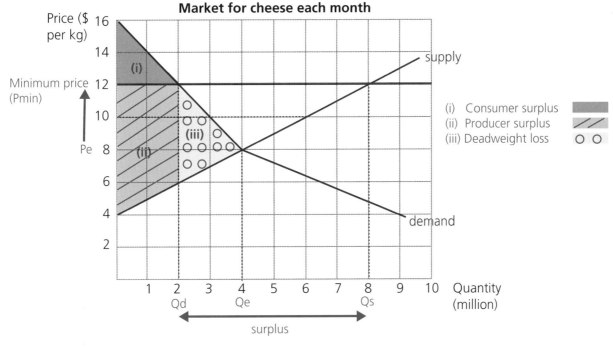

b What difficulty does the government face with getting a price control of $12 per kg?

The government has to decide what to do with the resulting surplus, usually stockpile it and sell it at a later date.

c Why might a government impose a minimum price?

To protect producers from receiving unreasonably low prices for their output.

5 a On the graph of the Weekly market for organic eggs below, show the effect of a minimum price of $7 per dozen (labelled as Pmin).

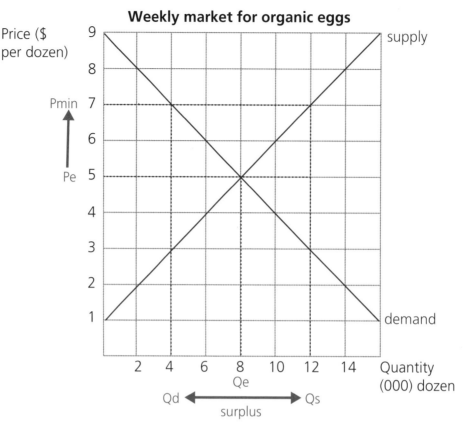

Weekly market for organic eggs

b Referring to the graph, identify:

- the price that consumers pay before and after the minimum price

  before: $5 per dozen (Pe)   after: $7 per dozen (Pmin)

- the price that producers receive before and after the minimum price

  before: $5 per dozen (Pe)   after: $7 per dozen (Pmin)

- the quantity that consumers buy before and after the minimum price

  before: 8 000 dozen (Qe)   after: 4 000 dozen (Qd)

c Referring to the graph, calculate the values before and after the minimum price.

	Before the minimum price	After the minimum price
Consumer surplus	0.5 x 8 000 x $4 = $16 000	0.5 x 4 000 x $2 = $4 000
Producer surplus	0.5 x 8 000 x $4 = $16 000	0.5 x 4 000 x $2 plus 4 000 x $4 = $20 000
Deadweight loss	Nil (zero)	0.5 x 4 000 x $4 = $8 000

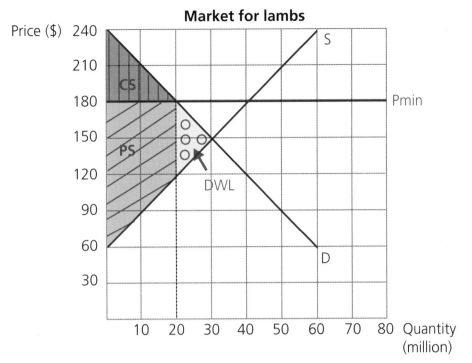

Market for lambs

6 a The government has imposed a minimum price of $180 per lamb. Label at the minimum price
   Consumer surplus   ‖‖‖‖
   Producer surplus   ⁄⁄⁄
   Deadweight loss (if any)   ○ ○

b Complete the table

	Value from the graph
(i) Change in consumer surplus	$\frac{(20m + 30m)}{2}$ x $30 = $750m (decrease)
(ii) Original producer surplus	0.5 x 30m x $90 = $1 350m
(iii) New producer surplus	(20m x $60) + (0.5 x 20m) x $60 = $1 800m
(iv) Change in producer surplus	$450m increase
(iv) Deadweight loss	0.5 x 10m x $60 = $300m

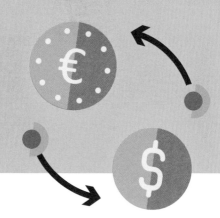

13 EFFICIENCY OF MARKET EQUILIBRIUM
Free trade and AE

Free trade is trade between countries without government intervention. Changes that take place in the market as a result of free trade allow the market to reach the equilibrium and the consumer surplus and producer surplus are still maximised. International free trade is more allocatively efficient than not trading, because the area of total surpluses increases.

Free trade – exports (X)

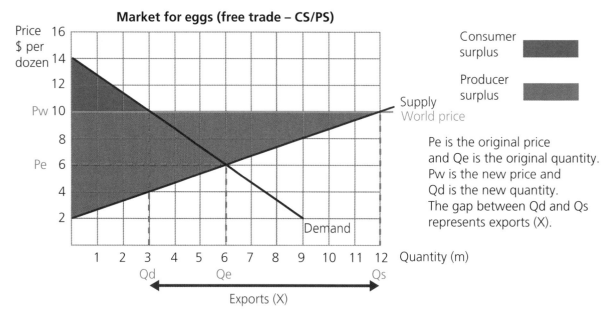

Market for eggs (free trade – CS/PS)

Consumer surplus

Producer surplus

Pe is the original price and Qe is the original quantity. Pw is the new price and Qd is the new quantity. The gap between Qd and Qs represents exports (X).

Exports (X)

	Original equilibrium	New equilibrium
Consumer surplus (CS)	0.5 × 6m × $8 = $24m	0.5 × 3m × $4 = $6m
Producer surplus (PS)	0.5 × 6m × $4 = $12m	0.5 × 12m x $8 = $48m
Deadweight loss (DWL)	Nil (zero)	Nil (zero)

With the free trade in eggs the increase in producer surplus of $36m offsets the decrease in consumer surplus of $18m. The market is allocatively efficient because the total surpluses increase by $18m.

The diagram shows that with free trade the price that consumers pay for eggs increases from Pe ($6 per dozen) to Pw ($10 per dozen). As the price increases the quantity demanded of eggs by local consumers decreases from Qe (6 million dozen) to Qd (3 million dozen). The value of sales to local consumers decreases from $36m to $30m. Consumer surplus decreases because consumers pay more and buy fewer eggs.

The producer now receives Pw ($10 per dozen) rather than Pe ($6 per dozen). They now sell 3m dozen eggs to local consumers and export 9m dozen eggs to overseas buyers. The revenue for the producer will increase from $36m to $120m, of which $30m comes from domestic sales and $90m from export sales. Producer surplus increases because producers receive a higher price and sell more eggs.

    ISBN: 9780170438100

Free trade – imports (M)

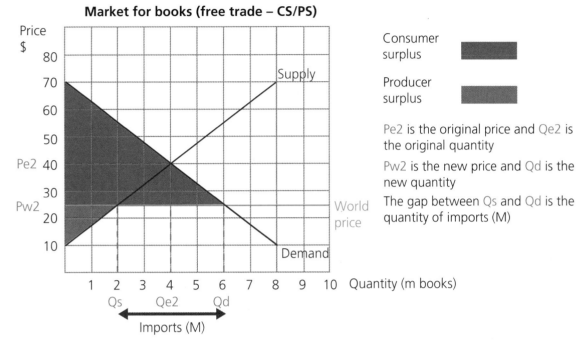

Market for books (free trade – CS/PS)

Consumer surplus

Producer surplus

Pe2 is the original price and Qe2 is the original quantity

Pw2 is the new price and Qd is the new quantity

The gap between Qs and Qd is the quantity of imports (M)

	Original equilibrium	New equilibrium
Consumer surplus (CS)	0.5 × 4m × $30 = $60m	0.5 × 6m × $45 = $135m
Producer surplus (PS)	0.5 × 4m × $30 = $60m	0.5 × 2m x $15 = $15m
Deadweight loss (DWL)	Nil (zero)	Nil (zero)

Overall net welfare increases because the decrease in producer surplus of $45m is more than offset by the gain in consumer surplus of $75m.

The diagram shows that the price that consumers pay for books decreases from Pe2 ($40) to Pw2 ($25). As the price decreases the quantity demanded of books by local consumers increases from Qe2 (4 million) to Qd (6 million). The value of sales decreases from $160m to $150m. Consumer surplus increases because they pay less and buy more.

Local producers have to lower the price to compete with cheaper imported books. They now receive Pw2 ($25) per book rather than Pe2 ($40), selling 2m books (Qs) rather than 4 million books. Their revenue will decrease from $160m to $50m. There is $100m spent on imported books because 4 million books are imported and sold at $25 per copy. Producer surplus decreases because they receive a lower price and sell less.

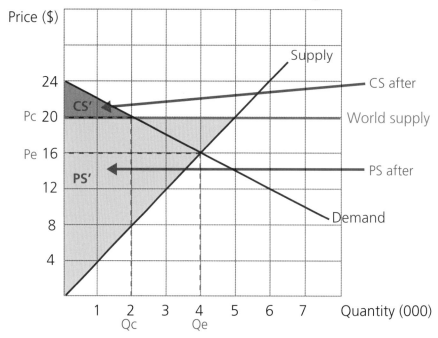

Free trade and allocative efficiency

1 a Assume **free trade** is taking place at a price of **$20**.
On the graph above label:
- the original equilibrium price (Pe) and quantity (Qe)
- the new equilibrium price (Pc) and quantity (Qc).

b Complete the table.

(i) Change in total consumer spending	($16 x 4 000) vs ($20 x 2 000) = $24 000 decrease
(ii) Change in suppliers' revenue	($16 x 4 000) vs ($20 x 5 000) = $36 000 increase
(iii) Change in consumer surplus	(0.5 x $8 x 4 000) vs (0.5 x $4 x 2 000) = $12 000 decrease
(iv) Change in producer surplus	(0.5 x $16 x 4 000) vs (0.5 x $20 x 5 000) = $18 000 increase
(v) The deadweight loss	nil (zero)

2 Study the diagram below and answer the questions that follow.

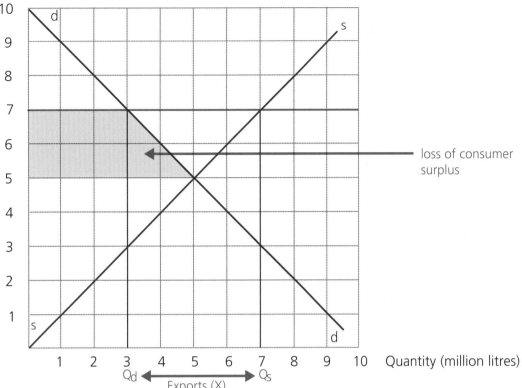

Trade diagram – New Zealand domestic market for milk weekly

a If the world price was $7, identify on the graph: **(i)** the quantity supplied and label it Qs.
   (ii) the quantity demanded and label it Qd.   **(iii)** the quantity exported or imported.

b Calculate at the world price:

   (i) the change in the total value of sales to the local market.

   (P x Q) vs (Pw x Qd) = ($5 x 5m) vs ($7 x 3m) = $4m decrease

   (ii) the quantity of milk exported. 4 million litres.

   (iii) State the total revenue at the world price of $7. Show your working. $7 x 7m = $49m

   (iv) How much revenue is from domestic sales? $7 x 3m = $21m

   (v) How much revenue is from export sales? $7 x 4m = $28m

c Calculate:

   (i) CS before $12.5m   **(iv)** PS before $12.5m

   (ii) CS after $4.5m   **(v)** PS after $24.5m

   (iii) Change in CS $8m decrease   **(vi)** Change in PS $12m increase

d Shade in the loss of consumer surplus.

3 Study the graph and answer the questions that follow.

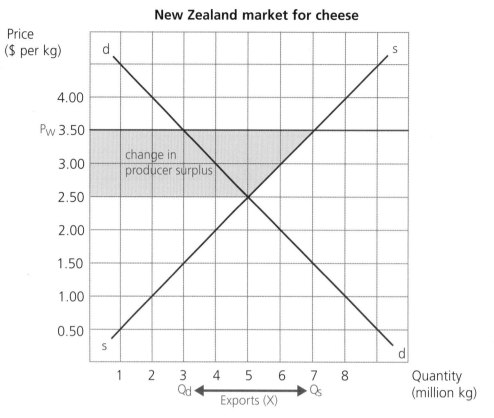

New Zealand market for cheese

a What is a quota? How does a quota on New Zealand cheese to Europe and the USA affect New Zealand cheese production?

A quota is a restriction on quantity, production, imports. The effect on New Zealand cheese production will be a decrease in supply.

b The world price for cheese is above the market equilibrium price and is the same for all levels of quantity.

(i) Draw the world price at $3.50 per kg and label it P_W.

(ii) What happens to the New Zealand market price if New Zealand is involved in the trade of cheese with other countries? Be specific. Increase to $3.50 per kg.

(iii) At a price of $3.50 per kg the New Zealand market has a surplus or excess supply. What will happen to this surplus? Exported, sold overseas, stockpiled.

(iv) Identify the new quantity of cheese sold in New Zealand at the world price. 3 million kg.

(v) Calculate the decrease in the quantity sold in New Zealand. 2 million kg.

(vi) Calculate the quantity of exports at the new world price. 4 million kg.

c Shade in and label the change in producer surplus.

 ISBN: 9780170438100

4 The world price for snapper is above the market equilibrium in New Zealand.

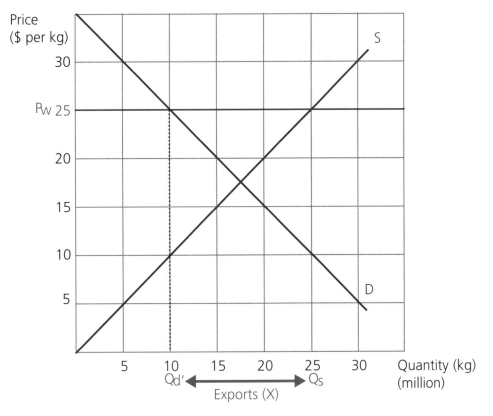

a Draw the world price at $25 per kg and label it P_W on the diagram above.

b What happens to the New Zealand domestic market price if New Zealand is involved in the trade of snapper?

It increases to $25 per kg.

c At a price of $25 per kg the New Zealand market has a surplus. What will happen to this surplus?

Exported.

d Identify the new quantity demanded in New Zealand at $25 per kg as Qd'.

Qd' as shown above. 10m kg.

e (i) State the total revenue at the world price of $25 per kg. Show your working.

$25 x 25m = $625m

(ii) How much revenue is from:

domestic sales $25 x 10m = $250m

export sales $25 x 15m = $375m

f Explain why international trade in snapper is allocatively more efficient for New Zealand than not trading.

International trade is allocatively more efficient than not trading, because the area of total surpluses (total gains from trade) increases. The gain in PS outweighs the loss of CS.

CS before = $153.125m   CS after = $50m   Change in CS = $103.125m decrease

PS before = $153.125m   PS after = $312.5m   Change in PS = $159.375m increase

5 Study the graph below and answer the questions that follow.

Trade diagram

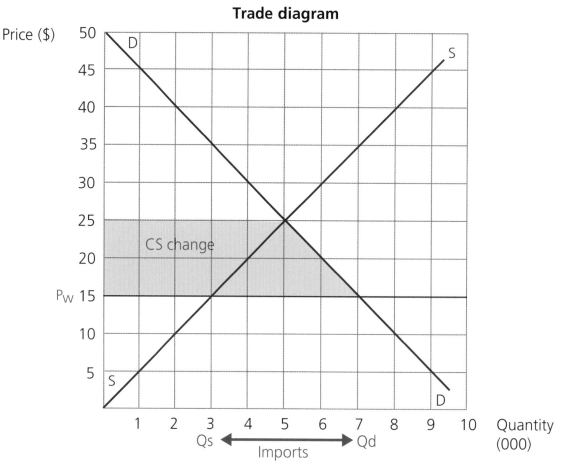

a If the world price is $15 and there were no trade restrictions, what would happen to the New Zealand domestic price? Explain why this would happen.

<u>The effect on domestic price in New Zealand is that it would fall, because imports become cheaper so</u>

<u>consumers buy them/competition from imports forces local price down.</u>

b (i) Draw on the diagram above a world price of $15 and label it P_W.

(ii) What is the new equilibrium price? <u>$15</u>

(iii) By what quantity has the sale of the product in New Zealand changed?

<u>Increased by 2 000.</u>

(iv) How many of the product do New Zealand firms supply to the market at the new price?

<u>3 000</u>

(v) Calculate the change in revenue for local (New Zealand) producers. Show your working.

<u>($25 x 5 000) difference ($15 x 3 000) = $80 000 decrease</u>

c Calculate:

(i) CS before <u>$62 500</u>   **(iv)** PS before <u>$62 500</u>

(ii) CS after <u>$122 500</u>   **(v)** PS after <u>$22 500</u>

(iii) Change in CS <u>$60 000 increase</u>   **(vi)** Change in PS <u>$40 000 decrease</u>

d Show and clearly label on the diagram above the change in consumer surplus that results from the world price of $15.

6 Assume New Zealand is a price taker in the market for mountain bikes and the current world price expressed in NZ dollars is $1 500.

Explain the impact of trade in the market. In your answer you should:

- Show on Graph 1 the world price for mountain bikes, label it Pw, the quantity of mountain bikes imported, label it M, and the increase in consumer surplus as a result of international trade in mountain bikes, shade it.
- Explain why international trade in mountain bikes is allocatively more efficient for New Zealand than not trading.

Graph 1: Market for mountain bikes in New Zealand

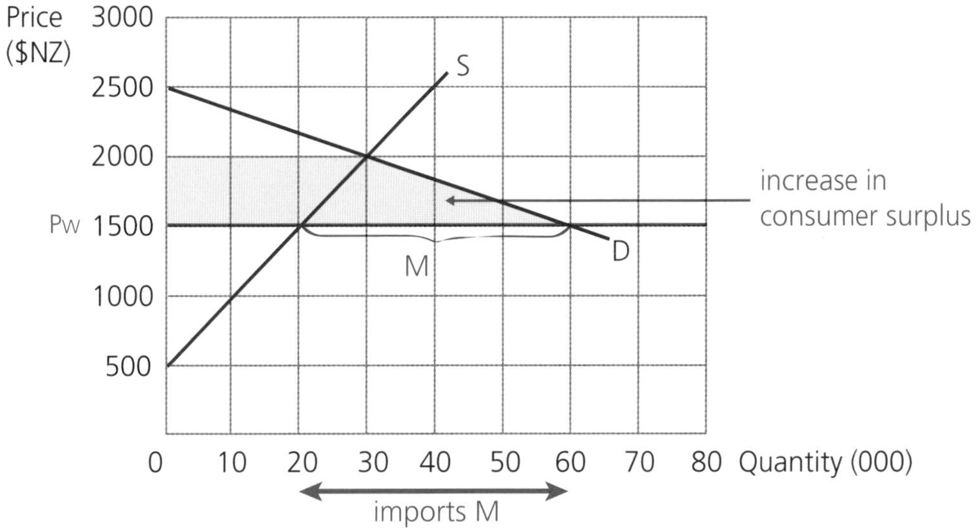

International trade is allocatively more efficient than not trading, because the area of total surpluses (total gains from trade) increases. Consumers are paying lower prices and consuming more, CS increases.

CS before trade was $7.5m and after $30m, therefore a gain of $22.5m. The PS before trade was $22.5m and after $10m, therefore a decrease of $12.5m. The gain in CS will offset the loss of PS.

7 The removal of trade barriers will improve allocative efficiency.

Explain how removing a trade barrier is allocatively efficient. In your answer you should use the diagram drawn and:

- Explain why the world supply curve is drawn as a horizontal line.
- Identify clearly areas of CS and PS before and after trade barriers are removed.
- Explain the effect of free trade on New Zealand consumers, producers and the allocation of labour resources.

Domestic market in New Zealand for bacon

The world supply curve is drawn as a horizontal line because the quantity of bacon imported by NZ is so small in relation to world output, so overseas suppliers can satisfy NZ needs without an increase in costs. NZ will pay Pw for any level of imports.

CS before = 1, after = 124, gain = 24

PS before = 23, after = 3, loss = 2

The gain in CS offsets the loss of PS.

The effect of free trade on consumers is price decreases and quantity demanded increases, CS overall increases, greater choice and higher standard of living. The effect on producers is they will receive a lower price and quantity supplied will decrease from Q to QL, they will receive less revenue, less profit and PS falls.

There will be a reallocation of resources in the economy, because fewer workers are needed to produce bacon in NZ because of the lower output (this is a derived demand) then unemployment in this industry will increase. Workers will be reallocated to relatively more profitable areas of production.

8 Exporters expect to benefit from free trade deals being signed, but consumers will lose.

Explain how removing a trade barrier is allocatively efficient. In your answer you should use the diagram drawn and:

Explain how exporters gain from a free trade deal. In your answer you should:

- Draw a sketch diagram to show changes in CS and PS as a result of exporting.
- Explain the effect of exporting on consumers and producers.
- Explain the possible effects of exporting on government revenue.

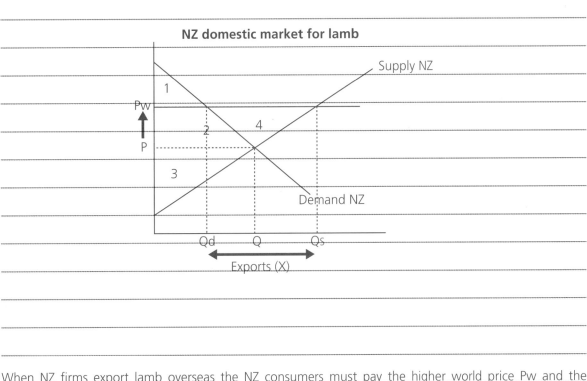

When NZ firms export lamb overseas the NZ consumers must pay the higher world price Pw and the quantity demanded falls from Q to Qd, CS falls from areas 1 and 2 to area 1, they will have less choice.

NZ producers of lamb will get a higher price and produce more, they will receive greater revenue and profits. PS will increase from area 3 to areas 2, 3 and 4. Firms will hire extra workers (derived demand) because of the need to increase output.

Direct tax collected by government will increase because the increase in revenue earned by lamb producers will result in an increase in company profits and company tax paid. More workers employed in the sheep industry will see an increase in income tax collected.

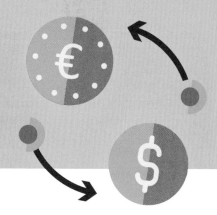

14 EFFICIENCY OF MARKET EQUILIBRIUM
Protectionism and AE

Protectionism refers to government measures (quotas and tariffs) that limit international trade. Protectionism will alter the market equilibrium in a way that results in a loss of allocative efficiency (termed deadweight loss).

Tariff & DWL

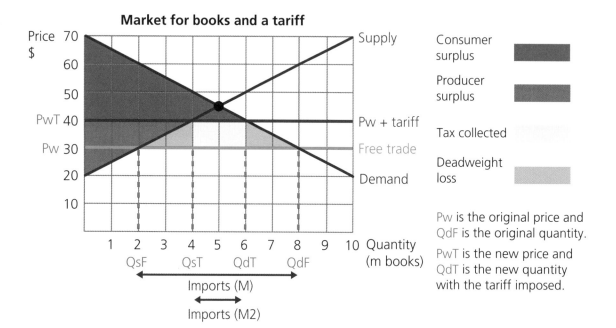

Market for books and a tariff

Pw is the original price and QdF is the original quantity.

PwT is the new price and QdT is the new quantity with the tariff imposed.

	Original equilibrium	New equilibrium
Consumer surplus (CS)	0.5 × 8m × $40 = $160m	0.5 × 6m × $30 = $90m
Producer surplus (PS)	0.5 × 2m × $10 = $10m	0.5 × 4m × $20 = $40m
Deadweight loss (DWL)	Nil (zero)	2 x (0.5 x 2m x $10) = $20m

With a per unit tariff of $10 placed on books, the equilibrium price increases from $30 (Pw) to $40 (PwT) and the equilibrium quantity decreases from 8m (QdF) to 6m (QdT). The quantity produced by local firms will now be 4m books (QsT) rather than 2m (QsF). The change in local firms' revenue is the difference between $60m ($30 x 2m books) and $160m ($40 x 4m books), which is an increase of $100m.

With the tariff in place, the quantity of books imported is now 2m books rather than the 6m previously imported when the price was $30. Part of the total value of consumer spending on books of $240m ($40 multiplied by 6m) will be $80m on imported books (imports multiplied by the world price), while the remaining $160m is with domestic (local) firms. The revenue received by the government is equal to the quantity imported multiplied by the per unit tariff imposed, (2m x $10), which is $20m.

There is a deadweight loss from the tariff that represents the loss of allocative efficiency because part of the original consumer surplus and producer surplus is not picked as part of the tariff imposed.

PHOTOCOPYING OF THIS PAGE IS RESTRICTED UNDER LAW. ISBN: 9780170438100

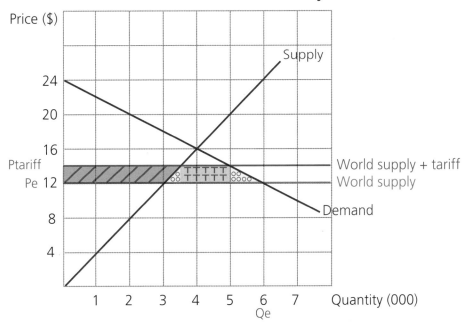

Protectionism and allocative efficiency

1 a On the graph above label the original free trade equilibrium price (Pe) and quantity (Qe)

b Assume that a **per unit tariff of $2 is imposed**. Draw and label the new supply curve.

Shade the gain in producer surplus

Label the tax revenue collected

Shade the loss of allocative efficiency

c Complete the table.

(i) Change in total consumer spending	($12 x 6 000) vs ($14 x 5 000) = $2 000 decrease
(ii) Change in suppliers' revenue	($12 x 3 000) vs ($14 x 3 500) = $13 000 increase
(iii) Change in consumer surplus	(5 000 x $2) plus (0.5 x 1 000 x $2) = $11 000 decrease
(iv) Change in producer surplus	(3 000 x $2) plus (0.5 x 500 x $2) = $6 500 increase
(v) The deadweight loss	(0.5 x 500 x $2) + (0.5 x 1 000 x $2) = $1 500

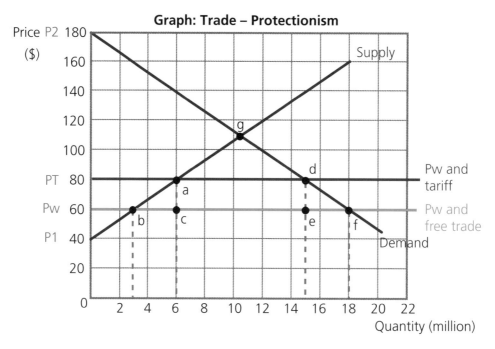

Graph: Trade – Protectionism

2 **a** Complete the table, using figures. Show your working.

	Free trade	Protectionism
Price	$60	$80
Local firms' output	3m	6m
Consumer expenditure	$60 x 18m = $1080m	$80 x 15m = $1 200m
Imports	15m	9m
Consumer surplus	(0.5 x 18m x $120) = $1080m	(0.5 x 15m x $100) = $750m
Producer surplus	(0.5 x 3m x $20) $30m	(0.5 x 6m x $40) = $120m
Deadweight loss (DWL)	Nil (zero)	2 x (0.5 x 3m x $20) = $60m

b Explain why there is a change in consumer surplus and producer surplus.

Producer surplus increases by $90m because producers receive a higher price ($80) and produce more (6 million units rather than 3 million units). Consumer surplus falls by $330m because they pay a higher price ($80 rather than $60) and consume less (15 million units rather than 18 million units).

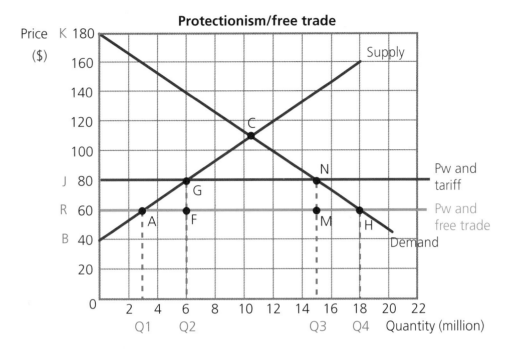

Protectionism/free trade

3 Study the diagram then use letters to complete the table below.

	Protectionism	Free trade
a Price	OJ	OR
b Local firms' output	Q2	Q1
c Imports	Q2 to Q3	Q1 to Q4
d Consumer surplus	KNJ	KRH
e Producer surplus	JGB	RAB
f Deadweight loss (DWL)	AGF plus NMH	Zero (nil)

4 Explain, using figures, the changes to consumer surplus, producer surplus and allocative efficiency as the result of government imposing a per unit tariff of $15.

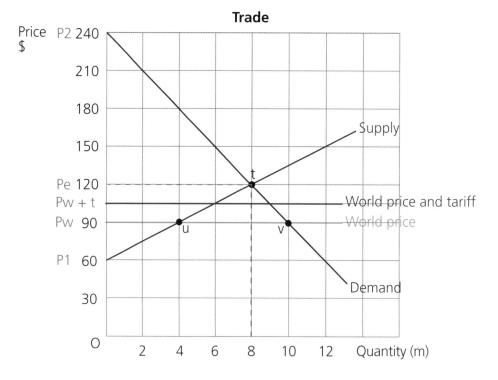

At the world price ($90), consumer surplus is $750m and producer surplus is $60m, the market is allocatively efficient.

When a tariff (a tax on imports) is levied on imported goods or services it will raise the price thereby making locally-made products relatively more competitive. The tariff lifts the price to $105 and local firms' output increases from 4 million to 6 million. Producer surplus for domestic producers will now be $135m, which is a gain of $75m. Consumer surplus with the tariff is $607.5m because consumers now pay a higher price ($105 instead of $90) and consume less (9m instead of 10m). There is a loss of consumer surplus of $142.5m as a result of the tariff.

The government raises tax revenue of $45m because this equals the tariff per unit ($15) multiplied by imports (3 million). When the government imposes a tariff, part of the consumer surplus and producer surplus from free trade is lost. This loss of allocative efficiency (DWL) in this instance is $22.5m (0.5 x 1m x $15 plus 0.5 x 2m x $15).

5 Referring to the graph below, fully explain (using letters) the impact on consumers, producers, the government and allocative efficiency of a tariff imposed on this market.

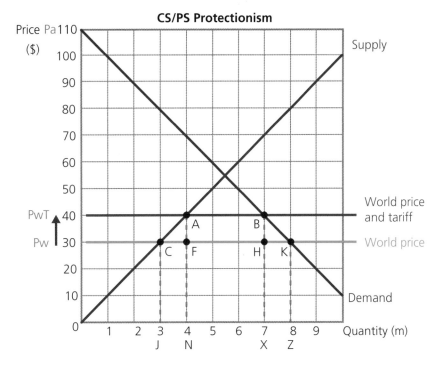

CS/PS Protectionism

At the world price (Pw), consumer surplus is the area PwKPa and producer surplus is the area PwCO, the market is allocatively efficient.

When a tariff (a tax on imports) is levied on imported goods or services it will raise the price thereby making locally-made products relatively more competitive. The effects of a tariff per unit are shown on the diagram. The tariff lifts the price to PwT ($40) and local firms' output increases from OJ (3 million) to ON (4 million). The quantity sold at PwT is OX (7 million) while imports are represented by the gap between ON and OX (3 million). The government raises tax revenue equal to the tariff per unit ($10) multiplied by imports (3 million), represented by the area AFHB, which is $30 million.

Consumer surplus with the tariff is the area PwTBPa because consumers now pay a higher price (PwT instead of Pw) and consume less (OX instead of OZ). The area PwKBPwT represents the loss of consumer surplus as a result of the tariff. At PwT domestic producers will now sell ON instead of OJ, and the producer surplus will now be PwTAO. The area PwCAPwT represents the gain of producer surplus that results from the government imposing a tariff.

When the government imposes a tariff, part of the consumer surplus and producer surplus from free trade is lost. This loss of allocative efficiency is termed a deadweight loss (DWL). In the diagram, it is the area represented by the the two triangles either side of the government revenue collected, these are CFA and HKB. They represent a loss of welfare by an individual or group that is not offset by welfare gain to some other individual or group.

15 REVISION/STUDY
Tasks and activities

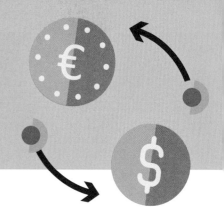

Exam hints

Preparation

Prepare for the exam by completing all exericises in this book, doing old papers or the written questions on eLearneconomics.com website.

In the exam

- Use appropriate economic language, examples and terms in your answers.

- Make accurate references in your answers to the resource material and/or graphs drawn, i.e., provide details in your descriptions, such as figures or names of individuals/firms/products.

- Take care and construct well-labelled, accurate graphs (with a title, graduated scales) using a ruler to plot curves. Refer to these graphs explicitly in your explanations, e.g., D1 to D2, P to P'.

- Write structured answers that link ideas, keep your answers on track and do not contradict what you have written.

- Read questions carefully and add reasons, causes and effects in your explanations.

- Flow-on effects need to be valid, explained in full and kept in context with the event that led to it, rather than a restatement of the initial event itself.

- Attempt all questions.

- Present answers in a legible form.

- Use a pen (not a pencil) on your script to ensure answers are clear.

- Do not use abbreviations or text language because these are not appropriate in a formal exam.

    ISBN: 9780170438100

Notes

Question one: Maximum price

a Using market forces, explain how the market equilibrium is restored. Refer to the diagram in your answer.

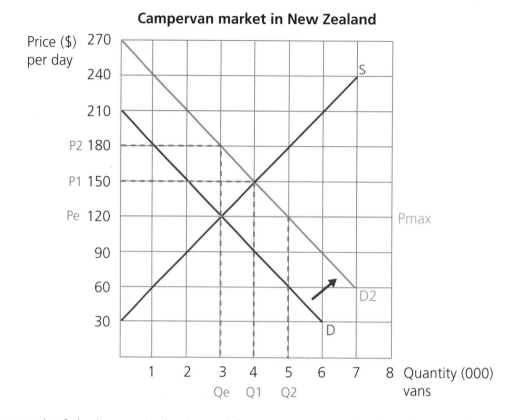

Campervan market in New Zealand

<u>As a result of the increase in the demand for campervans per day there is now a shortage (excess demand) at the original equilibrium price Pe ($120). Consumers will bid up the price. The quantity supplied by firms increases because hiring a campervan to consumers becomes more profitable for the firm (supplier), since revenue is higher they are more able to cover costs. The difference between revenue and costs is greater. The equilibrium is restored at P1 ($150) per day because quantity demanded equals quantity supplied of 4 000 vans/or because the excess demand is removed.</u>

b Compare and contrast the situation of the government leaving the market at the new equilibrium with the effect of imposing a maximum price of $120 per day on campervan rentals. Explain the impact on consumer surplus, producer surplus and allocative efficiency.

A maximum price is a price control set by government prohibiting the charging of a price higher than a certain level. At the maximum (ceiling) price of $120 per day consumers want 5 000 vans (Q2) but firms are only willing to provide 3 000 vans (Q1), this creates a shortage of 2 000 vans. Because there is a maximum price in place the market will not clear and the shortage of vans will continue to exist. Some consumers will miss out on getting a campervan.

If the market was allowed to operate without government intervention at $150 per day, both the consumer surplus and producer surplus would be $240 000 (.5 x $120 x 4 000) each. At the free market equilibrium of $150 per day, CS and PS are maximised and the market is allocatively efficient.

When the government imposes a maximum price of $120 per day on campervans the total value of consumer surplus increases by $75 000 because consumer surplus at P1 is $240 000 and at Pmax it is $315 000 (0.5 x $90 x 3000 plus ($60 x 3 000).

The total value of producer surplus decreases by $105 000 because producer surplus at P1 is $240 000 and at Pmax it is $135 000 (0.5 x $90 x 3 000).

The total surplus at P1 is $480 000 while it is only $450 000 at Pmax of $120. Overall the maximum price at $120 causes a deadweight loss of $30 000 (0.5 x $60 x 1 000) because it is that part of the maximum price that is not picked up as either consumer surplus or producer surplus.

Question two: A tariff

Study the diagram and answer the questions that follow.

Market for New Zealand clothes

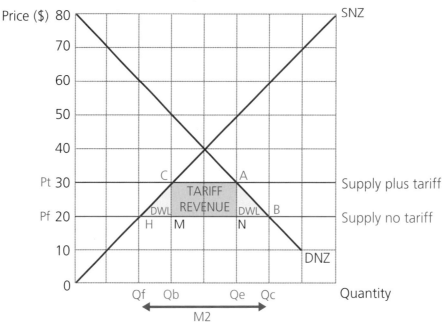

a Discuss the impact on allocative efficiency in the Market for New Zealand Clothes if the government removes the tariff on clothes. In your answer:

(i) Illustrate the removal of a per unit tariff of $10, label your new curve as Supply no tariff. Label the new equilibrium price as **Pf**, the new equilibrium quantity as **Qc**, local firms' output as **Qf** and the new level of imports as **M2**.

(ii) Explain in detail the changes made on your graph.

When a tariff (a tax on imports) levied on imported goods or services is removed it will lower the price of imported clothes into New Zealand, the price falls from Pt to Pf. The supply curve falls from Supply plus tariff to Supply no tariff. As the price falls local firms' output decreases from Qb to Qf because at the lower price it is less profitable for New Zealand firms to make clothes. The consumption of clothes increases from Qe to Qc because at a lower price buying clothes is more affordable. Imports increase from the gap between Qb to Qe to the gap shown as M2 (Qf to Qc).

 ISBN: 9780170438100

b Compare and contrast the impact of the government removing the tariff on consumers, producers, the government, and allocative efficiency. Refer to your diagram in your answer.

Because the price for consumers falls from Pt to Pf the quantity purchased by consumers increases from Qe to Qc. The consumer surplus increases by the area PtABPf. The consumer surplus increases because the price paid is lower and the quantity purchased greater.

At Pf domestic producers will now produce and sell Qf instead of Qb. The producer surplus will now be PfHO rather than the area PtCO. The area PtCHPf represents the loss of producer surplus that results from the government removing the tariff.

Because the tariff is removed the government no longer collects the tariff revenue ANMC shown on the diagram. The two triangles either side of the government revenue collected (CHM and ANB) represent the DWL from a tariff that is now picked as part of the new consumer surplus.

Allocative efficiency requires production efficiency, and it is not possible for one person to be made better off without making anyone else worse off. This means there is no possible reallocation of resources that will make someone better off without making someone else worse off. Allocative efficiency occurs at the free market equilibrium where the total consumer surplus and the total producer surplus are maximised. With the removal of the tariff on the market clothes it is now allocatively efficient at Pf because there is an overall gain in total surpluses, because the CS has increased to include the loss of PS, loss of tariff revenue and DWL (which had existed at Pt).

Question three: Sales tax and elasticity

Complete **a** and **b** to explain the impact of a sales tax on allocative efficiency in the market when goods or services are either price elastic or price inelastic.

Diagram 1: Elastic demand

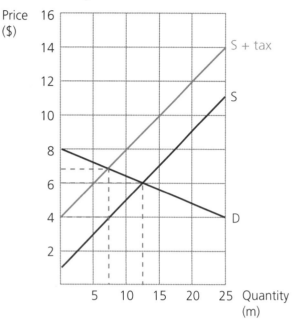

Diagram 2: Inelastic demand

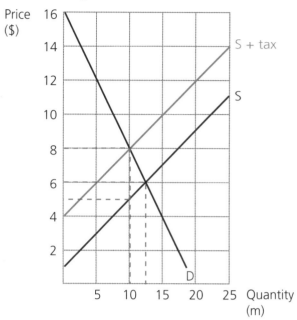

a Complete the table below, use figures and show your working:

		Diagram 1	Diagram 2
(i)	The new price	$7	$8
(ii)	The new quantity	7.5m	10m
(iii)	The change in consumer surplus	($1 x 7.5m) + (.5 x $1 x 5m) = $10m decrease	($2 x 10m) + (.5 x $2 x 2.5m) = $22.5m decrease
(iv)	The change in producer surplus	($2 x 7.5m) + (.5 x $2 x 5m) = $20m decrease	($1 x 10m) + (.5 x $1 x 2.5m) = $11.25m decrease
(v)	The deadweight loss	(.5 x $3 x 5m) = $7.5m	(.5 x $3 x 2.5m) = $3.75m
(vi)	The tax revenue for government	$3 x $7.5m = $22.5m	$3 x 10m = $30m

b Compare and contrast the impact of a per unit sales tax on allocative efficiency when goods or services have different elasticities.

Explain the change in consumer surplus, producer surplus and allocative efficiency. Refer to both graphs.

An indirect tax is a payment to the government that is added to the price of the good or service. The tax adds to the costs of production and as a result firms will decrease supply. The supply curve shifts vertically upwards to Supply and Tax, as illustrated on both diagrams. The tax per unit is represented by the vertical distance between the two supply curves, on both graphs there is a $3 per unit tax. The firm is able to pass on part of the tax to the consumer, on Diagram 1 it is $1 with the price paid by the consumer rising to $7 and on Diagram 2 the firm passes on $2 to the consumer with the price rising to $8. The increase in price to the consumer is greatest on diagram 2 because demand is inelastic with producers more able to pass the tax on to the consumer.

On both diagrams there is a loss in consumer surplus because consumers pay a higher price and consume less. The total value of consumer surplus decreases, in Diagram 1 it is by $10m and $22.5m in Diagram 2. More of the tax is passed onto the consumer in Diagram 2 because demand is inelastic, consumers will continue to buy the same quantity of the good or service (relatively) when compared with Diagram 1.

On both diagrams there is a loss in producer surplus from the tax because producers receive a lower price and sell less. The total value of producer surplus decreases by $20m in Diagram 1 and by $11.25m in Diagram 2. Because more of the tax is passed on in Diagram 2 than Diagram 1, the loss of producer surplus to the producer is greater in Diagram 1 than Diagram 2.

The government collects tax revenue on both diagrams. On Diagram 1 it is $22.5m and on Diagram 2 it is $30m. Because Diagram 2 is price inelastic the government receives greater tax revenue since the increase in price has had a proportionately smaller decrease in the quantity when compared with Diagram 1.

When the government imposes an indirect tax, part of the original consumer surplus and producer surplus is not being picked up, therefore causing a loss to society. This loss of allocative efficiency is termed a deadweight loss (DWL), this is a loss of welfare by an individual or group that is not offset by welfare gain to some other individual or group. In Diagram 1 it is $7.5m and Diagram 2 it is $3.75m. The DWL is greater in Diagram 1 because it is price elastic, so the proportionately larger decrease in the quantity means that the combined loss of PS and CS is more than on Diagram 2. A tax imposed on a good or service is more allocatively inefficient for a price elastic product than a price inelastic good or service.

Question four: Subsidy and elasticity

Complete **a** and **b** to explain the impact of a subsidy on allocative efficiency in the market when goods or services are either price elastic or price inelastic.

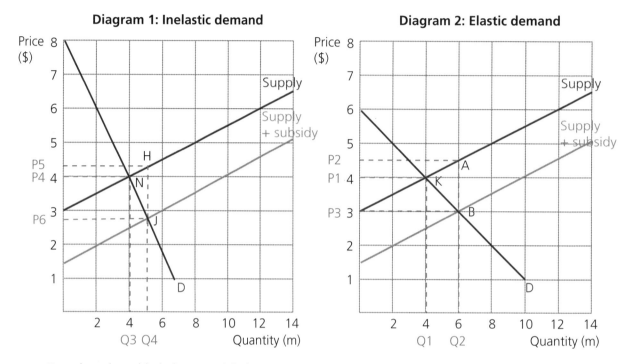

Diagram 1: Inelastic demand

Diagram 2: Elastic demand

a Complete the table below, use labels:

	Diagram 1	Diagram 2
(i) The new price	P6	P3
(ii) The new quantity	Q4	Q2
(iii) The change in consumer surplus	P4NJP6	P1KBP3
(iv) The change in producer surplus	P5HNP4	P2AKP1
(v) The deadweight loss	HNJ	ABK
(vi) The cost of the subsidy to the government	P5HJP6	P2ABP3

       ISBN: 9780170438100

b Compare and contrast the impact of a per unit sales tax on allocative efficiency when goods or services have different elasticities.

Explain the change in consumer surplus, producer surplus and allocative efficiency. Refer to both graphs.

A subsidy is a payment by the government to firms to keep costs down. The subsidy reduces the costs of production and as a result firms will increase supply. The supply curve shifts vertically downward to S and subsidy, as illustrated on both diagrams. The subsidy per unit is represented by the vertical distance between the two supply curves, on both graphs there is a $1.50 per unit subsidy. The firm passes on part of the subsidy to the consumer. On Diagram 1 it passes on $1.25 with the price paid by the consumer falling to P6 ($2.75). On Diagram 2 the firm passes on $1.00 and the consumer now pays $3 (P3). The decrease in price to the consumer is greatest on Diagram 1 because demand is inelastic.

On both diagrams there is an increase in consumer surplus because consumers pay a lower price and consume more. The total value of consumer surplus increases, in Diagram 1 by P4NJP6 and by P1KBJ3 in Diagram 2. More of the subsidy is passed on to the consumer in Diagram 1 because demand is inelastic.

On both diagrams there is an increase in producer surplus from the subsidy because producers receive a higher price and sell more. The total value of producer surplus increases by P5HNP4 in Diagram 1 and P2AKP1 in Diagram 2. Because less of the subsidy is passed onto the consumer in Diagram 2 than Diagram 1, the gain in producer surplus is greater in Diagram 2 than Diagram 1.

With a subsidy there is a loss of allocative efficiency (termed a deadweight loss) because part of the subsidy is not picked up as part of the new CS or PS. There is a loss of welfare by an individual or group that is not offset by welfare gain to some other individual or group. In Diagram 1 it is HNJ and Diagram 2 it is ABK. The DWL is greater in Diagram 2 because it is price elastic, so the proportionately larger increase in the quantity means that the combined loss of PS is more than Diagram 1.

A subsidy on a good or service is more allocatively inefficient for a price elastic product than a price inelastic good or service.

Question five: Trade and different time periods

a Explain fully the change in consumer surplus and producer surplus in the **short run** when there is an increase in the world price. Use labels and refer to your diagram.

Diagram 1: Short run (inelastic) supply for a product

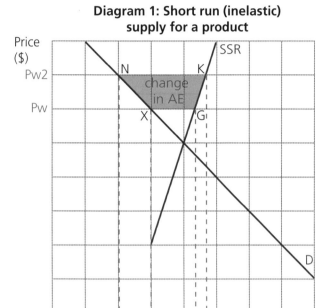

Diagram 2: Long run (elastic) supply for a product

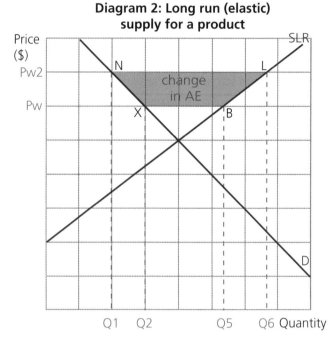

In Diagram 1 as the world price increases from Pw to Pw2, consumer surplus will decrease because consumers now pay a higher price (Pw2) and consume less (Q1 rather than Q2). The loss in consumer surplus is the area Pw2NXPw. Producer surplus will increase because producers now receive a higher price (Pw2) and supply more (Q4 rather than Q3). The increase in producer surplus is the area Pw2KGPw.

b Contrast and compare the impact on allocative efficiency in the **short run** with the **long run** that results from an increase in the world price to Pw2.

Explain the impact on allocative efficiency in both time frames and shade the change in allocative efficiency on both diagrams.

Explain why there is a greater change in allocative efficiency in the long run when compared to the short run.

Support your answer and refer to the labels on both diagrams.

Allocative efficiency requires production efficiency, and it is not possible for one person to be made better off without making anyone else worse off. This means there is no possible reallocation of resources that will make someone better off without making someone else worse off. Allocative efficiency occurs at the free market equilibrium where the total consumer surplus and the total producer surplus are maximised.

In the short run and long run allocative efficiency increases because the increase in producer surplus offsets any loss of consumer surplus, resulting in a net gain in surpluses. The increase in AE in the short run (on Diagram 1) is NKGX and in the long run (on Diagram 2) is NLBX. The increase in allocative efficiency is greater in the long run than the short run because in the long run producers are more able to respond to the increase in the world price because in the long run producers can change all the inputs used in the production process, which results in a proportionately larger increase in output. In the short run firms have at least one fixed factor of production and are restricted in their ability to increase output. The increase in producer surplus in the long run (Pw2LBPw) is greater than the increase in the short run (Pw2KGPw), this results in a larger increase in AE. The change in AE in the long run represented by the area NLBX is more than the increase of the area NKGX shown in the short run.

Question six: Subsidy

Subsidy and the market

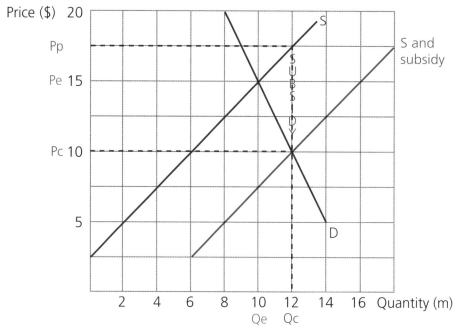

a (i) On the diagram illustrate the effect of a $7.50 per unit subsidy. Label the new equilibrium price as **Pc**, the new quantity as **Qc** and the price that producers now receive per item as **Pp**.

(ii) Explain how market forces move the market to the new equilibrium. Refer to the diagram in your answer.

A subsidy is a payment by government to firms to keep their costs down, and as a result firms will increase supply. As supply increases the equilibrium price will decrease and the equilibrium quantity will increase. At the original price of $15 (Pe) there is a surplus of 6m. Producers will now accept a lower price to get rid of unsold stock. The quantity demanded by consumers increases as the price falls. The equilibrium is restored at $10 (Pc) where the quantity demanded equals the quantity supplied at a quantity of 12m (Qc).

b Calculate the values of:

(i) Change in consumer surplus ($5 x 10m) plus (.5 x $5 x 2m) = $55m

(ii) Change in producer surplus ($2.5 x 10m) plus (.5 x $2.5 x 2m) = $27.5m

(iii) Cost of the subsidy to the government $7.5 x 12m = $90m

(iv) Deadweight loss (.5 x $7.5 x 2m) = $7.5m

c Explain the impact of a subsidy on consumer surplus, producer surplus and allocative efficiency. Refer to your calculations in **b**.

Consumer surplus (CS) is the difference between the maximum amount that a person is willing to pay for a good or service and its current market price. It represents the benefit consumers receive over and above what they actually pay (Pe) for a good or service. The price paid by the consumer falls by $5 and the quantity purchased increases by 2m. There is a gain in consumer surplus because consumers pay a lower price of $10 and consume 12m units. The gain in CS with this subsidy is $55m.

Producer surplus (PS) is the difference between the total earnings of suppliers for a certain quantity sold and the total costs required to put that quantity on the market. Producer surplus occurs in the market for a good or service because firms are willing to supply each unit for a lower price than they receive in the market. Producers receive an extra $2.5 per unit and sell 2m more. There is a gain in producer surplus from the subsidy because producers receive a higher price ($17.50) and sell 12m units. The gain in producer surplus with this subsidy is $27.5m.

Allocative efficiency occurs at the free market equilibrium ($15) where the total consumer surplus and the total producer surplus are maximised. Some of the subsidy is, however, not being picked up as part of the new consumer surplus and producer surplus, therefore causing a loss to society. This loss of allocative efficiency is termed a deadweight loss (DWL), which is a loss of welfare by an individual or group that is not offset by welfare gain to another individual or group. With this subsidy it is $7.5m.

Question seven: Goverment decisions

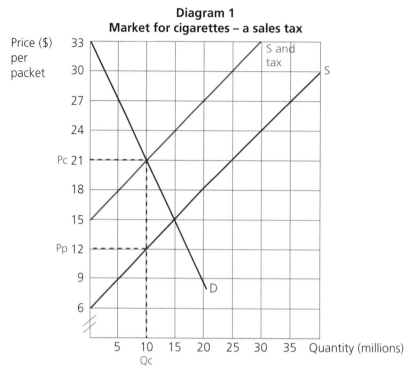

Diagram 1
Market for cigarettes – a sales tax

Price ($) per packet

Quantity (millions)

a On Diagram 1 illustrate the effect of a per unit tax that results in an equilibrium price of $21 per packet of cigarettes. Label the new equilibrium price as **Pc**, the new quantity as **Qc** and the price that producers now receive per item as **Pp**.

b Complete the calculations of the government imposing an indirect tax (show your working) for **Diagram 1**:

   (i) The change in consumer surplus ($6 x 10m) + (.5 x $6 x 5m) = $75m decrease

   (ii) The change in producer surplus ($3 x 10m) + (.5 x $3 x 5m) = $37.5m decrease

   (iii) The tax revenue for the government $9 x 10m = $90m

c The government decides to set a minimum price at $21 per packet of cigarettes. Complete the calculations (show your working) for **Diagram 2**:

   (i) The change in consumer surplus ($6 x 10m) + (.5 x $6 x 5m) = $75m decrease

   (ii) The change in producer surplus (.5 x $9 x 15m) difference ($9 x 10m) + (.5 x $6 x 10m)

       = $52.5m increase

   (iii) The change in consumer spending ($15 x 15m) difference ($21 x 10m) = $15m decrease

d Compare and contrast the impact of a minimum price with a policy of an indirect tax on the market for cigarettes, on consumer surplus, producer surplus and the government. Use the calculations you have made.

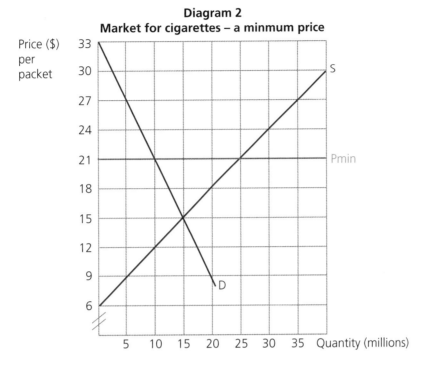

Diagram 2
Market for cigarettes – a minmum price

Consumer surplus (CS) is the difference between the maximum amount that a person is willing to pay for a good or service and its current market price. It represents the benefit consumers receive over and above what they actually pay for a good or service. For the minimum price and the indirect tax on both diagrams, the consumer surplus decreases by $75m because consumers pay a higher price ($21) and consume less (10m).

Producer surplus (PS) is the difference between the total earnings of suppliers for a certain quantity sold and the total costs required to put that quantity on the market. Producer surplus occurs in the market for a good or service because firms are willing to supply each unit for a lower price than they receive in the market. Producer surplus with the indirect tax decreases by $37.5m because producers receive a lower price ($12) and sell less (10m). With the minimum price the producer surplus increases by $52.5m because the increase in price of $6 received by producers offsets the fall in sales of 5m.

The government raises $90m in tax revenue from the imposition of the $9 per unit indirect tax, this revenue could be spent on smoking-related health issues or campaigns assisting people to stop smoking. There is no direct tax revenue raised from the minimum price, but the government will receive less GST receipts from the new consumer spending of $210m. The government might receive less company tax from the producers of cigarettes because their revenue will fall from $225m to $210m, which could reduce the profits they make.

Question eight: Goverment policies

Market for milk – maximum price

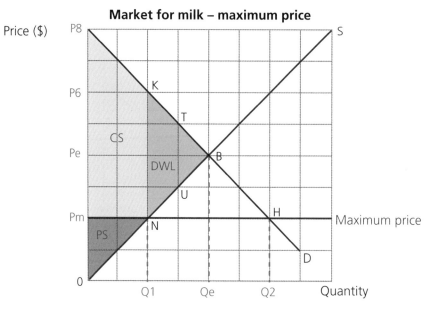

a On Diagram 1 above show the impact of a maximum price by shading and labelling **(i)** the new consumer surplus **(ii)** the new producer surplus and **(iii)** any loss of allocative efficiency.

b Explain the change in consumer surplus, producer surplus and allocative efficiency.

Consumer surplus (CS) is the difference between the maximum amount that a person is willing to pay for a good or service and its current market price. It represents the benefit consumers receive over and above what they actually pay for a good or service. Consumers will consume less milk because firms only supply Q1 at the maximum price. The original CS was P8BPe and the new CS is P8KNPm.

Producer surplus (PS) is the difference between the total earnings of suppliers for a certain quantity sold and the total costs required to put that quantity on the market. Producers will be selling less milk at a lower price, so the producer surplus will fall. Before the maximum price the producer surplus was PeBO and with the price control in place the producer surplus is PmNO.

Allocative efficiency occurs at the free market equilibrium (Pe/Qe) where the total consumer surplus and the total producer surplus are maximised. Some of the maximum price is, however, not being picked up as part of the new consumer surplus and producer surplus, therefore causing a loss to society. This loss of allocative efficiency is termed a deadweight loss (DWL), on the diagram it is the area BKN.

   ISBN: 9780170438100

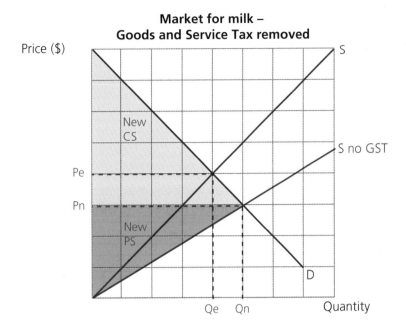

**Market for milk –
Goods and Service Tax removed**

Price ($)

New CS

Pe

Pn

New PS

S

S no GST

D

Qe   Qn

Quantity

c   Compare and contrast the impact of a maximum price with a policy of removing GST on the milk market on consumer surplus, producer surplus and allocative efficiency. In your answer:

(i) Label the original equilibrium price Pe and original equilibrium Qe. Label the new equilibrium price as Pn and new equilibrium quantity Qn on Diagram 2 above.

(ii) Shade and label the new consumer surplus and producer surplus.

(iii) Explain the change in CS, PS and allocative efficiency when the GST is removed.

(iv) Explain why removing GST would be more allocatively efficient that imposing a price control.

Refer to both diagrams.

Consumer surplus (CS) is the difference between the maximum amount that a person is willing to pay for a good or service and its current market price. It represents the benefit consumers receive over and above what they actually pay for a good or service. When the GST is removed from milk, the consumer surplus increases because consumers will pay less (Pn rather than Pe) and consume more (Qn rather than Qe).

Producer surplus (PS) is the difference between the total earnings of suppliers for a certain quantity sold and the total costs required to put that quantity on the market. Producer surplus occurs in the market for a good or service because firms are willing to supply each unit for a lower price than they receive in the market. When the GST is removed the producer surplus will increase to the shaded area because producers are selling more and no longer paying GST.

Allocative efficiency occurs at the free market equilibrium (Pe/Qe) because now total consumer surplus and total producer surplus are maximised. The deadweight loss that would exist with the maximum price is removed. A maximum price is allocatively inefficient because CS and PS are not maximised, the loss in PS is not offset by the gain in CS.

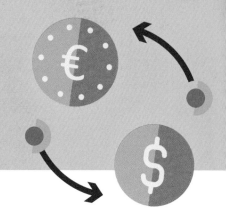

16 COSTS Basic concepts

Fixed, variable and total costs

Costs for a firm			
Output or quantity (Q)	Fixed Costs ($) FC	Variable Costs ($) VC	Total Costs ($) TC = FC + VC
0	250	–	250
1	250	70	320
2	250	120	370
3	250	140	390
4	250	160	410

The table above shows the typical costs faced by a firm. **Fixed costs (FC)** are **independent of output**, they must be paid whether or not the firm is producing, e.g., rent, mortgage repayments, rates. These are costs that a firm cannot avoid and must pay because they involve contractual arrangements with other parties, even if the firm closes down. Fixed costs (FC) are a constant amount regardless of the level of output (that is, they will not change).

Fixed costs can possibly change in the long run, e.g., the council sets new rates, firms arrange new terms of interest and repayment on loans or mortgages, or rent arrangements come up for review.

Variable costs (VC) represent **costs directly related to production** and will change as output increases or decreases, for example, power, raw materials, postage, wages. If there is no production, variable costs will be zero.

Total cost (TC) refers to the total expense firms incur to produce a certain level of output. Total cost is made up of total fixed costs (TFC or FC) and total variable costs (TVC or VC). When a firm is not producing (zero output) total costs are made up entirely of fixed costs because fixed costs are independent of output. The firm does not have any variable costs at zero output because variable costs are dependent on production and therefore are only incurred when a firm is producing.

The drawing of the typical-shaped curves for variable cost, fixed cost and total costs is shown in the diagram below. The total cost (TC) curve is similar in shape to the variable cost (VC) curve, but starts at the fixed cost (FC) curve. The vertical distance between TC and VC at any level is equal to FC. The fixed cost (FC) curve is drawn as a horizontal line.

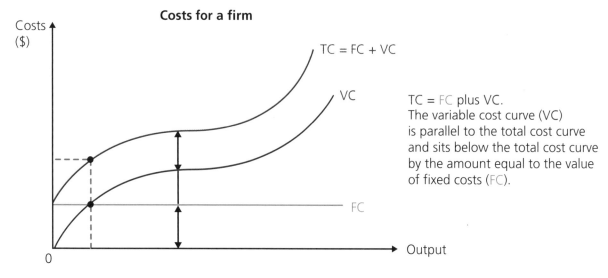

Costs for a firm

TC = FC plus VC.
The variable cost curve (VC) is parallel to the total cost curve and sits below the total cost curve by the amount equal to the value of fixed costs (FC).

 ISBN: 9780170438100

QUESTIONS & TASKS

1 a Complete the table.

Quantity	FC ($)	VC ($)	TC ($)
1	400	320	720
2	400	600	1 000
3	400	830	1 230
4	400	1 000	1 400
5	400	1 100	1 500
6	400	1 500	1 900
7	400	2 400	2 800

b Label the curves using the information from the table, use the small boxes for your answers.

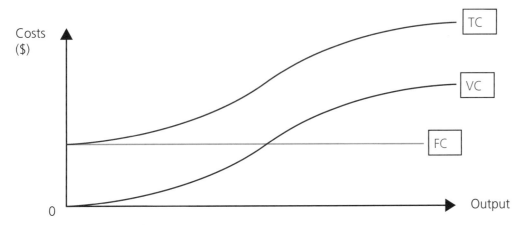

c What are a firm's variable costs (VC)?

A firm's variable costs are expenses directly related to production, e.g., wages, raw materials, stationery. The firm does not have any variable costs at zero output because variable costs are dependent on production and therefore are only incurred when a firm is producing.

d What are a firm's fixed costs (FC)?

Fixed costs (FC) are independent of output, they must be paid whether or not the firm is producing, e.g., rent, mortgage repayments, rates. These are costs that a firm cannot avoid and must pay because they involve contractual arrangements with other parties, even if the firm closes down. Fixed costs (FC) are a constant amount regardless of the level of output (that is, they will not change). Fixed costs can possibly change in the long run, e.g., the council sets new rates, firms arrange new terms of interest and repayment on loans or mortgages, or rent arrangements come up for review. Debt servicing is a fixed cost of paying interest on loans.

2 a Complete the table.

Quantity	FC ($)	VC ($)	TC ($)
0	400	nil/zero	400
1	400	640	1 040
2	400	750	1 150
3	400	800	1 200

b Draw the typical shapes of the total cost, fixed cost and variable cost curves.

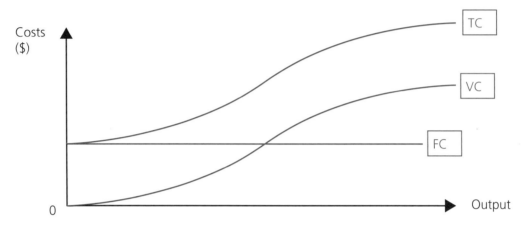

c Write whether the following 'costs' are fixed or variable.

(i) Rates _____ FC _____   **(vii)** Toll calls _____ VC _____

(ii) Hire purchase repayments _____ FC _____   **(viii)** Salaries _____ FC _____

(iii) Electricity _____ VC _____   **(ix)** Interest repayments on a mortgage _____ FC _____

(iv) Workers' wages _____ VC _____   **(x)** Insurance payments _____ FC _____

(v) Raw materials _____ VC _____   **(xi)** Gas for cars _____ VC _____

(vi) Stamps, postage requirements _____ VC _____   **(xii)** Rent for an office _____ FC _____

d What is meant by the term total cost (TC)?

Total cost (TC) refers to the total expense firms incur to produce a certain level of output. Total cost is made up of total fixed costs (TFC or FC) and total variable costs (TVC or VC). When a firm is not producing (zero output) total costs are made up entirely of fixed costs because fixed costs are independent of output. The firm does not have any variable costs at zero output because variable costs are dependent on production and therefore are only incurred when a firm is producing.

ISBN: 9780170438100

Costs for a firm			
Output Q	Fixed Costs FC ($)	Variable Costs VC ($)	Total Costs TC ($)
0	5 000	–	5 000
1	5 000	1 400	6 400
2	5 000	2 400	7 400
3	5 000	2 800	7 800
4	5 000	3 200	8 200
5	5 000	3 800	8 800
6	5 000	4 600	9 600

3 a Complete the table.

  b Give a formula that could be used to calculate total fixed costs.

    Fixed costs equals total costs minus variable costs or fixed costs equals average fixed costs multiplied by quantity.

  c Give a formula that could be used to calculate total variable costs.

    Variable cost equals total cost minus fixed costs or variable costs equals average variable costs multiplied by quantity.

  d Give a formula that could be used to calculate total cost.

    Total cost equals fixed costs plus variable costs or total cost equals average costs multiplied by quantity.

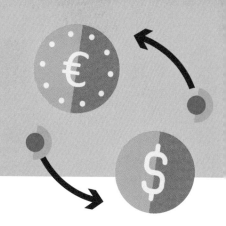

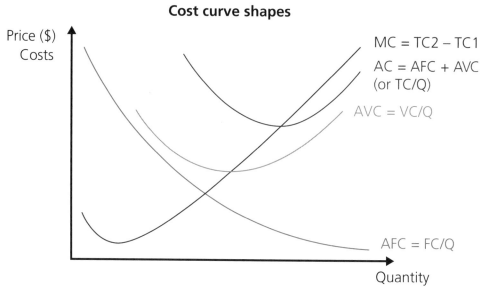

Cost curve shapes

Price ($)
Costs

MC = TC2 – TC1

AC = AFC + AVC
(or TC/Q)

AVC = VC/Q

AFC = FC/Q

Quantity

The average fixed cost (AFC) curve

Fixed costs (FC) are **independent of output**, they must be paid whether or not the firm is producing, e.g., rent, mortgage repayments, rates. These are costs that a firm cannot avoid and must pay because they involve contractual arrangements between other parties, even if the firm closes down. Fixed costs (FC) are a constant amount regardless of the level of output (that is, they will not change).

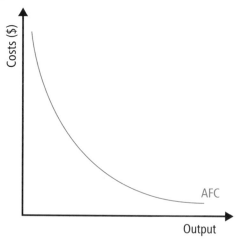

Costs ($)

AFC

Output

Output (Q)	Fixed costs ($)	Average fixed costs (AFC = FC/Q) ($)
0	800	–
1	800	800.00
2	800	400.00
3	800	266.67
4	800	200.00
5	800	160.00
6	800	133.33
7	800	114.29

Average fixed costs (AFC) equals fixed costs divided by quantity. Therefore, average fixed costs multiplied by quantity equals fixed cost. A change in a component of fixed costs will shift the fixed cost curves (total fixed costs and average fixed costs), total cost curve and average cost curve but leave the variable cost curve and the marginal cost curve unchanged.

As output increases, the average fixed cost curve (AFC) continuously falls from a maximum and tends towards zero because fixed costs are spread over a greater output.

Marginal cost (MC)

Marginal cost (MC) is the addition to total costs of an extra unit of output.

The typical **shape of the MC curve** is shown in the graph. Initially increasing returns and the more efficient use of resources leads to falling marginal costs. However, in the short run eventually marginal costs increase because of diminishing returns. The law of **diminishing returns** refers to the idea that as more and more of a factor (input) is used, with at least one fixed factor, there is some point at which the increase in output will be at a decreasing rate. Each variable unit produces less when diminishing returns are occurring, so the production of extra units of output will require more and more of the variable inputs (compared to earlier units). Therefore, it follows that the cost of each additional unit produced (ie, MC) must increase because more inputs are being used to produce it.

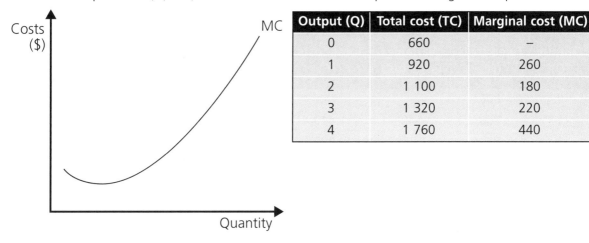

Output (Q)	Total cost (TC)	Marginal cost (MC)
0	660	–
1	920	260
2	1 100	180
3	1 320	220
4	1 760	440

To calculate marginal cost you work out the difference between total cost and the previous total cost. **Marginal cost will equal (Total Cost 2) minus (Total Cost 1)**. The marginal cost of the third unit in the table is $220 because it is the difference between the total cost of the third unit ($1320) and the total cost of the previous (second) unit produced ($1100).

If the total cost of 121 units is $12 093.95 and the total cost of production of 120 units is $12 000, the marginal cost is the difference between the total cost of 121 units and the total cost of the previous 120 units produced. In this instance the marginal cost will equal $12 093.95 minus $12 000 which is $93.95.

Given that total costs equals average costs multiplied by quantity, then marginal costs will equal (AC2 multiplied by Q2) minus (AC1 multiplied by Q1). For example, if the AC of 101 units is $19.95 and the average cost of 100 units is $20, the marginal cost equals (101 multiplied by $19.95) minus (100 multiplied by $20). Therefore, marginal costs equals $2 014.95 minus $2 000 which is $14.95.

Total costs equals fixed costs plus variable costs (TC = FC plus VC). Fixed costs are independent of output and do not change while variable costs are dependent on production, then the difference in total costs, which equals marginal cost, must be the difference between variable costs of the current output and the previous output. Given that marginal costs (MC) equals (FC plus VC2) minus (FC plus VC1), then MC must equal VC2 minus VC1. Marginal costs contain no fixed costs because fixed costs are a constant, the change in total costs must equal the change in variable costs.

Average total costs (ATC or AC) and average variable costs (AVC)

Variable costs (VC) represent **costs directly related to production** and will change as output increases or decreases, for example, power, raw materials, postage, wages. If there is no production, variable costs are zero.

A change in a component of variable costs will shift the variable cost curves (total variable costs and average variable costs), marginal costs and the total cost curve but leave the total fixed cost curve and the average fixed cost curve unchanged.

Variable costs divided by quantity equals average variable costs (AVC). Therefore, average variable costs multiplied by quantity equals variable costs.

Output (Q)	Fixed costs (FC)	Variable Costs (VC)	Total Costs (TC)	Average fixed costs (AFC = FC/Q)	Average variable costs (AVC = VC/Q)	Average costs (AC = TC/Q)
0	800	–	800	–	–	
1	800	640	1 440	800.00	640.00	1 440.00
2	800	1 200	2 000	400.00	600.00	1 000.00
3	800	1 660	2 460	266.67	553.33	820.00
4	800	2 000	2 800	200.00	500.00	700.00
5	800	2 200	3 000	160.00	440.00	600.00
6	800	3 000	3 800	133.33	500 00	633.33
7	800	4 800	5 600	114.29	685.71	800.00

Average total costs (ATC or AC) are the total costs divided by output.

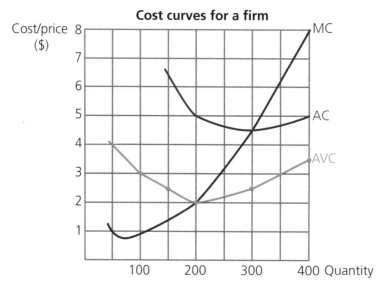

The average cost curve (ATC) is equal to average fixed costs (AFC) plus average variable costs (AVC). The **shape of the ATC (AC)** is therefore **derived from the shapes of the AFC and AVC curves**, and is **typically U shaped**.

As output increases, the AFC continuously falls because fixed costs are spread over a greater output. Intially, the AVC falls due to efficient resource use but at some stage diminishing returns set in causing the AVC to increase (because additional inputs are required to produce the additional output). Since both AFC and AVC fall initially, this causes the ATC curve to slope downward. At some stage however, as output increases, the AVC increases faster than the AFC falls, causing the ATC curve to slope upward.

As output increases the gap between AC and AVC narrows (gets closer). Average fixed costs (AFC) declines with increasing output because fixed costs (FC) are spread over a greater number of units of output. Since AC equals AFC plus AVC, a higher proportion of total costs (TC) will be made up of variable costs (VC) as output rises, so the gap narrows.

The rising section of the marginal cost curve intersects both the average cost curve and the average variable cost at their minimum (lowest) points. The AC and AVC curves must be drawn cutting MC at their minimum (lowest) points.

Average and marginal cost curve

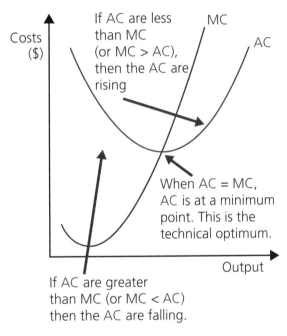

When marginal costs are less than average costs, then average costs must be falling because the extra cost of producing the next unit is less than the average cost.

When marginal costs are greater than average costs, then average costs must be rising because the extra cost of producing the next unit is greater than the average, therefore where AC equals MC, AC is minimised (the technical optimum).

Cost curve relationships

Cost curve relationships		
Cost curve to calculate	**Formula**	**Rearranging the formula**
Average fixed costs (AFC)	AFC = FC/Q	AFC x Q = FC
Average variable costs (AVC)	AVC = VC/Q	AVC x Q = VC
Average costs (AC or ATC)	AC = TC/Q	AC x Q = TC
Marginal costs (MC)	MC = TC2 − TC1	MC + TC1 = TC2 TC1 = TC2 − MC

QUESTIONS & TASKS

1 Complete each table and label the curves indicated by the title of each graph.

Output units	FC ($)	AFC ($)
0	100	–
1	100	100
2	100	50
3	100	33.33
4	100	25
5	100	20

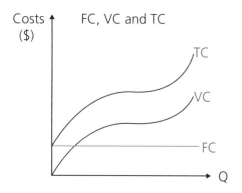

Output units	FC ($)	VC ($)	TC ($)
0	100	0	100
1	100	100	200
2	100	160	260
3	100	200	300
4	100	225	325
5	100	235	335
6	100	290	390
7	100	420	520

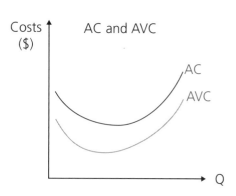

Output units	VC ($)	TC ($)	AVC ($)	AC ($)
0	0	100	–	–
1	100	200	100	200
2	160	260	80	130
3	200	300	66.67	100
4	225	325	56.25	81.25
5	235	335	47	67
6	290	390	48.33	65
7	420	520	60	74.29

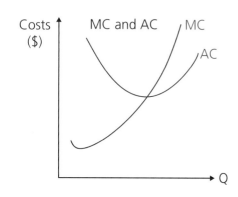

Output units	TC ($)	AC ($)	MC ($)
0	100	0	–
1	200	200	100
2	260	130	60
3	300	100	40
4	325	81.25	25
5	335	67	10
6	390	65	55
7	520	74.29	130

2 **a** Draw an accurate AFC cost curve and explain why AFC continually decline as output increases.

As FC are a constant then these fixed costs are spread over more units of output as production

increases.

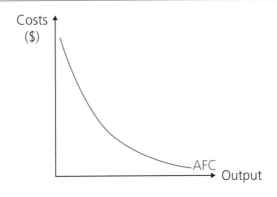

b Write correct or incorrect next to the following statements.

(i) TC = AC x Q _____correct_____   **(viii)** TC = AFC + AVC _____incorrect_____

(ii) TC = FC + VC _____correct_____   **(ix)** AFC = FC x Q _____incorrect_____

(iii) AFC = FC ÷ Q _____correct_____   **(x)** AC = TC ÷ Q _____correct_____

(iv) AC = AFC + AVC _____correct_____   **(xi)** AVC = VC x Q _____incorrect_____

(v) AVC = VC ÷ Q _____correct_____   **(xii)** FC + VC = AC _____incorrect_____

(vi) AFC + AVC = AC _____correct_____   **(xiii)** TC ÷ Q = AC _____correct_____

(vii) AC x Q = TC _____correct_____   **(xiv)** (AFC + AVC) x Q = TC _____correct_____

c If you were informed that the average cost was $9 and 100 units were produced, what is the total cost?

TC = AC x Q, $9 x 100 = $900

d Complete the table.

Quantity	Fixed costs ($)	Variable costs ($)	Total costs ($)	Average total costs ($) = $\frac{TC}{Q}$
400	200	3 200	3 400	8.5
500	200	4 000	4 200	8.4

e At 1 200 units AVC equals $10.16 and AFC are $0.83. Use this information to work out total costs, fixed costs and variable costs.

AC = AVC + AFC and TC = AC x Q, ($10.16 + 0.83) x 1 200 = $13 188.00

FC = AFC x Q = $0.83 x 1 200 = $996

VC = AVC x Q = $10.16 x 1 200 = $12 192

3 a Label all the curves in the graph.

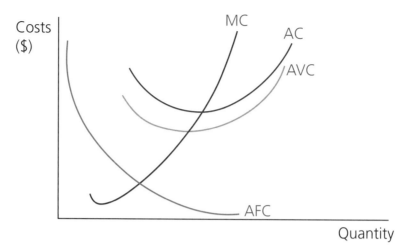

b Distinguish between marginal and average costs.

AC = TC ÷ Q or AC = AFC + AVC

MC is the addition to TC of an extra unit of output

c (i) What cost concept is represented by the vertical gap between AC and AVC? AFC

(ii) Explain why this gap narrows as output rises.

AFC decline with increasing output because the FC are spread over a greater number of units of

output. Because AC = AFC + AVC, a higher proportion of TC will be made up of VC as output rises

and so the gap narrows.

d Why does the MC curve intersect the AC curve at its minimum point?

Where MC is greater than AC then AC must be rising because the extra cost of producing the next unit

is greater than the average. Therefore where AC = MC, AC is minimised.

e Complete each table.

(i)

Quantity	AC ($)	TC ($)	MC ($)
100	20.00	2 000	
101	19.95	2 014.95	14.95

(ii)

Quantity	TC ($)	MC ($)	AC ($)
6	48	13	8
7	63	15	9

4 **a** Explain the shape of the marginal cost curve.

<u>Initially increasing returns and the more efficient use of resources leads to falling MC but in the short</u>

<u>run eventually diminishing returns will occur causing MC to increase.</u>

b Work out the marginal cost if the average cost of 2 000 units is $200 and of 2 001 units $199.95.

<u>$MC_2 = TC_1 - TC$ and TC = AC x Q, (2 001 x 199.95) diff (2 000 x 200) = $99.95</u>

c Use the table to answer the questions that follow.

   (i) Complete the table.

Output (Q)	Total costs (TC) ($)	Average costs (AC) ($)	Marginal cost (MC) ($)
0	660	–	–
1	920	920	260
2	1 100	550	180
3	1 320	440	220
4	1 760	440	440
5	2 420	484	660
6	3 960	660	1 540

  (ii) What is the technical optimum output of this firm, and how did you establish this position?

<u>minimum AC = 4 units and MC = AC</u>

 (iii) Complete these formulae.

   TC ÷ Q = <u>AC (ATC)</u>   AC x Q = <u>TC</u>

   FC + VC = <u>TC</u>   (AFC + AVC) x Q = <u>TC</u>

  (iv) At zero output what is the value of FC and VC for this firm? Give reasons for your answer.

<u>FC = $660 and VC = zero, because VC are zero when output is zero, all TC is made up of FC. VC</u>

<u>are directly related to output and there is no output.</u>

d Define 'marginal cost'.

<u>Marginal cost is the addition to total costs of an extra unit of output.</u>

Typical costs for a firm					
Output (Q)	Fixed costs (FC) ($)	Variable costs (VC) ($)	Total costs (TC) ($)	Marginal costs (MC) ($)	Average costs (AC) ($)
0	100	–	100	–	–
1	100	100	200	100	200
2	100	160	260	60	130
3	100	200	300	40	100
4	100	224	324	24	81
5	100	235	335	11	67

5 Compare and contrast the typical cost curves for a firm. In your answer you should:

- Complete the missing values in the table above and draw a sketch to show the following cost curves: MC, AC, AVC and AFC.
- Distinguish between marginal and average costs.
- Explain why the gap between the AC and AVC cost curves narrows as output increases.
- Explain why the MC curve intersects the AC at its minimum point.

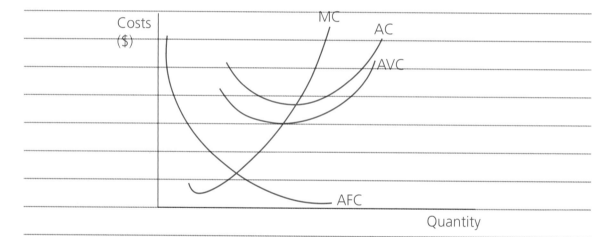

AC = TC ÷ Q or AC = AFC + AVC and MC is the addition to TC of an extra unit of output.

The cost concept represented by the vertical gap between the AC curve and the AVC curve is AFC. This gap narrows as output rises because AFC decline with increasing output because the FC are spread over a greater number of units of output. Because AC = AFC + AVC, a higher proportion of TC will be made up of VC as output rises and so the gap narrows.

The MC curve intersects the AC curve at its minimum point because where MC is greater than AC then AC must be rising because the extra cost of producing the next unit is greater than the average. Therefore where AC = MC, AC is minimised.

PHOTOCOPYING OF THIS PAGE IS RESTRICTED UNDER LAW.   ISBN: 9780170438100

6 A taxi driver is on duty at the airport one night. The usual taxi fare for the 50 kilometre trip from the airport to the city is $25.00. A potential passenger offers the taxi driver $15.00 for the trip. The driver has fixed costs of $500 per week and variable costs of 30 cents per kilometre.

Explain to the taxi driver about the typical costs for a firm. In your answer you should:

- Complete the missing values in the table below.
- Define fixed costs and variable costs and state a likely example of each for a taxi driver.
- Draw a sketch diagram to show a firm's MC, AC and AVC curves.
- Explain why the gap between the AC and AVC narrows as output rises.

Q	FC ($)	VC ($)	TC ($)	AC ($)	AFC ($)	AVC ($)	MC ($)
0	500	–	500	–	–	–	–
1	500	140	640	640	500	140	140
2	500	240	740	370	250	120	100
3	500	280	780	260	166.67	93.33	40
4	500	320	820	205	125	80	40
5	500	380	880	176	100	76	60
6	500	460	960	160	83.33	76.67	80

Fixed costs – (FC) costs of production that are independent of the level of output, e.g., fee to taxi company,

licence fees, insurance, interest on loan. They must be paid whether or not the firm is producing.

Variable costs (VC) – costs of production that are directly related to production. If the firm ceases to

operate, variable costs will be zero, e.g., wages, petrol, repairs, commission to the owner.

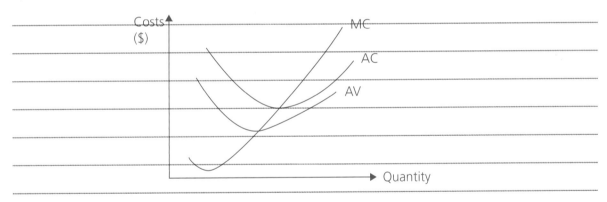

AFC declines with increasing output because FC are spread over a greater number of units of output. This

is because ATC = AFC + AVC, a higher proportion of TC will be made up of VC as output rises so the gap

narrows.

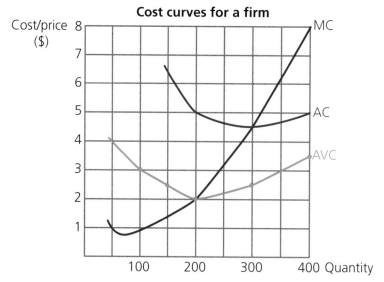

Cost curves for a firm

7 a Use the graph above to complete the statement. Justify your answer.

The total cost for a firm at 200 units is $1 000_____ and the total fixed costs are $600_____.

Total costs equal average total cost multiplied by the quantity produced. Therefore, at an output of

200 units, total costs equal $5 multiplied by 200 which equals $1000. Total fixed costs equal average

fixed cost multiplied by the quantity produced. Note the gap between the ATC (AC) and AVC equals

AFC. Therefore, at an output of 200 units, fixed costs equal $3 multiplied by 200 which equals $600.

b Complete the table.

Situation		Impact on average costs	Direction marginal cost curve will shift (inward, outward or not at all)
(i)	An increase in fixed costs.	increase	not at all
(ii)	An increase in salaries.	increase	not at all
(iii)	A decrease in rent paid when a new premises is found.	decrease	not at all
(iv)	A decrease in variable costs.	decrease	outward
(v)	A decrease in wages.	decrease	outward
(vi)	An increase in variable costs.	increase	inward
(vii)	An increase in the price of raw materials.	increase	inward

c Complete the statement. Justify your answer.

An increase in costs that are directly related to output for a firm will increase a firm's variable

costs_____ and marginal costs (or marginal costs and variable costs).

Variable costs (VC) represent costs directly related to production and will vary. If there is no production,

variable costs are zero, for example, power, raw materials, postage, wages. As costs directly related to

output increase a firm's variable costs and marginal costs will increase. Marginal cost (MC) is the addition

to total costs of an extra unit of output. Marginal cost contains no fixed costs. MC is the difference

between (FC plus VC1) and (FC plus VC2). Since fixed costs are constant, the difference in total costs,

which equals marginal cost, must be the difference between the variable costs, that is between VC1

and VC2.

       ISBN: 9780170438100

8 a Complete the statement. Justify your answer.

When the marginal cost is below average cost, average costs are <u>falling</u>. When the marginal cost curve is above average cost, average costs are <u>increasing</u>. Where average costs equal marginal costs, average costs are <u>minimised</u>.

<u>When marginal costs are less than average costs, then average costs must be falling because the extra cost of producing the next unit is less than the average. When the marginal costs are greater than average costs, then average costs must be rising because the extra cost of producing the next unit is greater than the average, therefore where AC = MC, AC is minimised.</u>

b (i) Label the curves below.

(ii) Draw a new average cost curve (AC2) to show the effect on a firm of an increase in fixed costs.

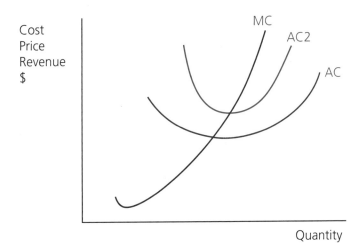

c (i) Label the curves below.

(ii) Draw a new average cost curve (AC2) and marginal cost curve (MC2) to show the effect on a firm of a decrease in variable costs.

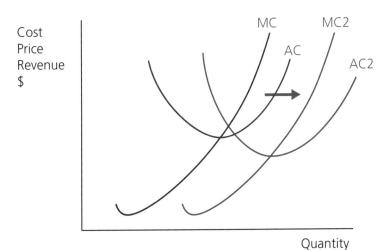

18 REVENUE CURVES
Perfect competition

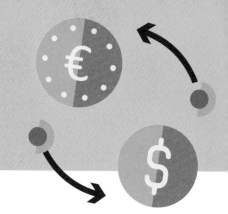

Features of perfect competition

Perfect competition is a market situation in which no firm or individual is able to influence the working of the market. Firms are small in size and exist in large numbers. Perfect competitors are **price takers**, because they are too small to influence price.

Firms produce **identical (homogeneous) products** and there are **no barriers to entry**, with anyone who wishes, able to set up in business.

The market structure also requires **perfect knowledge** meaning that firms know about prices of inputs and technology available and buyers have knowledge of price of finished goods and services, for example market gardens, orchardists, dairy farmers, maize growing. Christmas tree sellers might be considered perfect competitors if one tree is considered to be the same as the next.

An individual firm in perfect competition can sell as much as it desires at the ruling market price. Total revenue will increase steadily with sales, while the additions to total revenue (the marginal revenue) that results from each additional sale will be constant. Therefore, marginal revenue will equal price because all units are sold for the same price (MR = P). Average revenue is the same as price and doesn't change with output sales, since all units are sold at the same price.

The individual perfect competitor faces a horizontal demand curve because their supply is relatively small compared to the quantity supplied by the entire industry; they are able to sell all that they supply at the ruling market price. The industry demand curve is downward sloping because it represents the sum of all individual consumer demand curves at each price for the good of an industry and shows that additional quantities will be purchased at lower prices.

Revenue curves for perfect competition

Revenue for a perfect competitor can be divided into total revenue, average revenue and marginal revenue.

Total revenue (TR) is the revenue received from all sales. Total revenue equals price multiplied by the quantity (P × Q). A key relationship with revenue curves is that price equals average revenue (P = AR) because price and average revenue are calculated from total revenue.

Average revenue (AR) is the total revenue received from sales divided by the number of units sold. Average revenue equals total revenue divided by quantity (TR ÷ Q).

Marginal revenue (MR) is the change of total revenue resulting from increasing sales by one unit, that is, it's the addition to the total revenue of the firm as the result of the sale of an additional unit of output. Marginal revenue equals TR2 minus TR1.

An individual firm in perfect competition can sell as much as it is desires at the ruling market price. Total revenue will increase steadily with sales, while the additions to total revenue (the marginal revenue) that result from each additional sale will be constant. Marginal revenue will equal price because all units are sold for the same price (MR = P).

Average revenue is the same as price and doesn't change with output sales, since all units are sold at the same price (AR = P).

       ISBN: 9780170438100

Revenue for a firm in perfect competition is illustrated in the schedule and graph below.

Revenue for a perfect competitor				
Quantity Q	Price (P) $	Total revenue (TR) ($)	Average revenue (AR) ($)	Marginal revenue (MR) ($)
1	50	50	50	50
2	50	100	50	50
3	50	150	50	50
4	50	200	50	50
5	50	250	50	50

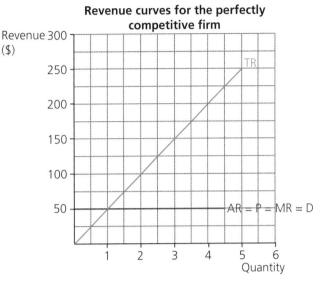

$TR = P \times Q$

$AR = TR/Q \quad P = TR/Q \quad AR = P$

$MR = TR2 - TR1$

$AR = P = MR = D$

The diagrams show that the individual firm in Graph two accepts the market price set in Graph one. The individual perfect competitor faces a horizontal demand curve because their supply is relatively small compared to the quantity supplied by the entire industry; they are able to sell all that they supply at the ruling market price. The industry demand curve is downward sloping because it represents the sum of all individual consumer demand curves at each price for the good of this industry.

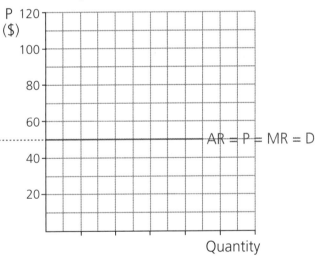

Marginal cost pricing is a feature of perfect competition. It is a situation in which price is equal to marginal cost (P=MC). Sellers cannot charge higher prices, i.e., mark-up price over cost, because they would immediately lose sales to competitors. This is called marginal cost pricing and occurs only in perfect competition.

QUESTIONS & TASKS

1 a Complete the table for a perfect competitor and then draw the curve indicated by the title of each graph.

Output	Price ($)	TR ($)	AR ($)	MR ($)
1	20	20	20	20
2	20	40	20	20
3	20	60	20	20
4	20	80	20	20
5	20	100	20	20

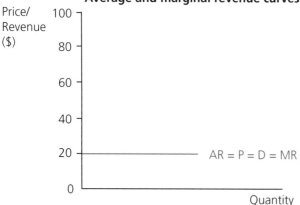

Average and marginal revenue curves

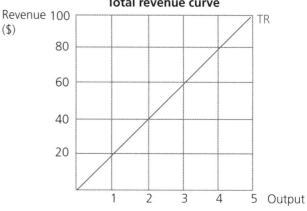

Total revenue curve

b Indicate which statements below are correct for perfect competition. (Use the table and graph in question **1a** to assist you.)

(i) All units are sold at $20. _____correct_____ **(ii)** MR > Price _____incorrect_____

(iii) Price = AR _____correct_____ **(iv)** AR = demand _____correct_____

(v) Price > MR _____incorrect_____ **(vi)** TR increases then falls. _____incorrect_____

c Explain why a perfect competitor's AR and MR curves are drawn as a horizontal line.

The firm is too small to influence price, it must accept the ruling market price. As a price taker it can

sell any amount at the market price therefore AR = MR.

d What are the features of an individual firm in perfect competition?

Homogeneous product (identical), no barriers to entry, price takers, perfect knowledge, large number

of firms.

       ISBN: 9780170438100

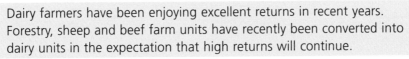

> Dairy farmers have been enjoying excellent returns in recent years.
> Forestry, sheep and beef farm units have recently been converted into
> dairy units in the expectation that high returns will continue.

2 a What is the relationship between a perfectly competitive dairy farm and the market supply of dairy products?

<u>Market supply comprises the total output of all individual dairy farms.</u>

b List three characteristics of a perfectly competitive firm that could apply to a dairy farm.

<u>Price takers, homogeneous product, no barriers to entry, firms have perfect knowledge of the market,</u>

<u>many producers in the industry.</u>

c Is the demand curve faced by an individual firm in perfect competition the same as the market demand curve? Why or why not?

<u>The firm's demand curve shows the demand for the firm's part of total industry output only. The</u>

<u>individual seller may sell as much as it wishes of its own production at the market price because the</u>

<u>quantity it can supply to the market only has a negligible effect on market price. No, the firm's demand</u>

<u>curve is not the same as the market demand curve. The market demand curve is determined by the</u>

<u>overall demand for the whole market and is downward sloping, i.e., showing that additional total</u>

<u>quantities will only be purchased at lower prices.</u>

d Use the diagram to explain how Graph 1 and Graph 2 illustrate perfectly competitive competition.

Graph 1: The individual firm

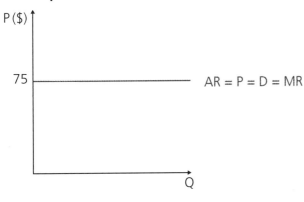

Graph 2: The market (industry)

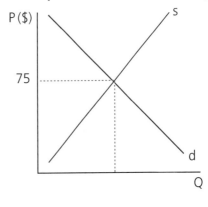

<u>The market (demand and supply) in Graph 2 sets the price that firms receive in Graph 1. The horizontal</u>

<u>AR curve in Graph 1 shows that the individual firm is a price taker, which is typical of perfect</u>

<u>competition.</u>

19 PROFIT

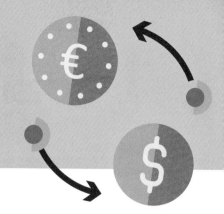

Economic and accounting costs

Accounting costs are the actual (or explicit) costs involved in the production process – mortgage, rent, power, office expenses, raw materials and wages. Accounting costs represent the costs of production that a firm will pay to other businesses. Accounting costs will always be less than economic costs.

Economic costs are the actual (explicit) or accounting costs as well as the opportunity costs (implied or implicit) of the resources used.

Implicit or implied costs are the opportunity costs of the resources used that are owned by the business. Economic costs represent the revenue that could be earned in alternative uses of assets that the firm owns, this would include the amount foregone by the owners that they could have earned working for a different business, for example, the lost salary of a teacher who starts a cafe. This would include the rent lost by the owner(s) of a factory whose firm currently uses the building, or the lost interest that could have been earned by the owner(s) if they had the funds in a bank account rather than being lent to the business.

Some producers will have higher economic costs than other producers because they own a larger proportion of the resources used in the production process when compared with other firms.

Economists use economic costs rather than accounting costs when determining the profit maximising level of output for a firm, because to calculate their profit maximising level of output, firms must know their total costs. Economic costs provide a total cost that includes all the costs of production including opportunity costs. Accounting costs do not cover opportunity costs, such as the return on the risk taken by the entrepreneur, and therefore do not cover all costs. Economic costs are always greater than accounting costs.

Economic and accounting profit

Explicit costs involve a monetary payment made by a firm to its suppliers, workers or others involved in running a business. Implicit costs, on the other hand, do not involve any payment being made to others.

Accounting profit is calculated as profit equals income minus expenses, where the expenses or costs are only the actual (or explicit) costs involved. So, in accounting terms, a 'profit' or surplus exists if the actual income of the business is greater than the actual expenses. Accounting profit is always greater than economic profit.

In economics, both actual costs and implied (or opportunity) costs are included in the calculation of profit. Therefore, economic profit equals the accounting profit minus the implicit or implied (opportunity) costs incurred by the business. There will always be opportunity costs involved in any business venture, so the economic profit for a business will always be less than the accounting profit.

For example, a teacher leaves his job and opens a cafe using his $100,000 from a savings account, that was earning 7% per annum. The teaching job had paid $60,000. The income from the cafe was $120,000 and costs were $40,000 after the first year. Therefore, the accounting profit is $80,000 because the accounting profit is the income of $120,000 minus the costs of $40,000.

The business has incurred two opportunity costs in operating the cafe, namely the lost salary of $60,000 by the owner and the interest lost of $7,000 (based on 7% of $100,000) that could have been earned on the savings had the savings not being used to start the cafe. The economic profit equals the accounting profit minus the opportunity costs. In this instance, the economic profit is $13,000 because economic profit equals the accounting profit of $80,000 minus the opportunity costs of $67,000. The economic profit of $13,000 is less than the accounting profit of $40,000.

Total revenue and total cost

The difference between total revenue (TR) and total cost (TC) is either a profit or loss. A firm that wants to maximise its profit or minimise its loss would operate at the output shown in the graphs.

Maximising profit

If a firm wants to maximise profit it would operate where there is the greatest vertical distance between TR and TC. This is shown on the graph as position Q. Any other position would result in a smaller profit, and if the firm operated beyond Q' it would make a loss.

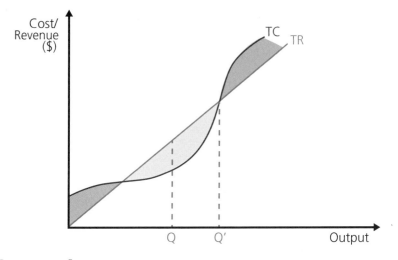

Minimising a loss

In the graph there is no position in which the firm can make a profit at this stage of its operation. To minimise its loss it would operate where the vertical distance between the total revenue (TR) and the total cost (TC) is the smallest. This is at output Q. Any other position would result in a greater loss.

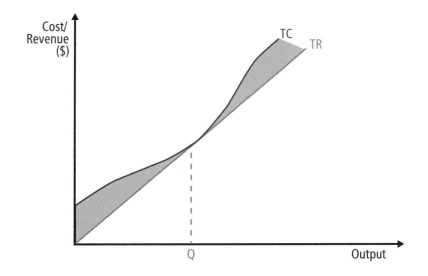

QUESTIONS & TASKS

1 a Complete the table below.

> Hagar Backpackers Accommodation was started by Hagar with $40 000 of his savings. Hagar had given up his job of teaching where he used to earn $35 000 per year. Market interest was 5% on deposits. After the first year's operation total revenue was $300 000 and total expenses $240 000. Use this information provided to work out the accounting and economic profit.

Accounting profit	$		Economic profit	$
Income	300 000		Income	300 000
Expenses	240 000		Less actual expenses	240 000
Net profit	$ 60 000		Less lost wages	35 000
			Less lost interest on savings	2 000
			Net profit	$ 23 000

b Why do economists use economic costs rather than accounting costs when determining the profit maximising level of output for a firm?

<u>To calculate their profit and therefore their profit maximising level of output, firms must know their total costs. Economic costs provide a total cost that includes all the costs of production including opportunity costs. Accounting costs do not cover opportunity costs such as the return to the risk taken by the entrepreneur and therefore do not cover all costs.</u>

c Economic costs cover more than accounting costs. Give two specific examples of non-accounting costs likely to be incurred by an owner of a backpackers.

<u>Any two answers that relate to normal profit earned or the opportunity cost of the owner's labour, capital or land use.</u>

d Define the following terms.

(i) Accounting profit: <u>Revenue minus total costs where costs are actual (or explicit) only.</u>

(ii) Economic profit: <u>Revenue minus total costs of both actual costs and implicit (opportunity) costs of alternative resource use.</u>

2 a (i) Complete the table and answer the questions that follow.

Quantity (000)	Total revenue ($000)	Total cost ($000)	Profit/Loss ($000)
0	–	145	loss 145
1	180	175	profit 5
2	320	200	profit 120
3	420	220	profit 200
4	480	250	profit 230
5	500	300	profit 200
6	480	370	profit 110
7	420	460	loss 40

(ii) According to the table, at what output would you recommend that this firm operate and why?

<u>4 000 units because this is where they make the greatest profit.</u>

b (i) Complete the table and answer the questions that follow.

Output (000)	TR ($000)	TC ($000)	Profit/Loss ($000)
5	25	40	15 loss
6	30	42	12 loss
7	35	45	10 loss
8	40	46	6 loss

(ii) According to the information in the table, what type of market structure is the firm? Give a reason for your answer.

<u>Perfect competition because AR = $5 for each level of output.</u>

(iii) From the information in the table, what would you recommend that this firm do and why?

<u>Either operate at 8 000 units (minimum loss) or possibly increase output and see if they make a</u>

<u>smaller loss.</u>

> Adrian's previous job as a real estate agent paid $60 000. Adrian uses $40 000 from a term deposit earning 5% per annum to start up a concrete pumping business.
> Accounting costs for the year $150 000   Total revenue $250 000

c Study the information given above then calculate the accounting profit and economic profit for Adrian who started off a business pouring concrete.

(i) Accounting profit: <u>Total revenue minus accounting costs $250 000 – $150 000 = $100 000</u>

(ii) Economic profit: <u>Total revenue minus accounting costs (minus opportunity costs)</u>

<u>$250 000 – $150 000 – $60 000 – $2 000 = $38 000</u>

d Which is greater, accounting profit or economic profit?

<u>Accounting profit</u>

e Which is greater – accounting costs or economic costs?

<u>Economic costs</u>

3 A business faces accounting costs and economic costs.

a Explain the difference between accounting costs and economic costs.

Accounting costs are the actual (explicit) costs involved in production – mortgage, rent, power, raw materials, wages, and so on.

Economic costs are the actual (explicit) or accounting costs as well as the opportunity costs (implied or implicit) of the resources used.

Economic costs would include the lost salary of a teacher who starts a lawn-mowing round. Rent lost by the owner of a factory whose firm currently uses the building is an economic cost. Economic costs include the lost interest that could have been earned by the owner(s) if they had the funds in a bank account rather than in a business.

Economic costs are always greater than accounting costs.

b Label the following costs explicit or implicit.

(i) Actual costs of production   explicit

(ii) Economic costs   implicit

(iii) Implied costs   implicit

(iv) Accounting costs   explicit

(v) Opportunity costs of interest foregone   implicit

(vi) Wages for factory workers   explicit

(vii) Rent lost for the building owned and used by the producer   implicit

(viii) Interest on the bank overdraft   explicit

(ix) Salary of the general manager   explicit

4 a Complete the table below assuming it represents a perfectly competitive firm and the current market price is $10.

Output (Q)	Average cost (AC) ($)	Total cost (TC) ($)	Total revenue (TR) ($)	Profit (or loss) ($)
8 000	2.10	16 800	80 000	63 200
10 000	2.50	25 000	100 000	75 000
12 000	5.00	60 000	120 000	60 000

b Why do economists use economic costs rather than accounting costs when determining the profit maximising level of output for a firm?

To calculate their profit and therefore their profit maximising level of output, firms must know their total costs. Economic costs provide a total cost that include all the costs of production including opportunity costs. Accounting costs do not cover opportunity costs such as the return for the risk taken by the entrepreneur and therefore do not cover all costs.

c Indicate whether the following statements are correct or incorrect.

Statement		Correct or incorrect?
(i)	Economic profit is always greater than accounting profit.	incorrect
(ii)	Accounting profit is always greater than economic profit.	correct
(iii)	Economic profit is always smaller than accounting profit.	correct
(iv)	The correct measure of economic cost includes explicit and implicit cost.	correct
(v)	The correct measure of economic cost includes accounting costs and opportunity costs.	correct
(vi)	Accounting profit is a firm's revenue minus explicit costs only.	correct
(vii)	Economic profit is a firm's revenue minus explicit costs only.	incorrect
(viii)	Actual costs are implicit costs of the opportunity costs in operating a business.	incorrect
(ix)	Implicit costs are the actual costs of a firm.	incorrect
(x)	Explicit costs are the actual costs of a firm.	correct
(xi)	Total revenue equals sales (or quantity) times price.	correct

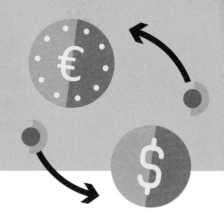

20 MARGINAL ANALYSIS
Perfect competition

Marginal analysis – Perfect competition

The **rule for maximising profit or minimising a loss (the equlibrium)** is where **marginal revenue (MR) equals marginal cost (MC)**. Any other position will result in a smaller profit or greater loss.

Therefore, the equilibrium output (determined from the intersection of the marginal cost and marginal revenue curves) is at a price of $200 and quantity Q (200). The **average revenue (AR)** equals $200 and the **average cost (AC)** equals $160.

Total revenue (TR) equals the quantity multiplied by the price or average revenue (**Q × AR**). In this case it equals 200 multiplied by $200 which equals $40 000.

Total cost (TC) will equal the quantity multiplied by the average cost (**Q × AC**). In this case it equals 200 multiplied by $160 which equals $32 000.

At the **equilibrium output Q** the firm is making a **supernormal profit** of $8 000. **Supernormal profit** is a return more than sufficient to keep the entrepreneur in their present activity. At the equilibrium output position where MR equals MC, the average revenue (AR) is greater than the average cost (AC). Supernormal profits will attract firms into a perfectly competitive industry because there are no barriers to entry.

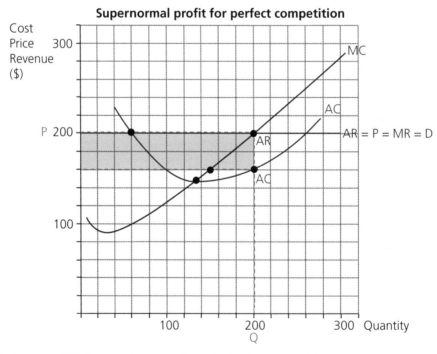

Supernormal profit for perfect competition

If output is **below equilibrium Q** (MR equals MC), the firm would be **missing out on marginal profits** because the revenue from producing the last article is greater than its cost of production, implying that the firm could increase output and increase profit.

However, increasing output **beyond Q** reverses the position. The firm will be **making marginal losses** because the revenue from one additional article is now less than the cost of its production. If increased output adds more to cost than to revenue, a firm has obviously passed the point of maximum profit (or minimum loss). Therefore the rule is adopted and applies in all circumstances where profit maximisation is the aim.

Subnormal profit

Subnormal profit is a return insufficient to keep the entrepreneur in their present activity. At the equilibrium output position where MR equals MC, average revenue (AR) will be less than average cost (AC). When a firm is making a subnormal profit it is likely that they will leave the industry.

Q (200) is the equilibrium output position because this is where MR equals MC. At an output of 200, the price (AR) is $200, the average cost (AC) is $260, the total revenue is $40 000 (AR multiplied by Q) and the total cost is $52 000 (AC multiplied by Q).

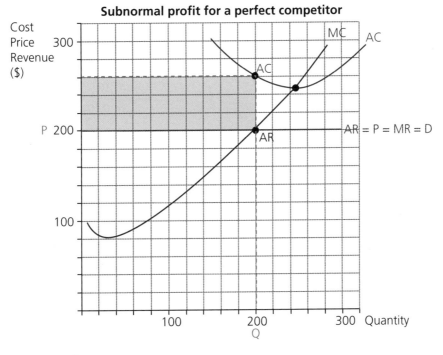

Subnormal profit for a perfect competitor

Normal profit

Normal profit in economic terms is a return to the entrepreneur sufficient to keep them in their present activity. At the equilibrium output position where MR equals MC, the average revenue (AR) will equal the average cost (AC).

Q (200) is the equilibrium output position because this is where MR equals MC. At an output of 200, the price (AR) is $200, the average cost (AC) is $200, the total revenue is $40 000 (AR multiplied by Q) and the total cost is $40 000 (AC multiplied by Q).

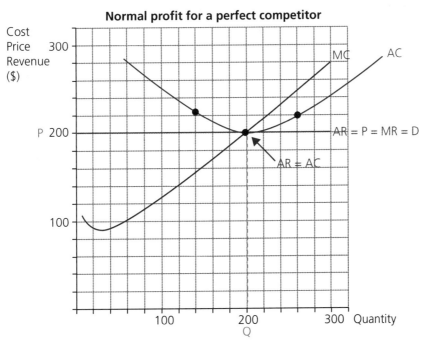

Normal profit for a perfect competitor

ISBN: 9780170438100 Marginal analysis – Perfect competition

QUESTIONS & TASKS

1 Work out the answers to the questions by using the graphs provided.

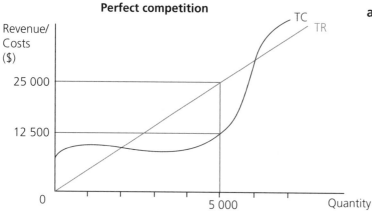

Perfect competition

a The maximum profit position is at an output of <u>5 000</u> because this is where the gap between the total revenue curve and the total cost curve is the <u>greatest</u> distance.

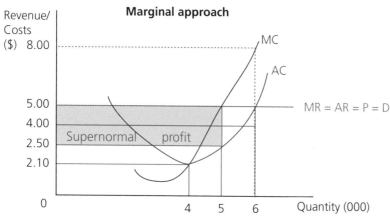

Marginal approach

b (i) Shade and label the appropriate level of profit made at the equilibrium level of output (maximum profit).

(ii) Complete the table.

Value	4 000 units	5 000 units	6 000 units
(i) MR/MC	$5/$2.10	$5/$5	$5/$8
(ii) AR/AC	$5/$2.10	$5/$2.50	$5/$5
(iii) TR (AR x Q)	$20 000	$25 000	$30 000
(iv) TC (AC x Q)	$8 400	$12 500	$30 000
(v) PROFIT	$11 600	$12 500	zero

c Using the idea of marginal analysis, explain why the firm would not want to operate at either 4 000 or 6 000 units.

<u>Producing at 4 000 units, the firm would be missing out on marginal profits because the revenue from producing the last article is greater than its cost of production, implying that the firm could increase output and increase profit. Operating at 6 000, the firm will be making marginal losses because the revenue from one additional article is now less than the cost of its production. If increased output adds more to cost than to revenue, a firm has obviously passed the point of maximum profit (or minimum loss).</u>

2 Use the graph to answer the questions that follow.

An individual firm's costs curves and revenue curve

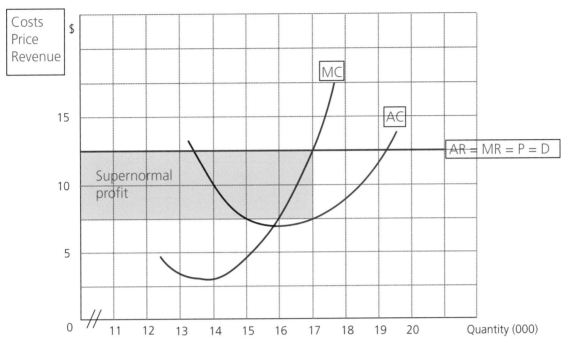

a Label all the curves and the vertical axes in the graph, using the small boxes for answers.

b Using a marginal analysis, what is the maximum profit position price and output?

Price: $12.50 _____   Output: 17 000 _____

c At the equilibrium output position calculate total revenue and total cost.

Total revenue (AR x Q): $12.50 x 17 000 = $212 500 _____

Total cost (AC x Q): $7.50 x 17 000 = $127 500 _____

d Shade in the area of profit.

e Work out the value of profit.

$5 x 17 000 = $85 000 _____

f (i) If the firm was operating at 15 000 units, what price would they charge?

$12.50 _____

(ii) Give values for MR and MC MR = $12.50 _____   MC = $4.80 (est) _____

(iii) What would the firm have to do to maximise profit in terms of price and output?

Increase output/price stays the same because operating at 15 000 units is below equilibrium of

17 000 units (where MR equals MC), the firm would be missing out on marginal profits because

the revenue from producing the last article is greater than its cost of production. The firm should

increase output to increase its profit. _____

_____

_____

_____

3 Use the graph to answer the questions below.

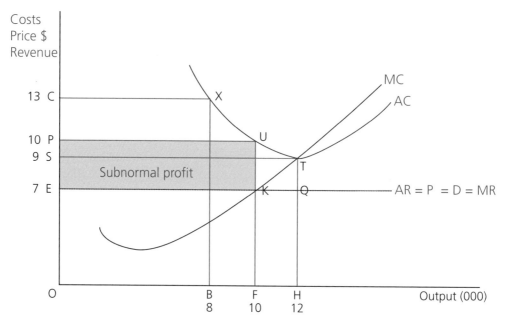

a Label the curves and axes in the graph.

b Give letters and values to identify at the equilibrium:

(i) Output <u>OF 10 000</u>

(ii) Price <u>OE $7</u>

(iii) TC <u>PUFO $100 000</u>

(iv) Quantity <u>OF   10 000</u>

(v) TR <u>FKEO $70 000</u>

(vi) Loss <u>PUKE $30 000</u>

(vii) AC <u>OP $10</u>

(viii) AR <u>OE $7</u>

c What made you choose the equilibrium output above?

<u>It's where MR = MC; any other position would be a greater loss.</u>

d In the graph, shade in the economic profit made.

e Define this type of profit.

<u>A return insufficient to keep entrepreneurs in their present activity.</u>

  ISBN: 9780170438100

4 Use the diagram to answer the questions that follow.

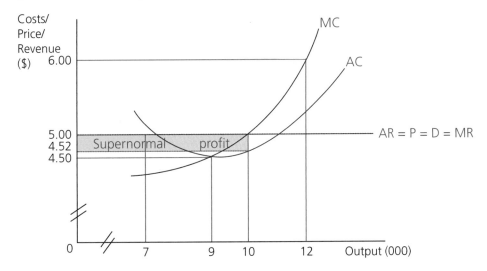

a Label all the curves and shade in the profit made.

b At the maximum profit (equilibrium output) position, what is the:

Price? $5.00   Total revenue? $50 000 (AR x Q = $5 x 10 000)

Output?   10 000   Total cost? $45 200 (AC x Q = $4.52 x 10 000)

Average revenue? $5.00

c By considering outputs 9 000, and 10 000 units, explain using marginal analysis the determination of the maximum profit output level.

• At 9 000 MR > MC (or MC < MR) and it is profitable to produce more, it is missing out on marginal

profits.

• At 10 000 MR = MC. This is maximum profit, any other position is a smaller profit.

d What type of profit is made in the diagram? Supernormal profit.

e Define this type of profit.

A return to the entrepreneur in excess (more than sufficient) of that required to hold them in their

present activity.

f Explain why the firm would not want to operate at 12 000 units.

At 12 000 units MC > MR the firm will be making marginal losses because the revenue from one

additional article is now less than the cost of its production. If increased output adds more to cost

than to revenue, a firm has obviously passed the point of maximum profit (or minimum loss) where

MR = MC.

5 Use the diagram to answer the questions that follow.

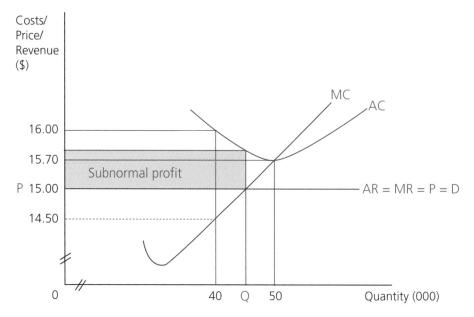

a Label the curves.

b (i) Identify the loss-minimising level of output as Q and price charged as P.

(between 40 000 and 50 000) shown

(ii) What made you choose this position?

MR = MC; any other position is a greater loss.

c Shade in the loss made.

d At 50 000 units:

identify average revenue	$15.00
identify marginal revenue	$15.00
calculate total revenue	50 000 x $15 = $750 000
calculate total cost	50 000 x $15.70 = $785 000
calculate loss made	$35 000

e At 40 000 units:

identify average revenue	$15.00
identify marginal revenue	$15.00
calculate total revenue	40 000 x $15 = $600 000
calculate total cost	40 000 x $16 = $640 000
calculate loss made	$40 000

6 Use the graph to answer the questions that follow.

a Define 'subnormal profits'.

<u>A return to entrepreneurs which is less than normal and which is insufficient to keep them in their</u>

<u>present activity.</u>

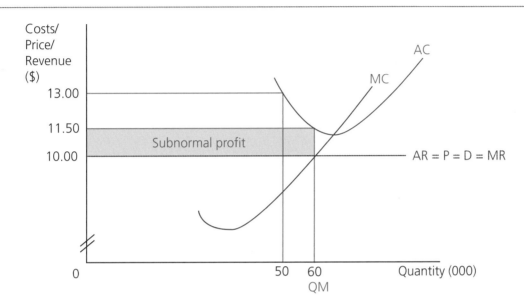

b Label the curves on the diagram above.

c (i) Identify loss minimising level of output as QM.

<u>Shown on diagram at 60 000.</u>

(ii) At the loss minimising level of output what is AR?   <u>$10</u>

TR?   <u>$10 x 60 000 = $600 000</u>

TC?   <u>$11.50 x 60 000 = $690 000</u>

loss?   <u>= $90 000</u>

d Shade in the loss made.

e (i) Why would the firm not produce at 50 000 units?

<u>Makes a greater loss (MR > MC). It could make a smaller loss by producing more.</u>

(ii) At 50 000 units what is AR?   <u>$10</u>

TR?   <u>$10 x 50 000 = $500 000</u>

TC?   <u>$13 x 50 000 = $650 000</u>

loss?   <u>$150 000</u>

21 REVENUE CURVES Monopoly

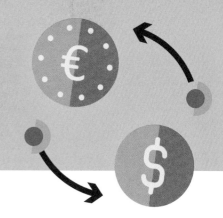

Imperfect competition

Firms are subdivided into monopolistic, oligopoly, duopoly, monopoly, and monopsony. Imperfect competitors produce differentiated products and have a varying degree of control over price. They are price makers because of their ability to make their products appear different, that is, relative to their competitors their products are not homogeneous. For any imperfect competitor to sell an additional unit they must lower the price. Therefore, as output increases, to sell an additional unit the price will fall. A decrease in output will see price increase.

Monopoly (or monopolist)

Single seller of good or service for which there are few if any substitutes, for example Kiwi Rail the only railway in New Zealand and New Zealand Steel the only steel producer in the country. Monopolies have strong barriers to entry in the same way that oligopolies do. Pure monopoly implies that there are no substitutes while a near monopoly is one with relatively few substitutes. For example Kiwi Rail has a pure monopoly in rail transport but it is only a near monopoly in transport. Limitations on monopolistic power include:

- due to consumers' incomes being limited, all commodities are in competition with each other so they cannot be too exorbitant in their pricing;
- government can break up monopolies or control their prices if they become too high; they could nationalise them and run them in the public's best interest.

A monopolist can set either price or quantity but not both in the market. If the monopolist sets the price the market will determine the quantity sold. If the monopolist determines the quantity then the market will determine the price. The monopolist has control over price or quantity produced, but not over both at the same time.

Barriers to entry — Monopoly power

Most firms face competition from existing firms that produce the good or provide the service. When barriers to entry to a market are either weak or non-existent new firms can enter the market, establish themselves and claim market share for the goods or service. This is not the case for a monopoly because they are the single seller of a good or service for which there are few, if any, substitutes, this situation arises because the strong barriers to entry restrict the entry of would-be competitors.

The strong barriers to entry for a monopoly range from **high establishment costs, technological expertise, legal monopolies** established by the government or barriers that arise from economies of scale in the instance of a natural monopoly.

Competitors are often kept out of an industry where a monopolist operates because of the enormous expense of setting up in the first place. In the case where a rail monopoly exists a would-be competitor would face the high capital cost of buying the land required for a rail corridor, laying down of tracks, building stations, buying trains and rolling stock, as well as any other associated expenses. The high capital cost involved in setting up would be a major deterrent to most firms.

Another barrier that protects a monopoly from competition is the technological expertise that a monopolist possesses. If a monopolist has developed technology by spending vast sums on Research and Development that only they have knowledge of and access to, this can make it difficult, if not impossible, for competitors trying to produce the same goods or provide the same service because they lack either the necessary skills needed or knowledge to do so. The time and expense for other firms to develop the expertise required helps maintain the monopolist's position in keeping competitors out of a market. Patents and copyright can protect a firm from competitors for a time, however, these measures may not be effective in the long term because new technology is developed or a competitor finds a way to circumvent a registered patent.

 ISBN: 9780170438100

Revenue curves

Revenue for an imperfect competitor can be divided into total revenue, average revenue and marginal revenue.

Total revenue (TR) is the revenue received from all sales. Total revenue equals price multiplied by the quantity (P × Q). A key relationship with revenue curves is that price equals average revenue (P=AR) because price and average revenue are calculated from total revenue.

Average revenue (AR) is the total revenue received from sales divided by the number of units sold. Average revenue equals total revenue divided by the quantity (TR ÷ Q). Average revenue (AR) falls in line with price changes, i.e., AR equals Price.

Marginal revenue (MR) is the change of total revenue resulting from increasing sales by one unit, that is, it's the addition to the total revenue of the firm as the result of the sale of an additional unit of output. Marginal revenue equals TR2 minus TR1. Marginal revenue should be plotted midway between consecutive units of output.

In any form of imperfect competition, to sell additional units requires that the price be lowered on all units. Therefore, for a decrease in price to sell an additional unit, the marginal revenue must be less than the price for which the prevoius unit is sold. The marginal revenue curve must lie beneath the average revenue curve for imperfect competition. It follows that average revenue (AR) or price (P) is always greater than marginal revenue (MR) in imperfect competition. A firm's demand curve in imperfect competition is its average revenue (AR) curve.

With the fall in price total revenue (TR) will reach a maximum and then fall thereafter. When total revenue (TR) reaches a maximum, marginal revenue (MR) equals zero (0). After this point, as output increases and the price decreases marginal revenue will become negative.

Revenue for a firm in imperfect competition is illustrated in the schedule and graph below. Note the marginal revenue curve cuts the output axis exactly halfway between the origin and where the average revenue curve cuts the output axis.

Revenue for an imperfect competitor

Quantity Q	Price (P) $	Total Revenue (TR) ($)	Average Revenue (AR) ($)	Marginal Revenue (MR) ($)
1	250	250	250	250
2	200	400	200	150
3	150	450	150	50
4	100	400	100	−50
5	50	250	50	−150

TR = P x Q

AR = TR/Q   P = TR/Q   AR = P

MR = TR2 − TR1

AR > MR

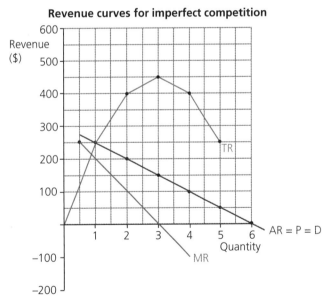

Revenue curves for imperfect competition

In **imperfect competition** the seller is able to charge a price in excess of marginal cost. This is called **mark-up pricing** and is where price is greater than marginal cost (P > MC).

QUESTIONS & TASKS

1 Complete the table by selecting your answer from the following: monopoly, AR (P), TR, imperfect competition, AR = MR, AR > MR or (MR < AR), MR, perfect competition, AR curve.

	Idea, formula, definition	Answer
a	To sell an additional unit the firm must lower its price	imperfect competition
b	Price stays the same for the individual firm because it is too small to influence price	perfect competition
c	P x Q	TR
d	TR ÷ Q	AR (P)
e	Demand curve of the perfect or imperfect competitor equals its …	AR curve
f	Many sellers of an identical product implies …	perfect competition
g	An industry consisting of only one firm	monopoly
h	The relationship for perfect competitors' AR and MR curves	AR = MR
i	The relationship for imperfect competitors' AR and MR curves	AR > MR (or MR < AR)
j	Any change in quantity results in no change in the price received by a firm	perfect competition
k	Additions to the total revenue of a firm as a result of sale of an additional unit of output	MR
l	Price multiplied by quantity	TR
m	Total revenue divided by quantity	AR (P)

2 Label the curves fully and give each diagram a title.

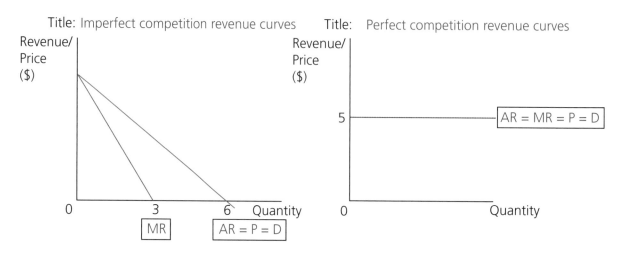

Title: Imperfect competition revenue curves   Title: Perfect competition revenue curves

3 a Complete the table and use the information to answer part **b**.

Quantity	Price ($)	TR ($)	MR ($)	AR = P ($)
1	36	36	36	36
2	32	64	28	32
3	28	84	20	28
4	24	96	12	24
5	20	100	4	20
6	16	96	−4	16
7	12	84	−12	12

b Label the curves and complete each statement.

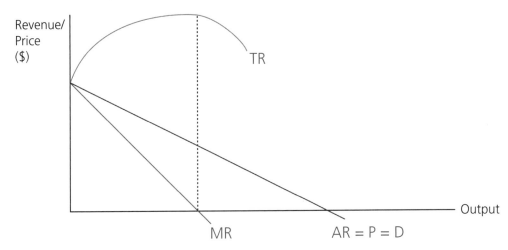

(i) When TR is a maximum, MR is <u>zero</u>.

(ii) When TR is falling, MR is a <u>negative</u> number.

c What are the features of a perfect competitor?

<u>Homogeneous product, no barriers to entry, large number of firms, perfect knowledge, price takers.</u>

d What are the features of a monopolist?

<u>Single seller of a product, few if any substitutes, strong barriers to entry. Can control price or quantity</u>

<u>but not both at the same time. If the monopolist sets the price the market will determine the quantity</u>

<u>sold. If the monopolist sets the quantity then the market will determine the price.</u>

4 Use the diagram to answer the questions that follow.

   a Draw an accurate MR curve.

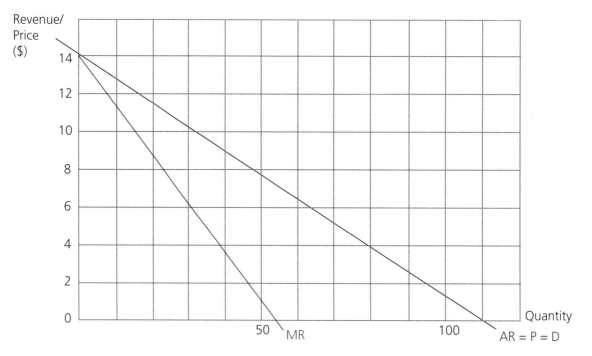

   b Complete the table.

Output	Price ($)	Total revenue ($)	AR ($)
20	11.50	230	11.50
50	7.80	390	7.80
80	3.90	312	3.90
95	2.00	190	2.00

   c Complete these statements.

      (i) In imperfect competition, as a firm increases its output price will <u>decrease</u>, e.g., an increase output from 20 to 95, price will <u>fall (decrease)</u> from <u>$11.50 to $2.00</u>.

     (ii) In imperfect competition, as a firm decreases output then price will <u>rise (increase)</u>, e.g., in decreasing output from 80 to 50 will see price <u>rise (increase)</u> from <u>$3.90 to $7.80</u>.

   d Complete the following statements.

      (i) An increase in output for an imperfect competitor will see price <u>decrease</u>.

     (ii) A decrease in output for an imperfect competitor will see price <u>increase</u>.

    (iii) The change in output and price for an imperfect competitor occurs in <u>opposite</u> directions.

    (iv) Price will rise in imperfect competition when output <u>decreases</u>.

     (v) Price will fall in imperfect competition when output <u>increases</u>.

    (vi) Price will not <u>change</u> for firms in <u>perfect competition</u> even if there is an increase or decrease in output.

5 Use the graph below to answer the questions that follow.

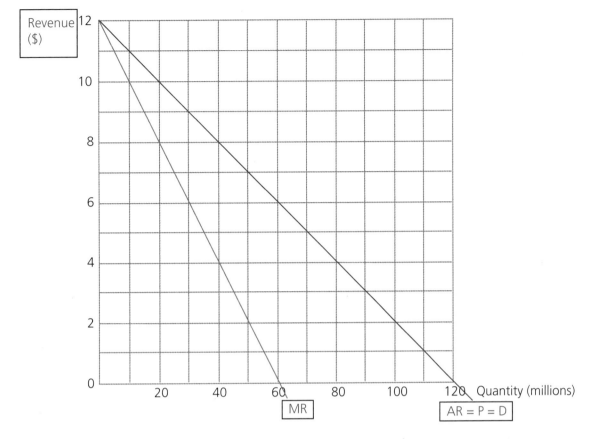

a Label all the curves and axes appropriately, using the small boxes for answers.

b Explain how the revenue curves illustrate imperfect competition.

To sell an additional unit the imperfect competitior must lower the price on all units sold, and the AR > MR.

c Define marginal revenue.

The additions to total revenue from increasing sales by one unit.

d (i) Complete the table using the information above.

Units	Price (AR) ($)	Total revenue (TR) ($)	Marginal revenue (MR) ($)
20 million	10	200m	8
40 million	8	320m	4
60 million	6	360m	0
80 million	4	320m	−4

(ii) Indicate at which level of output total revenue is a maximum and describe the relationship between TR and MR at this point.

Output: 60 million units

Relationship: When TR is a maximum the MR is zero.

6 a Label the curves and the axes and then answer the questions that follow.

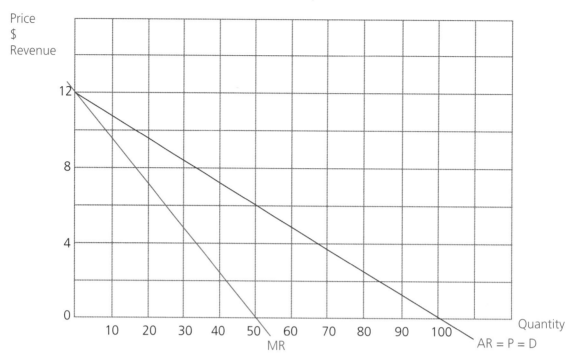

b What kind of demand curve does a monopolist face?

Downward sloping.

c At a price of $11, how many units can a monopolist sell? What is their total revenue?

Units sold = 10_____   TR = $110_____

d If the price is lowered to $6, how many units can the monopolist sell? What is their total revenue?

Units sold = 50_____   TR = $300_____

e Indicate if the following statements are correct or incorrect for the imperfect competitor.

Statement	Correct or incorrect?
(i) When a firm in imperfect competition increases output, price will increase.	incorrect
(ii) When a firm in imperfect competition increases output, price will decrease.	correct
(iii) When an imperfect competitor produces less, then price will decrease.	incorrect
(iv) When an imperfect competitor produces less, then price will increase.	correct

f Explain why a monopolist is able to set either market price or market quantity, but not both.

A monopolist can set either price or quantity but not both. If the monopolist sets the price the market will determine the quantity sold. If the monopolist determines the quantity then the market will determine the price. The monopolist has control over either price or quantity produced, but not over both at the same time.

7 Perfect competitors and imperfect competitors have different revenue curves.

Compare and contrast revenue curves for various market structures. In your answer:

- Label the curves and explain how the revenue curves illustrate imperfect competition.
- Explain why a monopolist is able to set either market price or market quantity, but not both.
- Explain why the average revenue curve is horizontal for a perfect competitor but slopes downward for a monopolist.

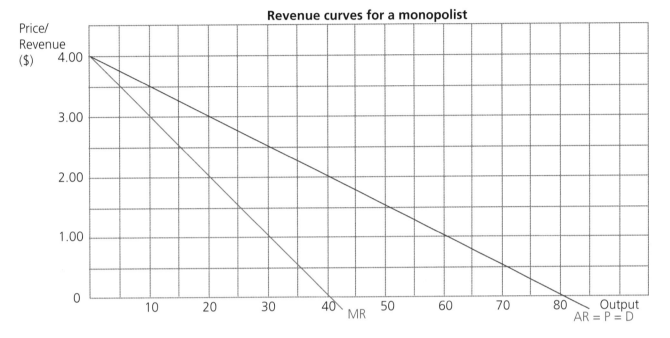

Revenue curves for a monopolist

The revenue curves above illustrate imperfect competition because to sell an additional unit the imperfect competitior must lower the price on all units sold, and the AR > MR.

A monopolist can set either price or quantity but not both. If the monopolist sets the price the market will determine the quantity sold. If the monopolist determines the quantity then the market will determine the price. The monopolist has control over either price or quantity produced, but not over both at the same time.

The perfect competitor is a price taker, and therefore must accept the market price or can sell any amount at the market price. The monopolist is the only producer; the demand curve for their product is the market demand, and the monopolist can only increase quantity by reducing the price on all sales.

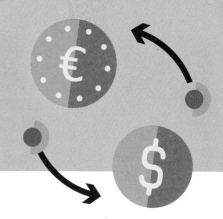
Marginal analysis – Monopoly

The **rule for maximising profit or minimising a loss (the equlibrium)** for a monopoly is the same as any other firm. The most profitable output or smallest loss is where **marginal revenue (MR) equals marginal cost (MC)**. Any other position will result in a smaller profit or greater loss.

Therefore, the equilibrium output (determined from the intersection of the marginal cost and marginal revenue curves) is at a price of **Pm** ($8) and quantity **Qm** (200m). The **average revenue (AR)** equals $8 and the **average cost (AC)** equals $5.

Total revenue (TR) equals the quantity multiplied by the price or average revenue **(Q × AR)**. In this case it equals 200m multiplied by $8 which equals $1600m.

Total cost (TC) will equal the quantity multiplied by the average cost **(Q × AC)**. In this case it equals 200m multiplied by $5 which equals $1000m.

At the **equilibrium output Qm** the monopoly is making a **supernormal profit** of $600m. Supernormal profit is a return to the entrepreneur more than sufficient to keep them in their present activity.

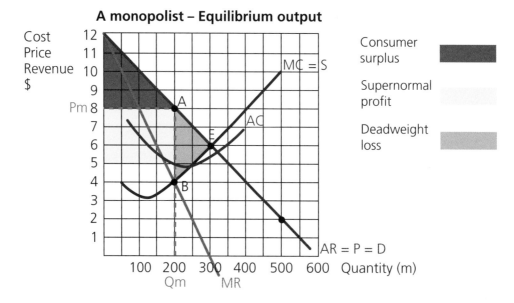

In imperfect competition, for a firm to sell an additional unit it must lower price. If the firm operates **below the equilibrium output**, it is **missing out on marginal profits** because its marginal revenue is greater than its marginal costs (or marginal costs are less than marginal revenue). Therefore, to maximise profits (or to minimise loss) the firm will need to increase output to where MR equals MC, as output increases price will fall.

If an imperfect competitor firm operates **beyond the equilibrium output**, it is **making marginal losses** because its marginal cost is greater than its marginal revenue (or marginal revenue is less than marginal cost). Therefore, to maximise profits (or to minimise loss) the firm will need to decrease output back to where MR equals MC, as output decreases the price will increase.

Subnormal profit

Subnormal profit is a return insufficient to keep the entrepreneur in their present activity. At the equilibrium output position where MR equals MC, average revenue (AR) will be less than average cost (AC).

Q (5m) is the equilibrium output position because this is where MR equals MC. At an output of 5m, the price (AR) is $9, the average cost (AC) is $11, the total revenue is $45m (AR multiplied by Q) and the total cost is $55m (AC multiplied by Q).

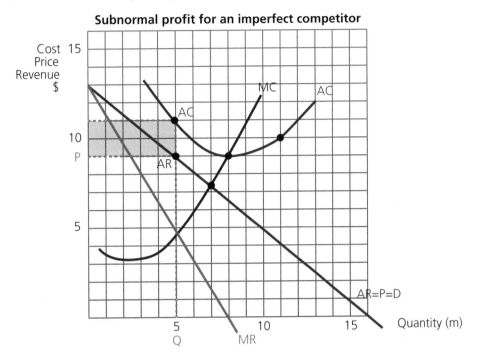

Subnormal profit for an imperfect competitor

Normal profit

Normal profit in economic terms is a return to the entrepreneur sufficient to keep them in their present activity. At the equilibrium output position where MR equals MC, the average revenue (AR) will equal the average cost (AC).

Q (5m) is the equilibrium output position because this is where MR equals MC. At an output of 5m, the price (AR) is $9, the average cost (AC) is $9, the total revenue is $45m (AR multiplied by Q) and the total cost is $45m (AC multiplied by Q).

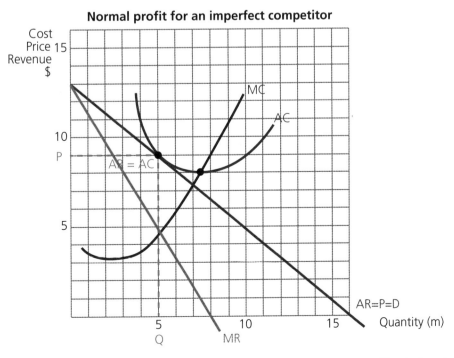

Normal profit for an imperfect competitor

1 Use the graphs to complete the tables.

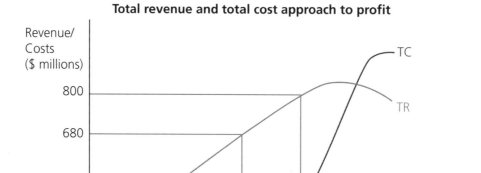

Total revenue and total cost approach to profit

a

Output (millions)	Total revenue (TR) ($m)	Total costs (TC) ($m)	Profit ($m)
4	680	440	240
5	800	500	300

Marginal approach to profit

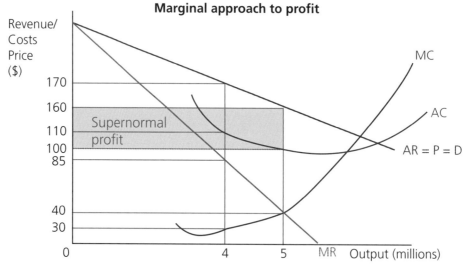

b

Value	Output of 4 million	Output of 5 million
MR	$85	$40
MC	$30	$40
AR	$170	$160
AC	$110	$100
TR (AR x Q)	$680 m	$800 m
TC (AC x Q)	$440 m	$500 m
Profit	$240 m	$300 m

c Shade in and label the area of profit at the equilibrium output.

2 Use the diagram to answer the questions that follow.

Costs and revenue curves for imperfect competition

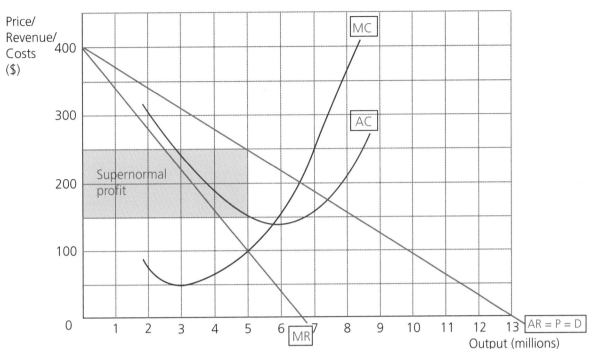

a Label the curves on the graph, using the small boxes for answers.

b According to the marginal analysis, at what output and price is profit maximised?

Output: <u>5 million</u>　　　　　　Price: <u>$250</u>

c At the equilibrium output position calculate total revenue and total cost.

Total revenue (AR x Q): <u>$250 x 5 m = $1 250 m</u>

Total cost (AC x Q): <u>$150 x 5 m = $750 m</u>

d Shade in the area of profit.

e Work out the value of profit.

<u>$100 x 5 million = $500 million</u>

f **(i)** If the firm was operating at 3 million units, what price would they charge?

<u>$320 (est)</u>

(ii) Give approximate values of MR and MC:

<u>MR = $225　　　　　MC = $50</u>

(iii) What must the firm do to maximise profits in terms of both price and output?

<u>The firm is missing out on marginal profits because MR > MC so should increase output and</u>

<u>decrease price.</u>

3 Use the diagram to answer the questions below.

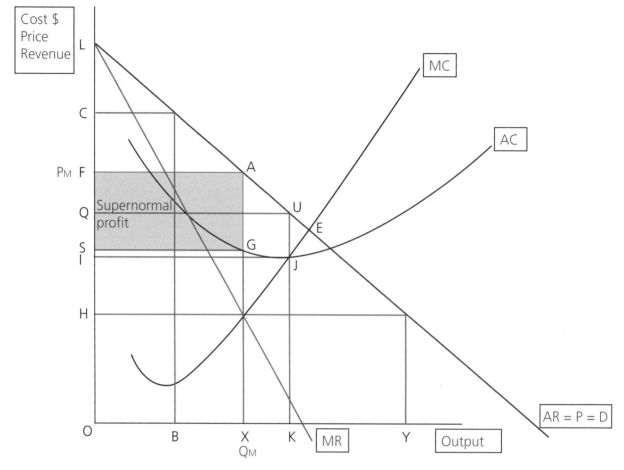

a Label the curves and axes, use the small boxes provided. Label the equilibrium price and quantity as PM and QM respectively. Shade and label the area of profit made.

b Give letters to represent the following at the maximum profit position.

Price:	<u>OF</u>	Total revenue	<u>FAXO (OXAF)</u>	Note: letters can be in any order but must give the area correctly.
Output:	<u>OX</u>	Total cost	<u>SGXO (XOSG)</u>	
Average cost	<u>OS</u>	Profit	<u>FAGS (AFSG)</u>	

c Explain, using the terms 'marginal losses' and 'marginal profits', why the firm would not choose to operate at OB or OY.

Operating at OB, the firm is missing out on marginal profits because its marginal revenue is greater than its marginal costs (or marginal costs are less than marginal revenue). Therefore, to maximise profits (or to minimise loss) the firm will need to increase output to where MR equals MC, as output increases price will fall.

At OY, the firm is making marginal losses because its marginal cost is greater than its marginal revenue (or marginal revenue is less than marginal cost). Therefore, to maximise profits (or to minimise loss) the firm will need to decrease output back to where MR equals MC, as output decreases the price will increase.

4 a Draw an imperfect competitor making supernormal profits in the diagram shown. Label the axes fully and then identify the equilibrium output as Q and price charged as P. Shade in the area of profit.

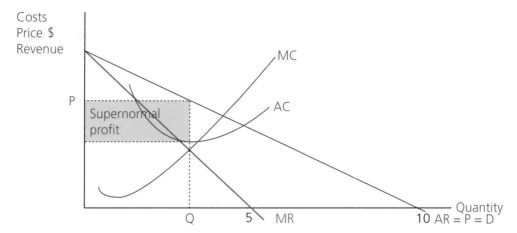

b Use the diagram below to answer the questions that follow.

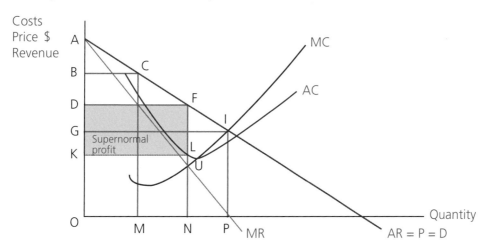

(i) Label the curves and axes.

(ii) Shade in the profit made.

(iii) Give letters to identify the following at the profit maximising position.

Output <u>ON</u>   TR <u>DONF</u>

Price <u>OD</u>   TC <u>KONL</u>

AR <u>OD</u>   Profit <u>DKLF</u>

(iv) In terms of profit maximising what is happening at OP?

<u>If an imperfect competitor firm is operating beyond the equilibrium output position where MR</u>

<u>equals MC, it is making marginal losses because its marginal cost is greater than its marginal</u>

<u>revenue (or marginal revenue is less than marginal cost). Therefore, to maximise profits (or to</u>

<u>minimise loss) the firm will need to decrease output back to where MR equals MC, as output</u>

<u>decreases from OP to ON the price will increase from OG to OD.</u>

5 Equilibrium output is where MR = MC.

Explain why equilibrium output is where MR = MC. In your answer you should:

- Label all the curves on the diagram below and calculate the monthly supernormal profit being made at the equilibrium output. Show your working.
- Show and label the area of supernormal profit made.
- Explain why the profit maximising price would be at the output you have indicated.

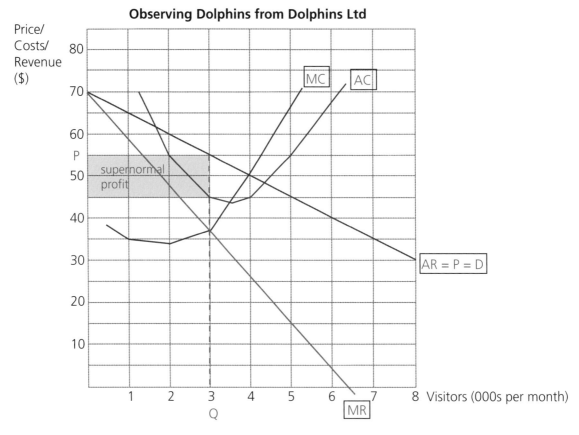

Observing Dolphins from Dolphins Ltd

The monthly supernormal profit made is $10 × 3 000 = $30 000.

The rule for maximising profit or minimising a loss is that the most profitable output or smallest loss is where marginal revenue (MR) = marginal cost (MC). On the diagram this is at 3 000 visitors per month.

If output is below equilibrium, the revenue from producing the last article is greater than its cost of production, implying that the firm could increase output and increase profit. However, increasing output beyond Q reverses the position. The revenue from one additional article is now less than the cost of its production. If increased output adds more to cost than to revenue, a firm has obviously passed the point of maximum profit. Therefore the rule is adopted and applies in all circumstances where profit maximisation is the aim.

The most profitable output is determined from the intersection of the marginal cost and marginal revenue curves. Any other position would result in a smaller profit (or greater loss if the aim is to minimise a loss).

_____

_____

_____

_____

6 The relationship between price and marginal revenue will determine a firm's market structure. Two firms have the following cost and revenue structures at an output level of 4 000 units.

Firm	Price	Marginal Revenue	Average Cost	Marginal Cost
X	$1.50	$1.20	$1.80	$2.00
Y	$0.75	$0.75	At its minimum level of $0.75	?

Explain how both firms can maximise profits. In your answer you should:
- Explain the profit maximising rule.
- Explain how we know Firm X is an imperfect competitor.
- Explain why Firm Y, a perfect competitor, should continue producing 4 000 units.

The rule for maximising profit or minimising a loss is that the most profitable output or smallest loss is where marginal revenue (MR) = marginal cost (MC).

If output is below equilibrium, the revenue from producing the last article is greater than its cost of production, implying that the firm could increase output and increase profit. However, increasing output beyond Q reverses the position. The revenue from one additional article is now less than the cost of its production. If increased output adds more to cost than to revenue, a firm has obviously passed the point of maximum profit. Therefore the rule is adopted and applies in all circumstances where profit maximisation is the aim.

The most profitable output is determined from the intersection of the marginal cost and marginal revenue curves. Any other position would result in a smaller profit (or greater loss if the aim is to minimise a loss).

Firm Y is a perfect competitor because AR equals MR while Firm X is an imperfect competitor because its marginal revenue is not equal to the average revenue (price), i.e., MR < AR and AR is greater than MR.

Firm Y, a perfect competitor, should continue producing at 4 000 units because as average cost is at its minimum level, it is equal to marginal cost; so the firm is operating at the point where MR = MC, which is the profit maximising level of output.

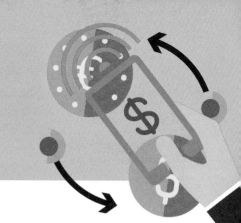

23 FIRMS AND PRICE

Pricing in perfect and imperfect competition

At the equilibrium output in **perfect competition** price and marginal cost are the same. Sellers cannot charge higher prices because they would immediately lose sales to competitors. This is called marginal cost pricing and occurs in perfect competition where price equals marginal cost (P = MC), and output is determined at the profit maximising position where MR = MC. This is shown in the diagram opposite.

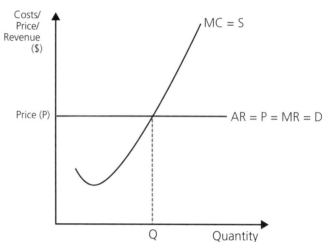

In **imperfect competition** the seller is able to charge a price in excess of marginal cost. This is called **mark-up pricing** and is where price is greater than marginal cost (P > MC), and the output is also at the profit maximising position where MR = MC. This situation is shown in the diagram opposite.

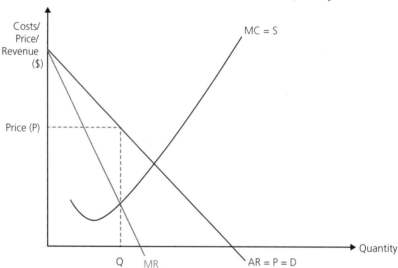

The outcome that is favoured by consumers is assumed to be that under perfect competition because this outcome is allocatively efficient and as such best represents the desires of society. A monopoly is deemed to restrict output and charge a higher price than would perfect competition; this is seen in the diagram opposite, where PmQm represents the monopoly situation and PpQp the perfect competition situation. A perfect competitor would have a lower price and greater quantity.

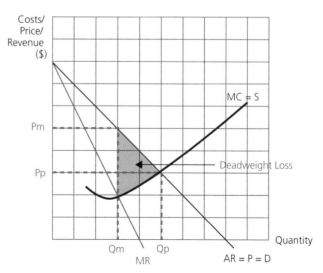

For society, insufficient resources are allocated to supply the quantity of goods or services that consumers demand; this is termed a loss of allocative efficiency or deadweight loss. This is shown as the shaded area in the diagram. This deadweight loss is a loss of welfare to individuals or society which is not offset by a welfare gain to some other individual or group.

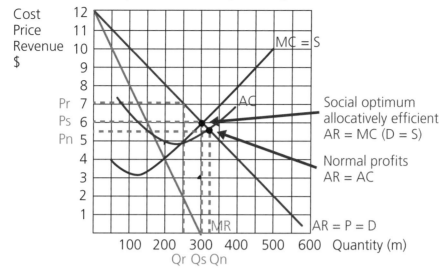

A monopolist – various price regulations

The government can regulate a monopoly by the administering of a price control that will not allow a monopolist to operate at the equilibrium. If a monopolist is regulated to a price of $7 (**Pr**) at an output of 250m (**Qr**) this is beyond the equilibrium position because marginal cost is greater than marginal revenue, the firm is making marginal losses on the increased output. The firm now makes a supernormal profit of $500m, this is less than the profit maximum position (or its most desired position). There is an increase in consumer surplus due to the lower price paid and higher quantity consumed by individuals. However, at Pr Qr the market is still not allocatively efficient because consumer surplus and producer surplus are not maximised but the deadweight loss is reduced.

A monopolist could be required or forced to **charge a price equal to marginal cost (P = MC)**. **Marginal cost pricing** results in the firm operating at the **social optimum** or **allocatively efficient** output position, in this case it is at a price of $6 (**Ps**) and an output of 300m (**Qs**). In a monopoly the average revenue curve is the market demand curve and the marginal cost curve is the supply curve for the good or service. At the new equilibrium position, the **deadweight loss is zero** (or eliminated) because the firm is operating where D (AR) = S (MC), the market is allocatively efficient because **consumer surplus and producer surplus are maximised**. At **Ps Qs** the monopolist is regulated to produce what a perfect competitor would produce and charge.

Average cost pricing regulates the firm to **charge a price equal to average costs (P = AC)**. In this instance the price would be $5.50 (**Pn**) and the quantity would be 325m units (**Qn**). The monopolist would not be maximising profits because the marginal revenue is less than marginal cost, the firm is making marginal losses on the increased output. The firm would make a **normal profit** instead of a supernormal profit. Normal profit is a return to the entrepreneur sufficient to keep them in their present activity.

Average cost pricing and marginal cost pricing both benefit consumers because they pay a lower price and receive a greater quantity than they would if the monopolist was allowed to operate at its preferred equilibrium output position.

Government ownership is an option, where a monopolist is owned and run by the government. The government can ensure that the monopolist acts in the public's best interest. In the private sector, inefficiency results in firms making a loss and leaving an industry. It is argued that state owned firms can be inefficient because there can be little incentive to be efficient and make profits. However, these enterprises today often operate along business lines and must return a dividend to the government, so they run as efficiently as any privatised firm.

1 a Complete the following statements, using marginal analysis (i.e., the relationship between MR and MC).

    (i) Firms maximise profit where <u>MR = MC</u>

    (ii) Firms minimise loss where <u>MR = MC</u>

    (iii) Firms make a greater loss or smaller profit if they do not produce at where <u>MR = MC</u>

    (iv) A firm will decrease or increase output to where <u>MR = MC</u>

b Complete the table.

Situation	Type of firm } Perfect / Imperfect	Relationship between MC and MR
(i) To maximise its profit the firm must decrease its output and raise prices	Imperfect	MC > MR (MR < MC)
(ii) To maximise its profit the firm must decrease its output and price remains the same	Perfect	MC > MR (MR < MC)
(iii) To maximise profit the firm must decrease output and increase price	Imperfect	MR < MC
(iv) To maximise its profit the firm has to lower its price and increase its output	Imperfect	MC < MR (MR > MC)
(v) To maximise its profit the firm has to leave output unchanged	Both	MR = MC
(vi) To maximise its profit the firm has to keep its price the same but increase its output	Perfect	MC < MR (MR > MC)

c Complete the table for imperfect competition that desires to achieve equilibrium output.

Change in price	Change in output	Relationship between MC and MR
(i) Do nothing	Do nothing	MC = MR
(ii) Increase	Decrease	MC > MR
(iii) Decrease	Increase	MR > MC

d Complete the table for a perfectly competitive firm that desires to achieve equilibrium output.

Change in price	Change in output	Relationship between MC and MR
(i) Remains unchanged	increase	MR > MC (MC < MR)
(ii) Remains unchanged	decrease	MR < MC (MC > MR)
(iii) do nothing	do nothing	MC = MR

2 **a** Label the curves and shade in the profit made.

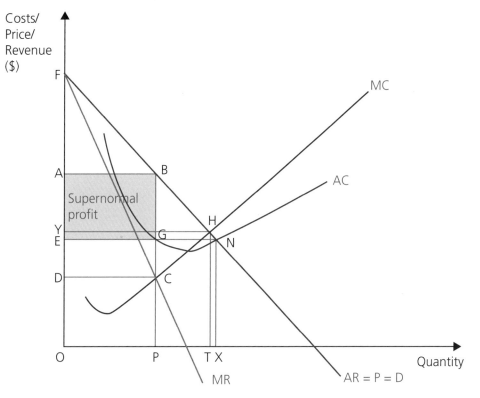

b Why are monopolies able to retain such supernormal profits?

Have strong barriers to entry, e.g., capital costs. These prevent other firms from entering the market and

increasing supply which will move prices down and so eliminate supernormal profit.

_____

_____

_____

_____

c Give letters to identify the following at the profit maximum level.

(i) Consumer surplus (CS) FAB   **(ii)** Average cost (AC)   OE

(iii) Total revenue (TR) OPBA   **(iv)** Total cost (TC)   POEG

(v) Price   OA   **(vi)** Deadweight Loss (DWL) BHC

(vii) Profit   BAEG

d Give letters to identify the price and output at the normal profit position.

Price OE   Output OX

e Give letters to identify the price and output at the social optimum position.

Price OY   Output OT

3 Use the diagram to answer the questions that follow.

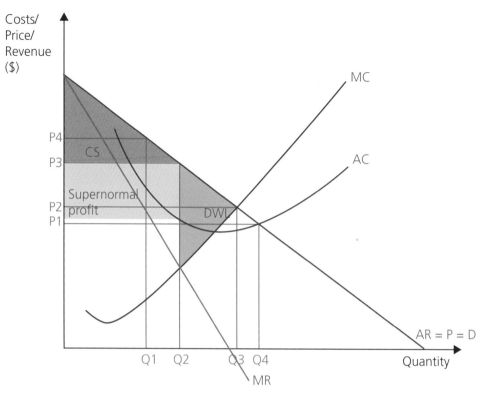

a Label the curves and shade in the profit where MR = MC.

b If the government was to regulate this monopoly into making normal profits, what price would they charge and what is the output?

Price P1 _____   Output Q4 _____

c At what price and output could the firm be regulated if price equals marginal cost?

Price P2 _____   Output Q3 _____

d At which price and output would this firm be regulated to produce the same level of output and price if it wanted to achieve the social optimum level of production?

Price P2 _____   Output Q3 _____

e Label the areas of consumer surplus (CS) and deadweight loss (DWL) and shade these in.

f Define deadweight loss.

A loss of welfare by an individual or group which is not offset by welfare gain to some other group or

individual. _____

_____

_____

_____

_____

4 Use the diagram to answer the questions that follow.

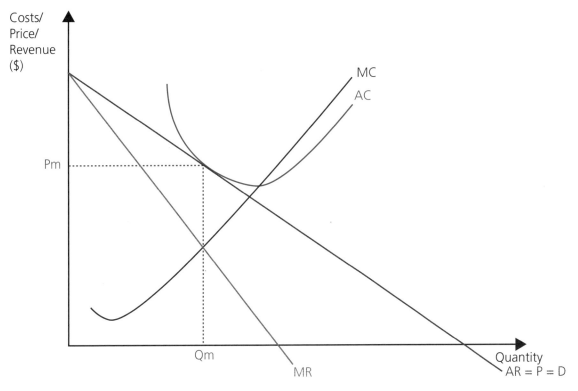

a   On the graph above:

   (i)   Label the profit maximising price (Pm) and quantity (Qm).

   (ii) Draw an appropriately positioned average cost curve (AC) showing the monopoly firm earning normal profit.

b   Justify the position of the average cost curve.

   Normal profit requires AR = AC (or TC = TR) at a given output level, so at Q the AC curve must cut (or be

   tangent) to the AR curve for them to have the same value, and so show normal profit being earned.

   _____

c   Explain why a monopolist is able to set either market price or market quantity, but not both.

   A monopolist can set either price or quantity but not both. If the monopolist sets the price the market

   will determine the quantity sold. If the monopolist determines the quantity then the market will

   determine the price. The monopolist has control over either price or quantity produced, but not over

   both at the same time.

   _____

   _____

d   Explain why the average revenue curve is horizontal for a perfect competitor but slopes downward for a monopolist.

   The perfect competitor is a price taker, and therefore must accept the market price or can sell any

   amount at the market price. The monopolist is the only producer; the demand curve for their product is

   the market demand, and the monopolist can only increase quantity by reducing the price on all sales.

   _____

   _____

5 Use the graph to answer the questions below.

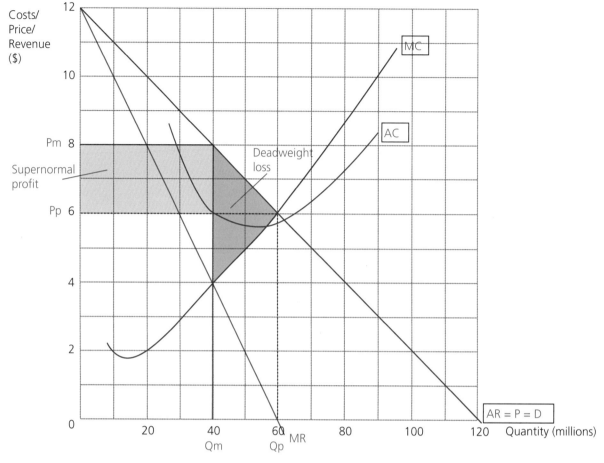

a (i) On the graph appropriately label all the curves and then identify the equilibrium level of output as **Qm** and identify the equilibrium price as **Pm**. Draw in an accurate MR curve and shade and label the profit made. Shade the deadweight loss.

(ii) Label the perfect competition price (**Pp**) and quantity (**Qp**).

b Explain, with reference to the diagram, why the outcome that is favoured by customers is **Qp**.

The outcome that is favoured by consumers is assumed to be that under perfect competition because this outcome is allocatively efficient and as such best represents the desires of society. A monopoly is deemed to restrict output and charge a higher price than would perfect competition; this is seen in the diagram, where PmQm represents the monopoly situation and PpQp the perfect competition situation. A perfect competitor would have a lower price and greater quantity.

For society, insufficient resources are allocated to supply the quantity of goods or services that consumers demand; this is termed a loss of allocative efficiency or deadweight loss. This is shown as the shaded area in the diagram. This deadweight loss is a loss of welfare to individuals or society which is not offset by a welfare gain to some other individual or group.

6 A monopoly is able to earn and retain supernormal profits in the long run.

Explain how a monoply is able to retain supernormal profits. In your answer you should:

- Label the curves on the diagram below and shade the supernormal profit made. Label the equilibrium output and price as **Qmax** and **Pmax**.
- Explain why long-run profits for a monopoly are likely to be different from those of a producer operating in perfect competition.
- Identify equilibrium price and quantity that would occur if the market was perfectly competitive.

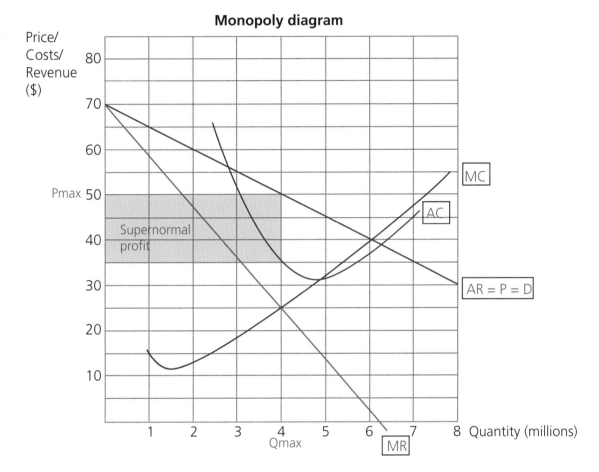

Monopoly diagram

Strong barriers to entry allow the monopoly to maintain control over price (or quantity) and make a supernormal profit in the long run. The perfect competitor has no such barriers and can only make normal profits in the long run since other firms are free to enter and leave the industry.

The equilibrium price and quantity if the market was a perfect competitor would be $40 and 6 million at the social optimum (allocatively efficient) position.

7 A firm will aim to produce where MR = MC.

Fully explain a firm's output decision using marginal analysis. In your answer you should:

- Label the profit maximising price (**Pe**) and quantity (**Qe**) on the graph and add an appropriately positioned average cost curve (AC) showing the monopoly firm earning normal profit.
- Justify your positioning of your average cost curve.
- Identify the market price (Pps) and market quantity (Qps) that would occur if the graph showed a perfectly competitive market.
- Explain using marginal analysis why a monopolist would not willingly operate at perfectly competitive market output.

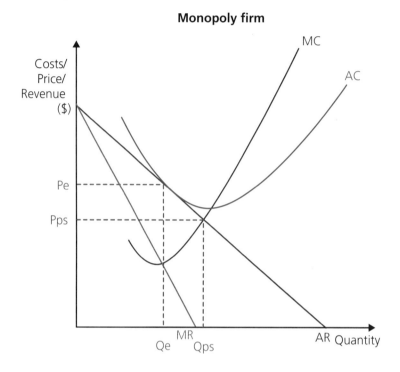

Monopoly firm

Normal profit requires AR = AC (or TC = TR) at a given output level, so at Qe the AC curve must cut (or be tangent) to the AR curve for them to have the same value, and so show normal profit being earned.

_____

_____

_____

At Qps, MC > MR. Therefore the firm is incurring marginal losses (negative marginal profit) on each additional unit of output. This reduces the maximum level of total profit the firm could earn. Therefore there is an incentive for the firm to reduce output (to where MR = MC). Consequently, the firm will not willingly produce at the perfectly competitive market level of Qps.

_____

_____

_____

_____

_____

 ISBN: 9780170438100

8 A monopolist will operate at the equilibrium output position.

Explain the equilibrium output position for a monopoly. In your answer you should:

- On Graph 1: draw a correctly positioned average revenue curve and label it AR = P = D; identify the monopoly firm's price (label it PM) and output (label it QM) and shade in the area showing the supernormal profit being earned.
- Show the effect that an increase in market demand has on the firm in the long run by carefully labelling any curve shifts, if necessary, to show the effect of an increase in market demand on a monopoly firm.
- Explain, using marginal analysis, the long-run output (i.e., QLR) shown on your diagram.

Graph 1: Monopoly firm

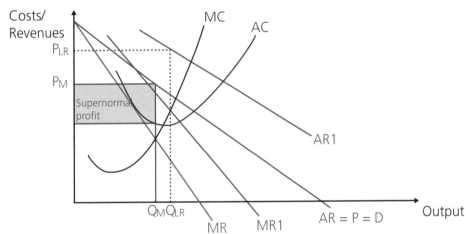

Shift AR and MR right and clearly label. Identify the new PLR as QLR. Label the long-run price PLR and output QLR.

Increased market demand increases both AR and MR, causing both to shift to the right.

At the initial output (QM), MR > MC and the monopoly firm is missing out on marginal profits (between QM and QLR).

So to maximise profits, the firm will increase output to QLR, i.e., where new MR = MC.

24 NATURAL MONOPOLY

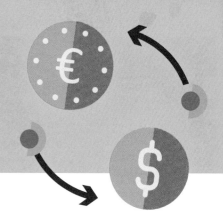

Features of a natural monopoly

A **natural monopoly** is when one firm has the ability to supply the entire market at lower prices than two or more firms.

A natural monopoly faces **downward-sloping average cost (AC)** for the entire range for which demand is applicable. The reason for its downward-sloping AC curve is usually that the initial investment in the infrastructure of the firm is large, but once it is in place, the **marginal cost (MC)** of production is **low**, for example hydro power. This high establishment cost is a strong barrier to entry and a natural monopoly could undercut any would-be competitor so they could not survive.

Natural monopolies often involve some kind of **network**, for example water, gas, phone, rail.

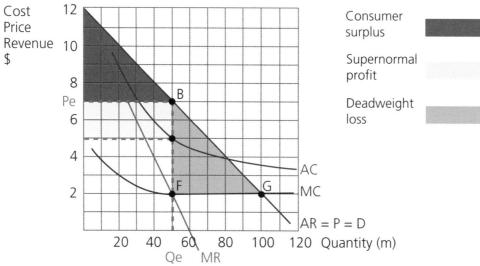

A natural monopoly – equilibrium output

The rule for maximising profit or minimising a loss (the equlibrium) for a natural monopoly is the same as any other firm. The most profitable output or smallest loss is where marginal revenue (MR) equals marginal cost (MC). Any other position will result in a smaller profit or greater loss. Therefore, the **equilibrium output** is at a price of **Pe** and quantity **Qe** (determined from the intersection of the marginal cost and marginal revenue curves).

If output is **below equilibrium Qe (where MR equals MC),** the firm would be **missing out on marginal profits** because the revenue from producing the last article (MR) is greater than its cost of production (MC), implying that the firm could increase output and increase profit.

However, **increasing output beyond Qe** reverses the position. The firm will be **making marginal losses** because the revenue from one additional article (MR) is now less than the cost of its production (MC). If increased output adds more to cost than to revenue, a firm has obviously passed the point of maximum profit (or minimum loss).

       ISBN: 9780170438100

Policies concerning natural monopoly

One way a government can regulate a monopoly is by administering **price controls** that do not allow a natural monopoly to operate at its preferred equilibrium output position where marginal revenue equals marginal cost. For this monopoly the equilibrium output is at a price of $7 (Pe) and quantity of 50m (Qe). The aim of price controls is to benefit the consumer with lower price and a greater quantity.

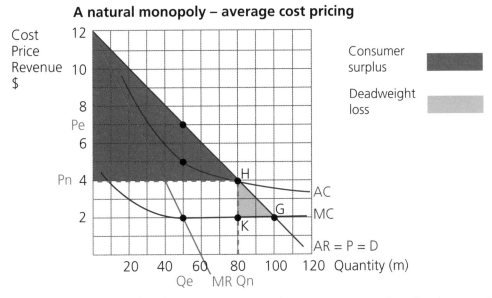

A natural monopoly – average cost pricing

Average cost pricing is a way that the government can improve resource allocation because it increases total surpluses in the market and reduces the deadweight loss that would be associated with a natural monopoly operating at its equilibrium position (MR = MC).

Average cost pricing regulates the firm to **charge a price equal to average costs (P = AC)**. In this instance the price would be $4 (**Pn**) and the quantity would be 80m units (**Qn**). The natural monopoly would no longer be maximising profits because the marginal revenue is less than marginal cost, the firm is making marginal losses on the increased output. The firm would make a **normal profit** instead of a supernormal profit. Normal profit is a return to the entrepreneur sufficient to keep them in their present activity. A natural monopoly regulated to a situation where price equals average cost is able to earn a fair rate of return.

The net **deadweight loss** to society is **reduced** but not eliminated, the deadweight loss is **now the area HKG**. The natural monopoly is making a normal profit so they may lack the funds to do R & D and be less innovative, this could be viewed as a negative impact on resource allocation of fixing the price. A price set to equal average cost is more socially desirable than the equilibrium output position because consumers experience a significant increase in consumer surplus due to the lower price and higher quantity consumed. Average cost pricing has the advantage over marginal cost pricing of not having to provide a subsidy to a natural monopoly to keep the firm operating.

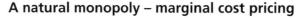

A natural monopoly – marginal cost pricing

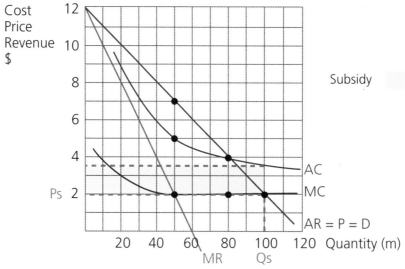

A natural monopoly could be required or forced to charge a price equal to marginal cost (P = MC). **Marginal cost pricing** results in the firm operating at the **social optimum** or **allocatively efficient** output position, in this case it is at a price of $2 (**Ps**) and an output of 100m (**Qs**). In a monopoly the average revenue curve is the market demand curve and the marginal cost curve is the supply curve for the good or service. At the new equilibrium position, the **deadweight loss is zero** (or eliminated) because the firm is operating where D (AR) = S (MC), the market is allocatively efficient because consumer surplus and producer surplus are maximised. At **Ps Qs** the natural monopoly is regulated to produce what a perfect competitor would produce and charge. However, the natural monopoly is making a **subnormal profit** shown by the shaded area. A subnormal profit is a return insufficient to keep the entrepreneur in their present activity, the firm would require a **subsidy** to continue operating in the long run.

Average cost pricing and marginal cost pricing both lower the price consumers pay and increase the quantity purchased. A natural monopoly operating at the equilibrium position creates a deadweight loss, average cost pricing reduces this deadweight loss while marginal cost pricing eliminates it. With marginal cost pricing a natural monopoly makes a subnormal profit and requires a subsidy to stay in business in the long run. Average cost pricing results in a natural monopoly making a normal profit that will mean it can stay in business in the long run without the need for a subsidy.

Government ownership is an option, where a natural monopoly is owned and run by the government. The government can ensure that the natural monopoly acts in the public's best interest. In the private sector, inefficiency results in firms making a loss and leaving an industry. It is argued that state owned firms can be inefficient because there can be little incentive to be efficient and make profits. However, these enterprises today often operate along business lines and must return a dividend to the government, so they run as efficiently as any privatised firm.

1 Use the graph to answer the questions below.

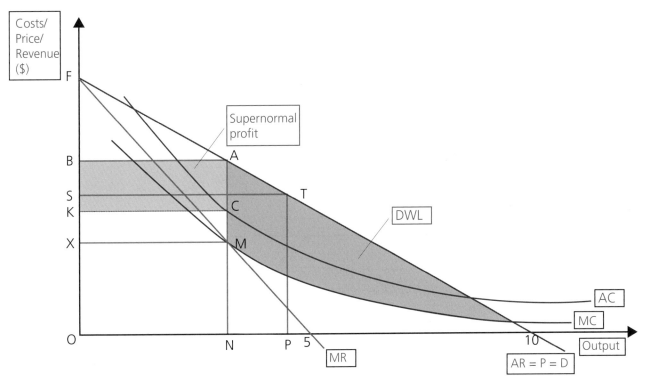

a Label the curves and axes, using the small boxes for answers. Shade in and label the area of profit made and DWL.

b Give letters to identify at the profit maximising level of output.

Price <u>OB</u>   Total cost <u>KONC</u>

Output <u>ON</u>   Profit <u>BACK/KCAB</u>

Average cost <u>OK</u>   Total revenue <u>BONA/ONAB</u>

c What is the distinguishing feature of a natural monopoly?

<u>A natural monopoly occurs when the AC of production for a single firm is falling over the entire market.</u>

<u>A single firm can produce at a lower price than two or more firms. High establishment costs but low</u>

<u>marginal costs. Involves a network.</u>

d Tick (✓) which of the following are likely to be natural monopolies.

    (i) New Zealand Steel   ☐   **(iv)** Water distribution network   ✓

    (ii) Rail   ✓   **(v)** Power generation   ✓

    (iii) Telecommunications   ✓

2 Use the graph to answer the questions below.

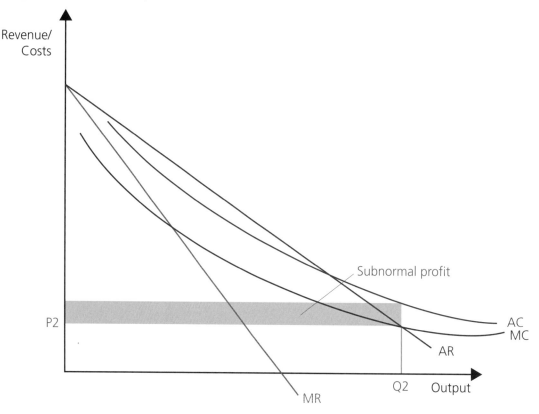

a (i) The government wishes to regulate the monopoly so that the socially optimum level of production is achieved. Identify the correct price and level of output. Label them P2 and Q2.

(ii) Shade and label the profit made at P2 and Q2.

(iii) What problem would be created in the long term? How could it be solved?

Problem At Q2 the monopolist is making a subnormal profit (AR < AC) and will not continue to operate

in the long run.

Solution Subsidise up to normal profits by government/nationalise and run in the public interest.

_____

b Outline another method (apart from price controls) that the government could use to regulate the monopolist.

Government could regulate the monopolist by taxing away any supernormal profit, removing statutory

barriers, encouraging competition, nationalising the industry.

_____

c Give a reason why natural monopolies may be socially desirable, despite the fact that superprofits often exist.

Lower prices to the consumers/research and development from the supernormal profits/avoids

unnecessary duplication of services and waste of resources.

_____

d Explain how economies of scale can lead to a natural monopoly.

Economies of scale will lead to average costs falling as output increases and so the firm can undercut

any would-be competition.

_____

3 Use the graph to answer the questions below.

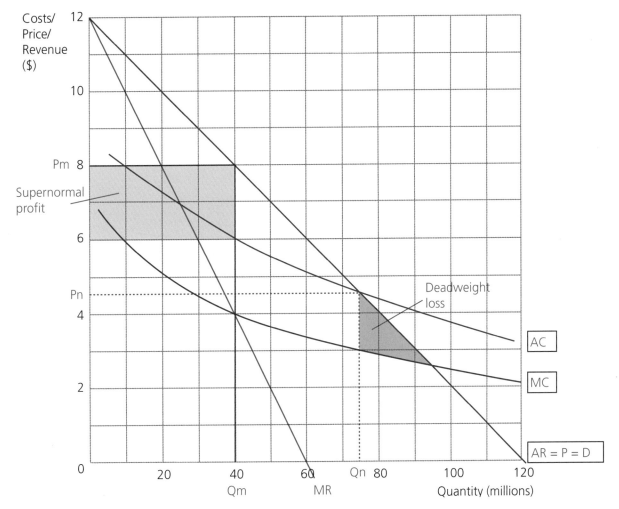

a On the graph appropriately label all the curves and then identify the equilibrium level of output as **Qm** and identify the equilibrium price as **Pm**. Draw in an accurate MR curve and shade and label the profit made.

b Calculate (and show your working):

   (i) the total revenue received by the phone company.   <u>P x Q $8 x 40 million = $320 million</u>

   (ii) the total cost.   <u>AC x Q $6 x 40 million = $240 million</u>

   (iii) the amount of profit.   <u>TR – TC $320 m – $240 m = $80 million</u>

   (iv) the amount of consumer surplus.   <u>½ x b x h = ½ x 40 m x $4 = $80 million</u>

c Define 'natural monopoly'.

<u>In a natural monopoly, the average cost curve slopes downward over the whole relevant output or</u>

<u>(alternatively) one producer can supply the entire industry demand for a lower price than two or more</u>

<u>producers.</u>

d On the graph identify the price a government could set to achieve normal profit. Label the price as **Pn** and quantity as **Qn**. Shade in the deadweight loss.

4 a Use the graph to answer the questions that follow. Draw an appropriately positioned average cost curve (label it AC) for the firm.

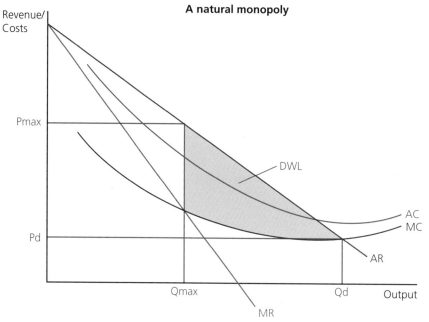

A natural monopoly

b (i) Identify and label the socially desirable price (Pd) and quantity (Qd).

(ii) Explain why the firm is unlikely to produce at this position.

<u>At this point the firm is not maximising its profit.</u>

c Describe a government policy that could be used to achieve the socially desirable level of output.

<u>Nationalise/regulate to P = MC/set price = MC and offer a subsidy as the monopoly would be making</u>

<u>a subnormal profit.</u>

d Label the equilibrium output as price Pmax and quantity Qmax. Shade the area of deadweight loss that results if the natural monopoly produces at the equilibrium level of output. Why is the equilibrium level of output less socially desirable than producing at Qd?

<u>At the equilibrium output the natural monopoly is making a supernormal profit and producing less than</u>

<u>what consumers or society wish. The good is overpriced and underproduced. At Qmax CS and PS are</u>

<u>not maximised and there is a DWL. At Qd total surpluses are maximised.</u>

e Indicate if the statements are correct or incorrect.

(i) A natural monopoly's key feature is that it owns patents that protect it from its competitors.	incorrect
(ii) A key feature of a natural monopoly is low establishment costs of setting up.	incorrect
(iii) A natural monopoly is when the government must grant the right to be a monopoly by statute.	incorrect
(iv) A natural monopoly must always earn supernormal profit.	incorrect
(v) A natural monopoly will always produce at a level where P = MC.	incorrect
(vi) A natural monopoly is when one firm can supply the entire market at lower prices than two or more other firms.	correct
(vii) A key feature of a natural monopoly is that it will be state owned.	incorrect
(viii) A firm is a natural monopoly if its average cost curve falls throughout its relevant output range.	correct
(ix) A natural monopoly always charges the highest possible price for its product.	incorrect
(x) A natural monopoly key feature is high establishment costs and some sort of infrastructure and network.	correct

 ISBN: 9780170438100

5 Market failure can result in underproduction and overpricing for a natural monopoly.

Explain market failure with reference to a natural monopoly. In your answer you should use the graph and:

- Draw an appropriately positioned AR curve and label it AR = P = D. Label the profit maximising price **Pn** and quantity **Qn**. Shade and label the profit made. Label the DWL. To improve resource allocation the government has set the price to equal average cost. Label the price position **Pac** and quantity **Qac**.
- Explain why a price set to equal average cost is more socially desirable than the profit maximising output position and the effect on resource allocation.
- Evaluate the effectiveness of average price controls as a government measure to improve resource allocation in a market controlled by a natural monopoly.

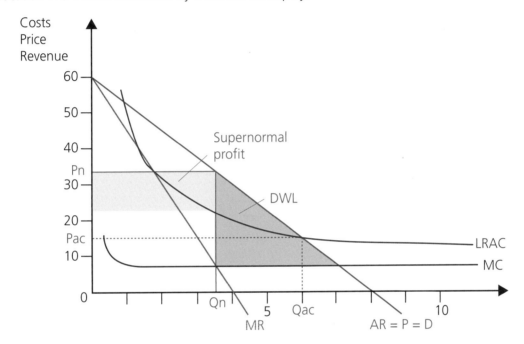

Setting a price to equal average cost is socially more desirable than the profit maximising because setting price equal to AC increases total surpluses, or reduces DWL. Makes natural monopolist earn normal profit so they stay in the market. Consumers experience a significant increase in consumer surplus due to the lower price and higher quantity consumed (compared to profit max). P = AC is socially more desirable than the profit max output (Qm). Gets closer to allocative efficiency. Setting a price equal to average cost can still negatively affect resource allocation because the firm still incurs a deadweight loss because they are not allocatively efficient at P = MC. OR With natural monopolists only making normal profit they may not have the funds to invest in R & D, so less innovation. OR Not operating at desired output, i.e., Qn and Pn.

To completely remove the DWL (or to maximise total surpluses), price needs to equal marginal cost. Natural monopolist will only produce QS if they receive a subsidy to cover the losses (subnormal profit). Taxes to fund the subsidy will come from non-consumers of this good, which is inequitable. Overall then, P = AC is a good compromise because it increases efficiency without the need for an inequitable subsidy.

25 THE LONG-RUN POSITION

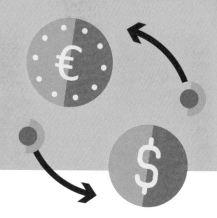

Monopoly and perfect competition

A monopolist (monopoly) is an imperfect market structure where there is a single seller of a good or service for which there are few, if any, substitutes, while in perfect competition there are many sellers of an identical (homogeneous) product.

Monopolies have strong barriers to entry while in perfect competition there are no barriers to entry and there is perfect knowledge or information. Perfect information (or perfect knowledge) is when consumers and producers in the market system are well informed so they are able to make rational decisions about the use of resources. This means producers are fully informed about the best and most efficient means of production. For consumers this requires that they are fully aware of the price and quantity of goods and service.

The demand curve faced by an individual firm in perfect competition is different from the market demand curve. The firm's demand curve is just one of the individual demand curves of firms that make up the market demand for the industry. The individual seller may sell as much as it wishes of its own production at the market price because the quantity it can supply to the market only has a negligible effect on market price. The demand curve faced by an individual firm is horizontal (perfectly elastic demand) because the firm is too small to influence price and is a price taker. Therefore, the firm's demand curve is not the same as the market demand curve. The market demand curve is determined by the overall demand for the whole market and is downward sloping since it represents the sum of all individual curves, i.e., showing that additional total quantities will only be purchased at lower prices. Because a monopoly is a single seller (producer) the demand curve it faces is the entire market demand curve, which is a downward sloping demand curve as per the law of demand.

The marginal revenue curves for a monopolist and perfectly competitive firm differ. In perfect competition firms are price takers because they are too small to influence price. Because all goods or services are sold for the same price (P) the average revenue (AR) will be equal to the marginal revenue (MR). A monopolist can only increase sales by decreasing the price on all commodities sold therefore marginal revenue (MR) will always be less than the price (P) or average revenue (AR). Therefore, in perfect competition AR = MR while AR is greater than MR for a monopolist (monopoly).

The equilibrium (profit maximising or loss minimising) level of output for both the perfect competitor and the monopolist is where marginal revenue equals marginal cost (MC = MR). The perfect competitor is a price taker but the monopolist can control the price or quantity sold. The marginal revenue is less than the average revenue for the monopolist and therefore the market output will be less and the price will be higher than for perfect competition (ceteris paribus). Pricing for a perfect competitor will involve marginal cost pricing. This is a situation in which price is equal to marginal cost. Sellers cannot charge higher prices, i.e., mark-up price over cost, because they would immediately lose sales to competitors. This is called marginal cost pricing and occurs only in perfect competition. Pricing for a monopolist involves mark up pricing. This is a situation where output is determined from MR = MC, but in which AR and P exceed MC. Sellers are able to charge a price in excess of marginal cost (P > MC). The price is marked up and this is a situation common in a monopoly market.

A monopoly is deemed to restrict output, charge a higher price and sell less than in perfect competition. A perfect competitor would have a lower price and greater quantity when compared with a monopolist. The outcome that is favoured by consumers is assumed to be that under perfect competition because this outcome is allocatively efficient. Therefore, a monopolist imposes a deadweight loss on society because it produces too little output at a higher price.

         ISBN: 9780170438100

Long-run equilibriums

A monopolist is able to make and retain supernormal profit in the long run because strong barriers to entry prevent other firms from entering the market and increasing supply, which will move prices down and so eliminate the supernormal profit. A perfect competitive firm cannot earn supernormal profits in the long run because there are no barriers to entry, therefore other firms will enter the industry resulting in an increase in market supply and a fall in price until normal profits are made in the long run.

The rule for maximising profit or minimising a loss is that the most profitable output or smallest loss is where marginal revenue (MR) = marginal cost (MC). Any other position will result in a smaller profit or greater loss.

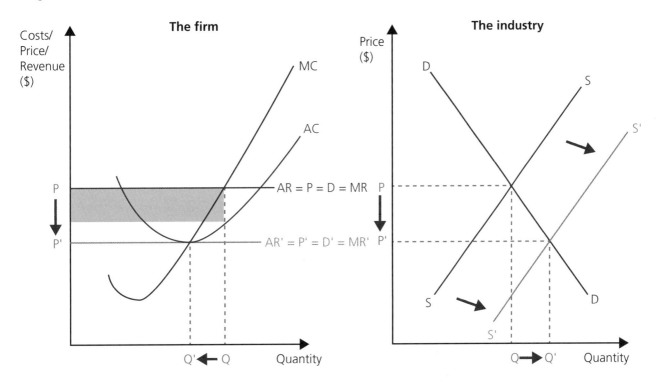

In **perfect competition** the long-run situation is one of normal profits where MR = MC and AR = AC. This is demonstrated by the following analysis. In the diagram the firm is making a supernormal profit at the equilibrium output positon Q. A supernormal profit is a return more than sufficient to keep the entrepreneur in its present activity. Supernormal profits attract other operators into the industry because there are no barriers to entry in perfect competition. Therefore, market supply for the industry will increase from S to S′ causing market price to fall from P to P′. Overall in the market, quantity increases from Q to Q′. Individual firms will now receive P′, make normal profits, this is the long-run equilibrium position. Because supernormal profits are eliminated, it removes the incentive for new operators to enter the industry.

QUESTIONS & TASKS

1 Equilibrium output for a natural monopoly and a perfect competitor are comparable.

Compare and contrast the output for perfect competition and a natural monopoly. In your answer you should:

- Complete the diagram by drawing in an accurate AR curve. Label the vertical axis and the MC and AC curves. Use dotted lines to identify the profit maximising output (**Q**) and price (**P**). Shade in and label the supernormal profit.

- On your completed diagram, identify the price a government could set to achieve a price and output comparable to what a competitive industry would achieve. Label it **Pg** and **Qg**.

- Compare and contrast the output and pricing decisions of a monopolist with those of a perfect competitor.

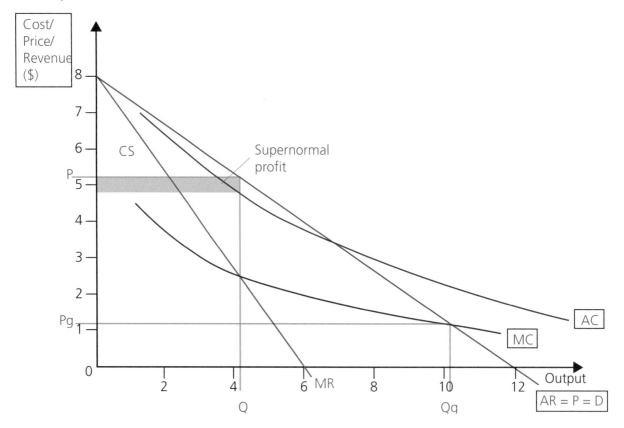

The profit maximising level of output for both perfect competition and the monopolist is where MR = MC.

The perfect competitor is a price taker and must accept the ruling market price because it is too small to

influence price; the monopolist can control the price OR the quantity sold. The monopolist has considerable

control. It is the market that determines the quantity if the monopolist sets the price, and if the monopolist

sets the quantity then market forces will determine the equilibrium price. The MR is less than AR for a

monopolist and therefore the market output will be less than for perfect competition and the price will be

higher (ceteris paribus).

_____

_____

2 Complete the statements using the diagrams provided.

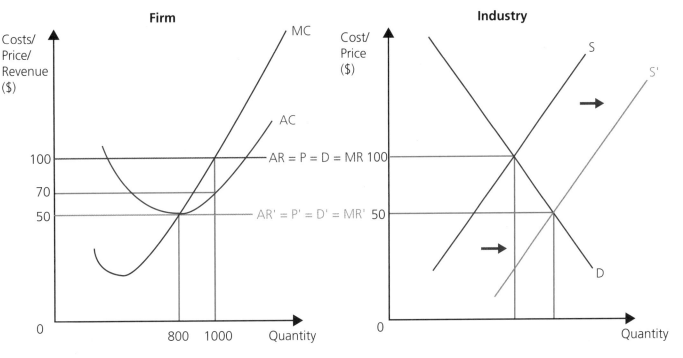

Firm

Costs/
Price/
Revenue
($)

MC

AC

100 ── AR = P = D = MR

70

50 ── AR' = P' = D' = MR'

0   800 1000   Quantity

Industry

Cost/
Price
($)

S

S'

100

50

D

0   Quantity

a At $100 (using AR = P = D = MR):

profit equals <u>$30 000</u> and will <u>attract</u> new firms and supply will <u>increase</u> and

price <u>decrease</u>.

b At $50 (using AR' = P' = D' = MR'):

profit is <u>normal (zero)</u> and the incentive for new firms to enter is <u>removed</u>,

because any further increase in <u>supply</u> and fall in price will see firms make a

<u>subnormal</u> profit.

c What are the characteristics of a firm competing in a perfectly competitive industry?

<u>Produce homogeneous (identical) products/no barriers to entry/perfect knowledge/price taker/small</u>

<u>relative to total market (not 'many sellers' because the question asks for the characteristics of a firm).</u>

_____

_____

d Define 'normal profit'.

<u>The return just sufficient to keep/hold entrepreneurs in their present activity.</u>

_____

_____

e Explain why a perfectly competitive firm cannot earn supernormal profits in the long run.

<u>No barriers to entry, therefore other firms will enter the industry, resulting in an increase in market</u>

<u>supply and a fall in price (and/or increase in average costs) until normal profits are made in the long</u>

<u>run.</u>

_____

3 Use the diagram to answer the questions that follow.

Graph 1

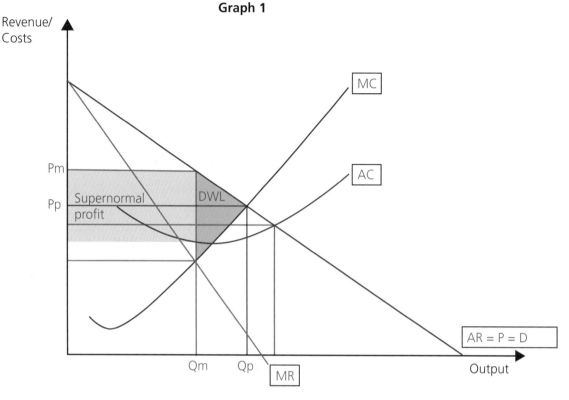

a On Graph 1:

  (i) Label the curves using the small boxes provided.

  (ii) Identify and label the quantity (**Qm**) and price (**Pm**) at which the monopolist will produce.

  (iii) Identify and label the equilibrium quantity (**Qp**) and price (**Pp**) that would occur if the market was perfectly competitive.

  (iv) Shade and label the deadweight loss (DWL) that results from the market being supplied by a monopolist, rather than by perfect competition.

b In Graph 1 the monopolist is making a supernormal profit at monopoly equilibrium.

  (i) Shade and label the supernormal profit.

  (ii) Explain why a monopolist is able to make a supernormal profit in the long run.

  Barriers to entry prevent other firms from entering the market and increasing supply, which will

  move prices down (and/or cause average costs to rise) and so eliminate the supernormal profit.

  _____

c What is one disadvantage to society of a firm being a monopoly?

  Higher prices and a lower output when compared with a perfect competitor and it creates a deadweight

  loss.

  _____

d Suggest one advantage to society if the government were to grant a license to only one operator to run deep sea mining.

  Protects resources from over-exploitation, keeps resources for future generations.

  _____

4 Use the diagrams to answer the questions that follow.

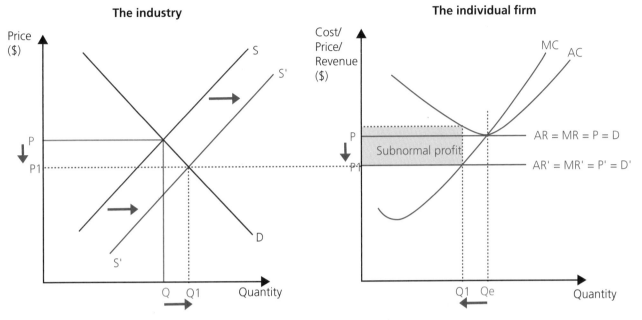

The industry

Price ($)

S

S'

P

P1

S'

D

Q   Q1   Quantity

The individual firm

Cost/
Price/
Revenue
($)

MC   AC

P

Subnormal profit

P1

AR = MR = P = D

AR' = MR' = P' = D'

Q1   Qe   Quantity

a Draw on the appropriate diagram an AC and MC curve to show the individual firm making normal profits at Qe.

b Show the effect of an increase in the number of firms starting up business. Label the new equilibrium P1 and Q1 on both diagrams.

c Assuming that there are no changes in costs faced by individual firms, shade in the level of profits now earned by each firm.

d Explain why a perfect competitor faces a horizontal AR curve.

<u>In a perfectly competitive market, there are many firms producing an identical product. No single firm</u>

<u>can influence price so firms must accept the ruling market price for all that they produce, so their AR</u>

<u>(and MR) is the same for every unit they sell.</u>

_____

_____

_____

_____

_____

_____

_____

_____

_____

_____

_____

_____

_____

5 Use the diagram to answer the questions that follow.

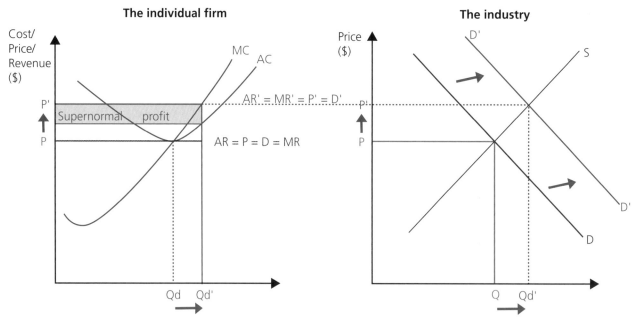

The individual firm

The industry

a On the appropriate diagram draw in average total costs to illustrate farmers making normal profits. Show the output as Qd.

b On both diagrams show what would have happened from increased demand (label both diagrams fully). Explain what has happened to the individual firm regarding:

(i) Profit (and shade this in): Increased to supernormal

(ii) Output: Increased

(iii) Price: Increased

c A perfectly competitive firm has marginal revenue of $2.50. The level of output is currently 10 000 units. Calculate:

(i) total revenue $25 000

(ii) average revenue $2.50

d List four characteristics of a perfectly competitive firm that could apply to a dairy farm.

Price takers

Homogeneous product.

Many producers in the industry.

No barriers to entry. Firms have perfect knowledge of the market.

 ISBN: 9780170438100

6 In perfect competition an individual firm produces a small fraction of total output and cannot influence market price.

Explain features of perfect competition. In your answer you should:

- On Graph 2 label all the curves appropriately, using the small boxes for answers.
- Explain how Graph 1 and Graph 2 illustrate perfectly competitive competition.
- On Graph 2 clearly label the equilibrium level of output as Qm. Show and label appropriately the amount of supernormal or subnormal profit being made at this level of output. Clearly label the shutdown point (S) and break-even point (B).
- Explain why the firm may continue to produce in the short run even if the price temporarily falls below the break-even price.
- On both Graph 1 and Graph 2 show the long-run equilibrium situation.

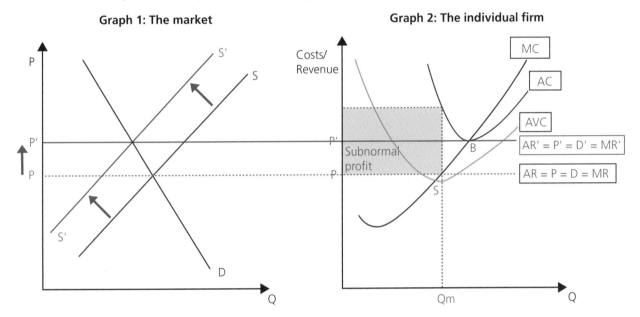

Graph 1: The market   Graph 2: The individual firm

The market (demand and supply) in Graph 1 sets the price for Graph 2. The horizontal AR curve in

Graph 2 shows the individual firm is a price taker, which is typical of perfect competition.

The firm will continue to produce in the short term, even if the price falls below the break-even price,

because the price is above minimum AVC the firm is covering all its VC and contributes something to its

FC. Although it is making a subnormal profit in the short run it would be making a greater loss if it closed

down.

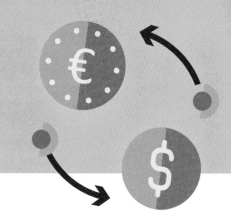

Question one: Long-run perfect competition

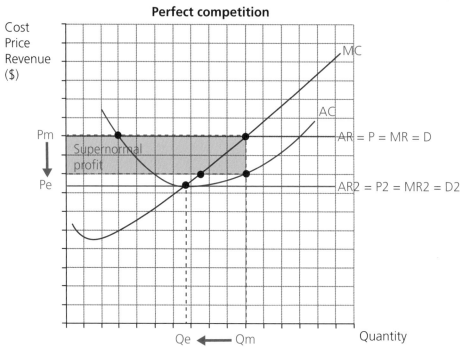

Perfect competition

a **(i)** Label all the curves.

(ii) Show the equilibrium output position on the diagram above, identify the price as **Pm** and quantity as **Qm**. Shade and label the economic profit made.

(iii) Explain in detail why Qm is the equilibrium position.

The rule for maximising profit or minimising a loss (the equilibrium) for a natural monopoly is the same as any other firm. The most profitable output or smallest loss is where marginal revenue (MR) equals marginal cost (MC). Any other position will result in a smaller profit or greater loss. Therefore, the equilibrium output is at a price of Pm and quantity Qm (determined from the intersection of the marginal cost and marginal revenue curves).

If output is below equilibrium Qm (where MR equals MC), the firm would be missing out on marginal profits because the revenue from producing the last article is greater than its cost of production, implying that the firm could increase output and increase profit.

However, increasing output beyond Qm the firm will be making marginal losses because the revenue from one additional article is now less than the cost of its production. If increased output adds more to cost than to revenue, a firm has obviously passed the point of maximum profit (or minimum loss).

b (i) On the diagram on the previous page label the long-run equilibrium position, identify the price as **Pe** and quantity as **Qe**.

(ii) Using marginal analysis explain the changes on your diagram.

In the diagram the firm is making a supernormal profit at Qm. A supernormal profit is a return more than sufficient to keep the entrepreneur in its present activity. Supernormal profits attract other operators into the industry because there are no barriers to entry in perfect competition. Therefore, market supply for the industry will increase causing market price to fall. Overall the firm will receive a lower price and make normal profits, this is the the long-run equilibrium position because as supernormal profits are eliminated, it removes the incentive for new operators to enter the industry.

If an individual firm operates at the old equilibrium position Qm (where MR equals MC) they will be making marginal losses because the marginal cost is greater than its new marginal revenue (or the new marginal revenue is less than marginal cost). Therefore, to maximise profits (or to minimise loss) the firm needs to decrease output to the equilibrium position. This is where the new marginal revenue equals marginal cost (MR2 = MC), this is shown as the decrease from Qm to Qe, where normal profits are made.

Question two: Allocative efficiency

a Explain equilibrium output for firms. In your answer you should:

- Calculate the values of the missing items in the table and put them in the spaces provided. Firm A is a perfect competitor and Firm B is a monopoly.

- Make a recommendation on the action they should follow to maximise profits. Justify your position.

	Price (P)	Marginal Revenue (MR)	Quantity (Q)	Total Revenue (TR)	Total Cost (TC)	Average Cost (AC)	Marginal Cost (MC)
Firm A	$1.50	$1.50	100	$150	$150	$1.50	$2.00
Firm B	$2.00	$1.50	1 000	$2 000	$1 750	$1.75	$1.50

Firm A: The firm is currently operating at a point where MC>MR.

The firm is making marginal losses on some units and these decrease maximum total profit.

The firm should reduce output to the level where MR=MC so that all these marginal losses would be avoided and the firm would be maximising profit.

Firm B: The firm is currently operating at the point of profit maximisation where MC=MR.

The firm should not reduce output; if it were to do so it would miss out on marginal profits because MR>MC for these output levels and so profit would not be maximised.

OR The firm is currently operating at the point of profit maximisation where MC=MR.

The firm should not increase output; if it were to do so it would miss out on marginal profits because MC>MR for these output levels and so profit would not be maximised.

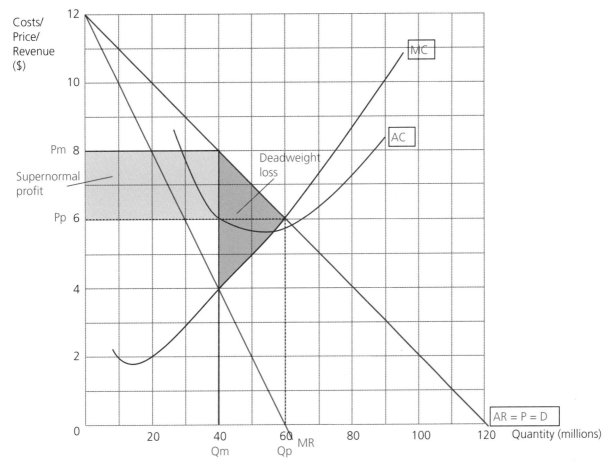

b (i) On the diagram appropriately label all the curves and then identify the equilibrium level of output as **Qm** and identify the equilibrium price as **Pm**. Draw in an accurate **MR** curve and shade and label the profit made.

(ii) Label the perfect competition price (**Pp**) and quantity (**Qp**).

(iii) Using the distinguishing feature of a monopoly, explain why a deadweight loss exists.

(iv) Using the distinguishing feature of a perfectly competitive firm, explain why it is allocatively efficient.

A monopoly is able to retain supernormal profits in the long run because monopoly markets have strong barriers to entry that discourage other firms setting up. At the equilibrium output where MR equals MC the monopolist charges more and produces less than would be the case if the firm operated as a perfect competitor. Operating at the equilibrium output position creates a deadweight loss shown by the shaded area because consumer surplus and producer surplus are not maximised, the market is not allocatively efficient

A perfectly competitive firm is a price taker, it is too small to have any influence on the market price and must accept the ruling market price. At the equilibrium output in perfect competition, price and marginal cost are the same. Sellers cannot charge higher prices because they would immediately lose sales to competitors. This is called marginal cost pricing and occurs in perfect competition where, at the equilibrium output position, price equals marginal cost (P = MC). A perfectly competitive firm is allocatively efficient meaning that consumer surplus and producer surplus are maximised, there is no deadweight loss.

Question three: Costs

A perfect competitor – increase in fixed costs

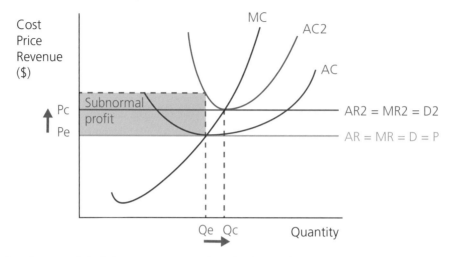

a **(i)** On the diagram, label the cost curves, identify the profit maximising price (**Pe**) and quantity (**Qe**).

(ii) Draw a new average cost curve (**AC2**) to reflect an increase in fixed costs. Shade in and label the new profit made in the short run (normal, subnormal or supernormal).

(iii) Show the effect that an increase in fixed costs will have on the price (**Pc**) and quantity (**Qc**) in the long run, label any curve shifts that will occur.

(iv) Using the distinguishing features of perfect competition explain the change in the market that takes place over the two time periods. Refer to marginal analysis and the diagram in your answer.

In the diagram the firm is making a normal profit at Qe. A normal profit is a return sufficient to keep the entrepreneur in its present activity. An increase in fixed costs will increase average costs but leave marginal costs unchanged. A perfectly competitive firm is a price taker, it is too small to have any influence on the market price and must accept the ruling market price. At the equilibrium, after the increase in fixed costs, the firm will make a subnormal profit in the short run. Some firms will exit the market causing supply to decrease and the price to increase from Pe to Pc.

If an individual firm operates at the old equilibrium position Qe (where MR equals MC) they will be missing out on marginal profits because the marginal revenue is greater than marginal cost. Therefore, to maximise profits the firm needs to increase output to the new equilibrium position. This is where the new marginal revenue equals marginal cost (MR2 = MC), this is shown as the increase in output from Qe to Qc, where normal profits are made in the long run.

A perfect competitor – decrease in variable costs

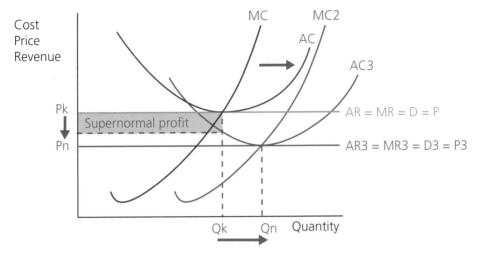

b **(i)** On the diagram, label the cost curves, identify the profit maximising price (**Pk**) and quantity (**Qk**).

(ii) Draw a new average cost curve (AC3) and marginal cost curve (MC2) to reflect a decrease in variable costs. Shade in and label the new profit made in the short run (normal, subnormal or supernormal).

(iii) Show the effect that a decrease in variable costs will have on the price (Pn) and quantity (Qn) in the long run, and label any curve shifts that will occur.

(iv) Using the distinguishing features of perfect competition explain the change in the market that takes place over the two time periods. Refer to marginal analysis and the diagram in your answer.

In the diagram the firm is making a normal profit at Qk. A decrease in variable costs will decrease average costs and decrease marginal costs, shown as an outward shift on the graph as MC2 and AC3. A perfectly competitive firm is a price taker, it is too small to have any influence on the market price and must accept the ruling market price. At the equilibrium output the firm will now, in the short run, make a supernormal profit rather than a normal profit. Some firms will enter the market because there are no barriers to entry and there is perfect knowledge of market conditions. This will cause supply to increase and the price to decrease from Pk to Pn. Firms now accept this new price and will make normal profits in the long run.

If an individual firm operates at the old equilibrium position Qk (where MR equals MC) they will be missing out on marginal profits because the marginal revenue is greater than its new marginal costs. Therefore, to maximise profits the firm needs to increase output to the new equilibrium position, (where MR3 = MC2), this is shown as the increase in output from Qk to Qn. In this situation the firm will make normal profits in the long run.

Question four: Monopoly

Monopoly firm

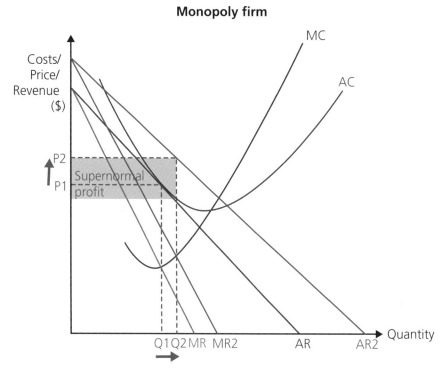

a (i) Using MR and AR identify the profit maximising price (**P1**) and quantity (**Q1**).

(ii) Show an increase in market demand as indicated by **MR2**, label the new demand as **AR2**. Label the new profit maximising price (**P2**) and quantity (**Q2**). Shade in and label the profit made.

(iii) Using marginal analysis explain the impact on price, profit and output decisions of the monopolist.

At Q1 the monopolist is earning a normal profit. The monopolist's demand curve is its average revenue curve, an increase in market demand shifts the average revenue curve from AR to AR2. If the monopolist remains operating at the original equilibrium position Q1 (where MR equals MC) it would be missing out on marginal profits because the new marginal revenue is greater than marginal costs, the new profit maximising output is where MR2 equals MC. The total revenue is now higher because the price received is higher (P2) and more is sold (Q2). Therefore, the monopolist now earns a supernormal profit, shown as the shaded area.

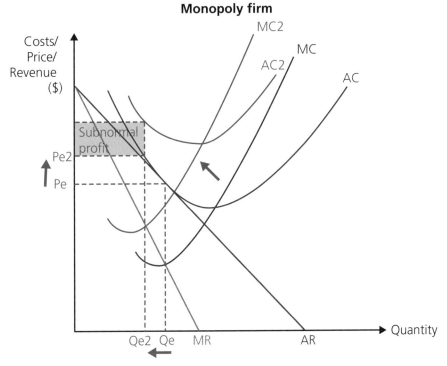

Monopoly firm

b **(i)** Using MR and AR identify the profit maximising price (**Pe**) and quantity (**Qe**).

(ii) Show an increase in variable costs. Label the new profit maximising price (**Pe2**) and quantity (**Qe2**). Shade in and label the profit made.

(iii) Using marginal analysis explain the impact on price, profit and output decisions of the monopolist.

An increase in variable costs for a monopolist will shift the MC curve upwards to the left from MC to MC2. It will also increase average costs so they will now be higher, shown as AC2.

At Qe, MC2 is now greater than MR so the monopolist will be making marginal losses. The equilibrium output position will be reduced to Qe2 (where MR = MC2), the price will rise from Pe to Pe2. The monopolist will now make a subnormal profit rather than the normal profit it was making previously.

Question five: Natural monopoly and allocative efficiency

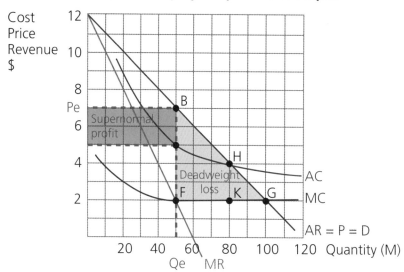

A natural monopoly – equilibrium output

a (i) Show the equilibrium output position on the diagram, identify the price as **Pe** and quantity as **Qe**.

(ii) Explain in detail why Qe is the equilibrium position.

(iii) Shade and label the profit and deadweight loss at Qe.

The rule for maximising profit or minimising a loss (the equilibrium) for a natural monopoly is the same as any other firm. The most profitable output or smallest loss is where marginal revenue (MR) equals marginal cost (MC). Any other position will result in a smaller profit or greater loss. Therefore, the equilibrium output is at a price of Pe and quantity Qe (determined from the intersection of the marginal cost and marginal revenue curves).

If output is below equilibrium Qe (where MR equals MC), the firm would be missing out on marginal profits because the revenue from producing the last article is greater than its cost of production, implying that the firm could increase output and increase profit.

However, increasing output beyond Qe reverses the position. The firm will be making marginal losses because the revenue from one additional article is now less than the cost of its production. If increased output adds more to cost than to revenue, a firm has obviously passed the point of maximum profit (or minimum loss).

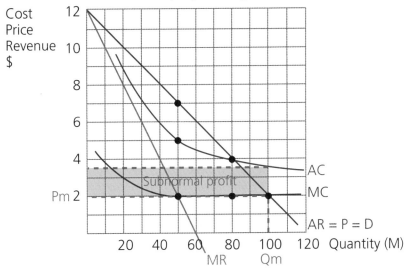

A natural monopoly – marginal cost pricing

Cost Price Revenue $

b (i) Show the equilibrium output position on the diagram if the government enforced marginal cost pricing. Identify the price as **Pm** and quantity as **Qm**.

(ii) Explain in detail the impact on allocative efficiency of Pm.

(iii) Use shading to illustrate further intervention that may be needed if the government uses marginal cost pricing. Explain why this intervention is required.

A natural monopoly could be required or forced to charge a price equal to marginal cost (P = MC). Marginal cost pricing results in the firm operating at the social optimum or allocatively efficient output position. In a monopoly the average revenue curve is the market demand curve and the marginal cost curve is the supply curve for the good or service. At the new equilibrium position, the deadweight loss is zero (or eliminated) because the firm is operating where D (AR) = S (MC), the market is allocatively efficient because consumer surplus and producer surplus are maximised. At Pm Qm the natural monopoly is regulated to produce what a perfect competitor would produce and charge. However, the natural monopoly is making a subnormal profit shown by the shaded area. A subnormal profit is a return insufficient to keep the entrepreneur in their present activity, the firm would require a subsidy to continue operating in the long run.

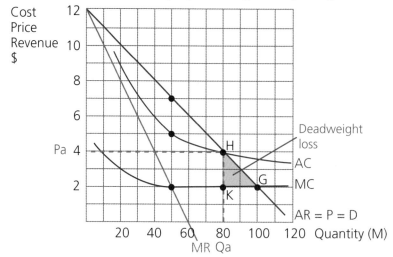

A natural monopoly – average cost pricing

c **(i)** Show the equilibrium output position on the diagram if the government enforced average cost pricing. Identify the price as **Pa** and quantity as **Qa**.

(ii) Explain in detail the impact on allocative efficiency of Pa. Shade and label in any loss in allocative efficiency if average cost pricing is used.

(iii) Explain why average cost pricing is more effective than marginal cost pricing.

Average cost pricing is a way that the government can improve resource allocation because it increases total surpluses in the market and reduces the deadweight loss that would be associated with a natural monopoly operating at its equilibrium position (MR = MC). Average cost pricing regulates the firm to charge a price equal to average costs (P = AC). The natural monopoly would no longer be maximising profits because the marginal revenue is less than marginal cost, the firm is making marginal losses on the increased output. The firm would make a normal profit instead of a supernormal profit. Normal profit is a return to the entrepreneur sufficient to keep them in their present activity. A natural monopoly regulated to a situation where price equals average cost is able to earn a fair rate of return. The net deadweight loss to society is reduced but not eliminated, the deadweight loss is now the area HKG.

The natural monopoly is making a normal profit so it may lack the funds to do Research & Development and be less innovative, this could be viewed as a negative impact on resource allocation of fixing the price. A price set to equal average cost is more socially desirable than the equilibrium output position because consumers experience a significant increase in consumer surplus due to the lower price and higher quantity consumed. Average cost pricing has the advantage over marginal cost pricing of not having to provide a subsidy to a natural monopoly to keep the firm operating.

Average cost pricing and marginal cost pricing both lower the price consumers pay and increase the quantity purchased. A natural monopoly operating at the equilibrium position creates a deadweight loss, average cost pricing reduces this deadweight loss while marginal cost pricing eliminates it. With marginal cost pricing a natural monopoly makes a subnormal profit and requires a subsidy to stay in business in the long run. Average cost pricing results in a natural monopoly making a normal profit that will mean it can stay in business in the long run without the need for a subsidy.

Question six

In the long run a perfect competitor will earn normal profits.

Explain why perfectly competitive firms make normal profit in the long run. In your answer you should:

- On Graph 1 below label the profit maximising level of output as **Qe** and shade and label the area of subnormal profit made.

- Explain why the marginal revenue curve for a perfectly competitive firm is drawn as a horizontal line.

- Explain why farmers who entered the dairy industry at the height of the 'boom' face the greatest risk of failure.

- Assuming this firm remains in the industry for the long run, explain how its profit maximising level of output will change.

Graph 1: The perfectly competitive firm

Perfect competitors are too small to affect the price so P = MR = AR, and the marginal revenue curve is drawn as a horizontal line.

Dairy farmers who were the last to enter the industry face increasingly scarce resources (herds, labour, suitable land) and therefore are likely to have relatively high costs/debt/interest payments, consequently, they are likely to be the most vulnerable to falling revenues and prices.

Making a subnormal profit will cause firms to leave the market until normal profit is made in the long run at minimum AC level of output above the current level. The profit maximising level of output increases as marginal revenue increases as a result of firms leaving the industry.

PHOTOCOPYING OF THIS PAGE IS RESTRICTED UNDER LAW.   ISBN: 9780170438100

   ISBN: 9780170438100